MW01673340

The Commands of Jesus

EXTRA LARGE PRINT

Jesus Christ's handbook for personal transformation and world change

Assembled and with notes
by Michael Phillips

Meister Eckhart wrote: "There are plenty to follow our Lord half-way, but not the other half. They will give up possessions, friends and honors, but it touches them too closely to disown themselves." It is just this astonishing life which is willing to follow Him the other half, sincerely to disown itself, this life which intends *complete* obedience, without *any* reservations, that I would propose to you in all humility, in all boldness, in all seriousness. I mean this literally, utterly, completely, and I mean it for you and for me—commit your lives in unreserved obedience to Him.

If you don't realize the revolutionary explosiveness of this proposal you don't understand what I mean. Only now and then comes a man or a woman who…is willing to be utterly obedient, to go the other half, to follow God's faintest whisper. But when such a commitment comes in a human life, God breaks through…

The first step to the obedience of the second half is the flaming vision of the wonder of such a life…Once having the vision, the second step to holy obedience is this: Begin where you are. Obey *now.* Use what little obedience you are capable of, even if it be like a grain of mustard seed. Begin where you are.

Thomas Kelly, *A Testament of Devotion*, 1941 "Holy Obedience"

The three volumes of *The Commands* and the five volumes of *The Eyewitness Bible* present a unity of vision and outlook on God's work and purposes through history and in the individual lives of his people. Their themes and messages form a single tapestry-perspective of the Bible as God's revelation. They are most profitably read in conjunction with each other, and with that overarching unity in mind.

The Commands of the Prophets
The Commands of Jesus
The Commands of the Apostles

The Eyewitness Old Testament, Volume 1
The Eyewitness Old Testament, Volume 2
The Eyewitness New Testament, Volume 1
The Eyewitness New Testament, Volume 2
The Eyewitness New Testament, Volume 3

Special Editions:
The Commands of the Prophets Extra Large Print Edition
The Commands of Jesus Extra Large Print Edition
The Commands of Jesus Journal Edition
The Prayers of the Commands
The Commands of Jesus Pocket Edition
The Commands of the Apostles Pocket Edition

10-14-2025

Scriptures are taken from the Revised Standard Version unless otherwise noted.

FIRST EDITION, *The Commands*. 2012
SECOND EDITION, *The Commands of Jesus*, 2014
THIRD EDITION, *The Commands of Jesus*, 2020
EXTRA LARGE PRINT, Sunrise Wise Path Books, 2025

ISBN 978-1-959666-94-3

Cover design by Joseph Dindinger

CONTENTS

The Commands of Jesus

1. ANDREW—*Love*

1 Obey my Commands.
2 Love.
3 Love God.
4 Love man.
5 Love the brethren.
6 Pray.
7 Be careful and watchful.
8 Remain alert and on guard.
9 Take heart, take courage.
10 Don't be afraid.

2. JAMES—*Purity*

11 Be pure.
12 Guard against ambition.
13 Commit no sexual sins.
14 Be patient, enduring, persevering.
15 Repent
16 Listen.
17 Listen carefully.
18 Be clear-minded, thoughtful, mentally diligent.
19 Apply yourself to think, learn, understand.
20 Think no impure thought.

3. PETER—*Humility*

21 Be humble.
22 Give when asked and do more than required.
23 Follow me.
24 Care for the suffering.
25 Give to the poor.
26 Believe.
27 Believe in God.
28 Believe in me.
29 Don't be anxious.
30 Believe that you will receive what you pray for.

4. MATTHEW—*Righteousness*

31 Be righteous.
32 If part of your body sins, get rid of it.
33 Be at peace, reconciled, and united with others.
34 Deny yourself.
35 Lose your life.
36 Be a servant.
37 De not defraud.
38 Be a son or daughter of God.
39 Pray, fast, give, and do good in secret.
40 Beware of practicing piety to be noticed.

5. PHILIP—*Forgiveness*

41 Forgive.
42 Forgive 70 x 7 times.
43 Do good, be good.
44 Seek first God's kingdom.
45 Store up treasure in heaven.
46 Be kind.
47 Love and pray for your adversaries.
48 Do good to those who hate you.
49 Do not exalt yourself.
50 Honor your father and mother.

6. JUDAS—*Hypocrisy*

51 Guard against hypocrisy.
52 Let your light shine before men.
53 If someone takes from you, do not demand back what you have given.
54 Seek no spiritual signs.
55 Be born again.
56 Do not justify or worry how to defend yourself.
57 Learn of me.
58 Receive the kingdom of God like a child.
59 Have salt in yourselves.
60 Be a good steward over what God has given you.

7. BARTHOLOMEW—*Trust*

61 Trust and have faith in God.
62 Do not be called teacher or leader.
63 Do not be diverted by externals, traditions, and doctrines, but look to the heart.
64 Don't fret about trifles.
65 Do not show goodness and hospitality only to those who are kind to you.
66 Worship the Lord and serve him only.
67 Do not desire more than God gives you.
68 Do not pray ostentatiously and with empty phrases.
69 Remain gratefully aware of your spiritual need.
70 Take up your cross.

8. JAMES SON OF ALPHAEUS—*The Golden Rule*

71 Do and think toward others as you would have them behave toward you.
72 Don't judge.
73 Deal with your own faults before thinking of the faults of others.
74 Ask, seek, knock.
75 Enter through the narrow gate.
76 Come to me with your burdens and find rest.
77 Take my yoke upon you.
78 Don't swear.
79 Judge rightly not by appearances.
80 Give the world its due and give God the things that are his.

9. THOMAS—*Truthfulness*

81 Love truth, speak truth, do truth.
82 Do not speak carelessly.
83 Acknowledge your discipleship.
84 Let your yes be yes and your no be no.
85 Do not doubt.
86 Speak graciously with words of peace.
87 Let people injure you without retaliating.
88 Show mercy.
89 Proclaim the kingdom of God.
90 Don't insult or call anyone a fool.

10. THADDAEUS—*Obedience*

91 Rule your life by the will of God.
92 Settle disputes promptly and privately.
93 Ask the Lord of the harvest to send workers.
94 Partake of the symbols of my body and blood.
95 Do for the least of humanity as you would for me.
96 Do not give way to anger.
97 Do not close your eyes to the Holy Spirit's work.
98 Give generously and not merely from your abundance.
99 Don't heed false prophets.
100 Obey the commandments.

11. SIMON THE ZEALOT—*Gladness*

101 Be glad in all circumstances.
102 Give up everything.
103 Don't resist evil men.
104 Do not lead others into sin.
105 Teach the nations to obey what I have commanded.
106 Do not follow the example of those who preach but do not practice.
107 Don't cast your pearls before swine.
108 Do not test the Lord.
109 Wash one another's feet.
110 Be wise as snakes and innocent as doves.

12. JOHN—*The Abiding Life*

111 Abide in me by obeying my commands.
112 Don't separate what God has joined.
113 Love me by having my Commands and words and keeping them.
114 Count the cost of single-minded devotion to God.
115 Don't look back on your past life.
116 Don't call me Lord and not do what I tell you.
117 Do as I do and become like me.
118 Bear fruit as my disciples.
119 Practice my words.
120 This is my Command: Love one another.

Introduction

Where lies the gospel power to transform ourselves and change the world?

This book has been compiled for anyone seriously interested in understanding more clearly the essence of the teachings of Jesus Christ.

What follows comes from no denominational or doctrinal slant. No agenda lurks between the lines other than to get to the bottom of what Jesus' life and teaching means. It is intended to speak uniformly to Catholics, Protestants, liberals, conservatives, Orthodox, Evangelicals, Mormons, Anglicans, Baptists, Presbyterians, Independents, Methodists, Episcopalians, Brethren, Nazarenes, Lutherans, Mennonites, Adventists, Pentecostals, even to those who perhaps do not consider themselves Christians in name at all…to any and all who are in earnest about knowing what the God-man Jesus Christ was all about. However this little book has chanced to come into your hands, that is its only purpose and we hope it is helpful in your life toward that end.

TWO QUESTIONS

Jesus made an absolutely remarkable claim that has gone almost unnoticed for two thousand years.

All Christians are familiar with Christ's Great Commission—his final charge to make disciples of all nations and take his gospel to the ends of the earth. What has gone undetected, however, is the roadmap he gave detailing exactly how this world-changing enterprise is to be carried out. Jesus told his disciples and followers throughout time specifically *how* to carry out the Great Commission with maximum effect, and how to transform their own characters in the process.

Imagine that we were to randomly query a room of a hundred people from a diverse spectrum of backgrounds and churches. We would pose two questions.

"What is the foolproof method for carrying out Christ's Great Commission that would *guarantee* success?"

"By what means will Christ's followers grow to reflect Christlikeness in their personal lives and receive the Lord's *Well done, good and faithful servant* at the end of life?"

Both questions have the same answer. There are not a variety of answers. There is *one* answer. Only one, without wiggle room. All other responses might point to a host of very good things. But they would be *wrong* answers.

What do we suppose would be the percentage of correct answers? We can almost be assured that the result would be a failing grade. 60%...50%. Would it even be as high as 30%?

You and I might take a moment to reflect how we would answer these questions.

Or imagine being told: "There is a simple prescription embedded in the heart of Jesus' teaching, overlooked, untaught in the churches, ignored by most pastors and all theologians, that will grow Christlikeness of character within you, and will fulfill the Great Commission in your life by the impact this powerful secret exercises on those with whom you come in contact."

Would you not do anything to discover that great secret of life? Such knowledge would truly represent the treasure hid in a field, the pearl of great price, the ultimate goal of spirituality.

In truth, such a secret exists. It sits right in front of our noses.

In light of the Lord's remarkable but unnoticed instructions about exactly *how* to "make disciples of all nations" and *how* to grow Christlikeness of character, the astonishing thing is that for two thousand years, Christianity has been attempting to carry out that commission, and Christians have been attempting to live the Christian life, by *different* means.

It is an unbelievable thing. Jesus told us, if we tapped into this powerful secret, that the world would come to know him. In response Christians down through the years have spent most of their efforts engaged in a myriad of other things that he said would *never* accomplish those high purposes. Christendom has been ignoring the one thing that *will* work, and doing a thousand things that will *not* successfully evangelize the world even if we do them for ten thousand years.

Are we really so dense as to have been ignoring his simple and straightforward formula for so long?

There is only one way for the world to come to know Christ. In the following pages, taking one element of Jesus' instructions at a time, we will look at that simple prescription for the making of disciples and for the infusing of Christlikeness of character within the lives of those who call themselves Christ's followers.

THE OUTSIDES AND INSIDES OF TRUTH

Before we look at Christ's instruction handbook, a caution is in order.

To play with the outsides of holy things is the surest and most serious way to impede spiritual growth. Pretended spirituality is more lethal than atheism. Spiritual blindness is the inevitable result of using God's truths as spiritual toys. This practice is taking place around us all the time. The old race of the Pharisees is by no means extinct in modern Christendom. It is much easier to analyze and study and discuss and preach and teach about the outer husks of truth than to *live* truth.

What lies before us is a holy quest. It is a quest that could change the world. It *should* have changed the world long before now, and would have done so had the truths been *lived,* not played with and analyzed and doctrinalized. Sadly, millions through the years have found it more pleasing to intellectualize Jesus' teachings than do what he said.

So count the cost of this quest. The Gospel of Jesus Christ is a holy handbook, not a toy.

A few years ago, it became the rage in certain circles to ask, "What would Jesus do?" Very few really wanted to *do* what Jesus did. But everyone wanted to talk about it. So they made bumper stickers and bracelets that reminded them of a phrase that somehow became "cool" among Christian youth, as if saying it was the same as doing it.

Most who were caught up on the WWJD bandwagon were playing with holy things. That WWJD fad was thus used to trivialize obedience to the example of Jesus Christ. How many of those cool Christian young people who wore the bracelets and emblazoned WWJD on their notebooks and binders are now walking in the daily self-denying relinquishment of Christlikeness? How many are thus truly changing the little corners of the world where they live because they took seriously *doing* what Jesus would do? One wonders. Surely there are some, and God bless those who had the courage to take it seriously.

BELIEF, DOCTRINE, THEOLOGY...OR CONDUCT AND CHARACTER?

Recently I began reading a book about the basics of Christianity by one of the renowned theologians of our generation. Most would recognize his name. He is a man I have highly respected for years.

This author embarked on his discussion of the basics of Christianity with a startling statement: "Christianity is not a code of conduct."

That simple sentence slammed into my head with magnum force. As he went on to discuss being "born again" and various doctrines of Christian "belief," including the necessity of "trusting Christ for salvation," that opening sentence remained seared on my brain.

Certainly he was trying to emphasize the truth that being a Christian involves more than simply "being a good person." That is true, of course, as far as it goes. Being a Christian is not synonymous with simply "living a good life." Being a *Christ-ian* means literally to be a "follower of Christ."

That means *following* him—doing what he said and heeding his example. It means being a *disciple.* There is a heavy price tag to calling oneself a "disciple" of anyone. There's a cost, a commitment. It is a serious word. It means following someone around so you can model your life after his.

The more I reflected on it, however, I could not escape the conclusion that Christianity is *precisely* a code of conduct. Jesus taught behavior and attitudes, *not* a doctrinal belief system. He did not teach ideas or theology…he taught conduct.

Christianity *is* a code of attitude and behavior. It is what we do and how we think. It is a *code of personal character.* Jesus laid out very succinctly and specifically what that code is. Then he told his listeners, "If you want to be my follower, if you want to be called my disciple, if you want to be identified with my name, do these things. Live by these principles. Think by these patterns. Behave in these ways. You cannot be my follower any other way than by adopting this code of conduct and character. To be *my* follower, you must live the Commands. Do so, and you will become like me, and the world will know that I came from the Father."

FOUR WORDS—DO WHAT JESUS SAID

The subject of this book are the Commands that Jesus laid upon his disciples and followers in the four gospels. What we will try to do is isolate what those Commands are. Then, with a brief challenge to us all, but without overmuch analysis and intellectualization, we will attempt to discover ways to live them more effectively.

At last we are in a position to answer the questions posed to the hundred hypothetical individuals. Believe it or not, both can be answered in four words.

The answers are simply:

The world will come to Christ as Christians DO WHAT JESUS SAID.

Christians will reflect Christlikeness in their personal lives as they DO WHAT JESUS SAID.

It's not rocket science. Jesus said with unambiguous clarity: Obey my teaching and the world will know that I came from the Father. Obey my teaching and you will become like me.

This is why his Great Commission contains the words, "…teaching them to observe *all that I have commanded you.*"

Not teaching them to study it…teaching them to *do* it. Teaching them to do it by observed example. It is not enough to ask *what* would Jesus do, we have to *do* what Jesus told us.

The example they will observe and learn from is yours: *Go to the nations and teach and example how to do what I said.* Believe it or not, the Great Commission says nothing about getting people saved or confirmed or taking them to Bible study or urging them to join a church. He tells us to teach people to *do what he said.*

It may be time that we collectively ask whether the doctrinal machinery of Christianity's ideas and belief systems is working as a basis for living and spreading the Gospel of Jesus Christ. Might it be time to refocus instead on *doing what Jesus said?*

The true gold of the Gospel. The treasure hid in the field. The pearl of great price.

The Commands.

Michael Phillips

Series One

"The Andrew Commands"

Love

God's Bull's Eye

We are generally familiar with six of the twelve disciples of Jesus—the three of his most intimate circle that were often together, Peter, James, and John, as well as Philip, Thomas, and Judas. The other six, though we know their names, remain mostly a mystery to us.

It is suggested but not widely known that Andrew was in all likelihood the first of the twelve to follow Jesus. Matthew recounts the first call in this way, "As he walked by the Sea of Galilee, he saw two brothers, Simon who is called Peter and Andrew his brother, casting a net into the sea; for they were fishermen. And he said to them, "Follow me, and I will make you fishers of men." (Matthew 4:18-19) Not only do we have the call of the first two disciples here, but we have one of the first of Jesus' Commands and surely one of the most important of all the Commands: *Follow me.* (It is actually the second Command given—the first came in the previous verse: *Repent.*)

John, however, records this chain of events differently.

Andrew was already a disciple of John the Baptist. The day after Jesus' baptism in the Jordan by John, Jesus walked by. John was standing talking with two of his disciples and John made his famous declaration, "Behold the Lamb of God." After John's statement, his two disciples began to follow Jesus. Jesus turned around and saw them and said, "What do you want?" They asked him where he was staying. Jesus replied, "Come and see." They went with him and spent the rest of the day with him.

One of these young men was Andrew. The other is not identified. It did not take Andrew long to realize that he was involved in something very special. The first thing he did was go find his brother Simon. "We have found the Messiah!" he told him excitedly. He then took Peter and introduced him to Jesus.

From that day on, Peter and Andrew were his disciples. Immediately it became Peter, not Andrew, who took center stage. As Andrew's first thought upon meeting Jesus was of his brother, he never begrudged Peter the spotlight. He was content to follow, to listen, to obey, to be one of the six "unknown disciples." We almost never hear of him individually again. He fades into the background.

But Andrew's example should never fade from our memory. He *loved* his brother as he *loved* Jesus. That was enough. James and John were ambitious. They wanted to be known as the greatest of the disciples. Andrew had no such ambition. He had fulfilled his part in God's plan. He had followed, then he had taken his brother to meet Jesus. He had obediently done what God gave him to do. And such he would continue to do for the rest of his life.

ἀγάπη: AGAPĒ—*Love*

In the Lord's call of Andrew and Peter we observe a wonderful example of both forms of New Testament love at work. Andrew's filial love for his brother (φιλέω: PHILEŌ—tender affection) moved him to bring Peter to meet Jesus. In him both brothers would discover the higher love, the very *ἀγάπη* that created the universe. In AGAPĒ is PHILEŌ fulfilled and glorified, for as their friend John later wrote: *God IS AGAPĒ.*

Love is God's bull's eye.

Series One

God's Bull's Eye

1. Obey my Commands.
2. Love.
3. Love God.
4. Love man.
5. Love the brethren.
6. Pray.
7. Be careful and watchful.
8. Remain alert and on guard.
9. Take heart, take courage.
10. Don't be afraid.

1. Obey My Commands

"If you love, me you will keep my commandments." (John 14:15)

This is truly the first of the Commands. Its importance is self-evident. The nature of a command requires obedience. A "command" is not a "suggestion." A command is a *command*. Obedience is compulsory. And yet…there remains such a thing as *dis*obedience.

Perhaps this is why Jesus often introduces the subject of obedience with the tiny but eternally significant word *If*. He recognizes that there are always two paths—obedience and disobedience. He commands obedience. But many will *not* obey.

The Bible focuses these two paths from beginning to end—always highlighting that the choice between the two lies within the will of the human mind and heart. We *choose* whether to obey or disobey, we *choose* light or darkness, we *choose* whether to live by God's principles or disregard them, we *choose* whether to exalt ourselves or deny ourselves. We each make that choice a hundred times every day.

At the end of his life, Moses issued this charge to the Israelites: *"I have set before you this day life and good, death and evil. If you obey the commandments of the Lord your God which I command you this day, by loving the Lord your God, by walking in his ways, and by keeping his commandments…then you shall live and multiply, and the Lord your God will bless you…But if your heart turns away, and you…are drawn away to worship other gods…I declare to you this day that you shall perish…I have set before you life and death, blessing and curse; therefore choose life, that you and your descendants may live, loving the Lord your God, obeying his voice, and cleaving to him; for that means life to you and length of days."* (Deut. 30: 15-20)

Jesus continually emphasizes this same *if*. He phrases his Command to obedience, not as a *direct* command, but as a natural outgrowth of love:

If you love me you will keep my commandments. (John 14:15)

He who has my Commands and keeps them, he it is who loves me. (John 14:21)

If a man loves me, he will keep my word. (John 14:23)

You are my friends if you do what I command you. (John 15:14)

Jesus is well aware of the games people play with spiritual things. He wants none to mistake what it means to be his follower. Many will claim to love him. Many will pretend to love him. Many will talk about loving him. Many will analyze what it means to love him.

But there exists only one validating sign. A Christian is distinguished and defined by that one, and *only* that one, thing. The progression is clear.

If you love me you will obey my commands. This is my commandment, that you love one another as I have loved you.

As it was for the Israelites to the commands of Moses, obedience to the Commands of Jesus is a daily, moment-by-moment choice. We make it over and over. We are *continually* making it. It is a progressive and ongoing choice that defines obedience to this Command, and to all the Commands. It defines what it means to love Jesus and be his follower.

Therefore...*choose life.* Choose to obey the Commands.

> Do you ask, "What is faith in him?" I answer, The leaving of your way, your objects, your self, and the taking of his and him; the leaving of your trust in men, in money, in opinion, in character, in atonement itself, *and doing as he tells you.* I can find no words strong enough to serve for the weight of this necessity—this obedience. It is the one terrible heresy of the church, that it has always been presenting something else than obedience as faith in Christ...
>
> It will be neither the church nor the world that will sit on the great white throne. He who sits there will not ask, "Did you go to church?"...but, "Did you do what I told you?"
>
> George MacDonald, *Unspoken Sermons, Second Series, The Elect Lady,* Ch. 11

God, bring to my remembrance this day the Command of Jesus to OBEY HIS COMMANDS. Protect me from the terrible scourge of Christianity—playing games with spirituality...pretending to love Jesus while disregarding what he tells me to do. Remind me every day, every hour, every moment, that love for Jesus is defined by obedience. Thus, heavenly Father, may I be an instrument in my small corner of the world for the ultimate salvation of mankind. Amen.

2. Love

"This is my commandment, that you love one another." (John 15:12)

It is surprising at first approach to the Commands of Jesus to discover that the Command to "love" is not the most frequently given injunction to fall from his mouth. But it is surely *the* most pivotal and central Command laid upon his followers which summarizes and incorporates and draws up into it *all* his teaching, and *all* the Commands.

The Command to *Love*—all men, all women, all people, all children, all life, all truth, the very creation itself and everything in it—and the love demonstrated and exampled by his own life and sacrificial death, is truly the single fact, the single teaching, the single Command, the single life-power, that distinguishes Jesus Christ from all other teachers. It is his love that separates Jesus from all other human beings that have ever walked this planet. That single Command is intended to set apart and differentiate his followers from the world and everything in it. Love is thus intended to be the visible mark and characteristic which Christians wear, which exudes from their very being. It is LOVE which will result in the transformation of the world, and the transformation of individual human character into the Christlikeness which is the image of Jesus himself, a reflection of God the Father, the Creator of heaven and earth.

Only *love* has the power to accomplish these mighty purposes of God, which Jesus came among men to make possible in the lives of those who came after him. For LOVE is the creative power of God himself, the essence of his nature and being. All love in the universe flows out of that infinite and eternal well of God's being-ness. When we love, we touch others and ourselves with God himself.

In only one verse of Scripture do we have an actual *definition* of who God is. That occurs in 1 John 4:16. What God *is*, in a word, is *love*.

> Where Love is, God is. He that dwelleth in Love dwelleth in God. God is love. Therefore LOVE. Without distinction, without calculation, without procrastination, love. Lavish it upon the poor, where it is very easy; especially upon the rich, who often need it most; most of all upon our equals, where it is very difficult, and for whom perhaps we each do least of all. There is a difference between *trying to please and giving pleasure*. Give pleasure. Lose no chance of giving pleasure. For that is the ceaseless and anonymous triumph of a truly loving spirit. "I will pass through this world but once. Any good thing therefore that I can do, or any kindness that I can show to any human being, let me do it now. Let me not defer it or neglect it, for I shall not pass this way again."
>
> Henry Drummond, *The Greatest Thing in the World*

God, bring to my remembrance this day the Command of Jesus to LOVE. Remind me that in loving, I show the world your character, your nature…who you are. Though no one around me may recognize its full implications, when I obey the Command to LOVE, I am stepping into my full discipleship as Christ's follower. To LOVE is to abide in him as he abided in you. Therefore, give me the strength to LOVE, the courage to LOVE, the insight to LOVE, the wisdom to LOVE, the humility to LOVE, the selflessness to LOVE, the patience to LOVE, the sensitivity to LOVE, the kindness to LOVE, and the compassion to LOVE as Jesus loved. Thus, heavenly Father, may I be an instrument in my small corner of the world for the ultimate salvation of mankind. Amen.

3. Love God

"Hear, O Israel: The Lord our God, the Lord is one; and you shall love the Lord your God with all your heart, and with all your soul, and with all your mind, and with all your strength."

(Mark 12:29)

The Command to "Love God" is at root vague and ambiguous. *How* are we to love God? Is such love something we *feel*? How many of us have read the words "with all your heart, and with all your soul, and with all your mind, and with all your strength," and not felt that perhaps our love for God is *not* filled with the all-consuming level of devotion that Jesus spoke of. The practicality of it is hard to get hold of.

This difficulty is multiplied many times over in a world where people hold so many wrong ideas that their first response to this Command might well be, "But I *don't* love God. I don't even like him! I could never believe in the kind of God that is commonly taught. If there is a God, he must be different than *that*."

The first step in being able to love God, therefore, is knowing him aright—knowing him as he truly is. In some cases this may be much different than we have been taught. The impasse blocking love for God is not limited to the non-Christian world. The vast majority of Christians as well have been taught doctrines whose implications are discordant to a right knowing of God. The implication of much Christian theology points to a deity whom only an *unloving* man or woman would worship. How then can we possibly *love* a being whose very essence, according to the worst of such doctrines, is the very antithesis of love.

George MacDonald's words about the false idea of God held by one of his characters probe deep: *The human niche where the idea of a God must stand, was...occupied by the most hideous falsity...The notion of a God is one from which naturally a thoughtful man must feel more or less recoil while as yet he knows nothing of the being himself, or of the nature of his...perfect...devoted fatherhood. It is one thing to seem to know with the brain, quite another to know with the heart.* (*There and Back,* Ch. 23)

We might consider reading Jesus' response to the scribe in Mark 12 with a single word altered: "The Lord our God, the Lord is one; and you shall *know* the Lord your God with all your heart, and with all your soul, and with all your mind, and with all your strength."

How many of us have dedicated all our heart, soul, mind, and strength to a right *knowing* of God? Such a simple shift in emphasis changes everything!

To love God, we have to *know* his being and character as Jesus taught us about his Father. Knowing him aright, love toward him will flow naturally from every corner of our being. Then we will indeed desire to love him and serve him and yield to him our all.

"Everything depend[s] on the kind of God believed in...How many ideas of God there might be, for every one who believe[s] in him must have a different idea…

"The best of men said he knew God; that God was like himself, only greater; that whoever would do what he told him should know that God, and know that he spoke the truth concerning him…

"No man is a believer…except he give his will, his life to the Master… no man, in a word, who does not obey him, that is, who does not do what he said…It seems preposterous that such definition should be necessary; but thousands talk about him for one that believes in him; thousands will do what the priests and scribes say…for one who will search to find what he says that he may do it—who will take his orders from the Lord himself, and not from other men…A man must come up to the Master, hearken to his word, and do as he says. Then he will come to know God, and to know that he knows him."

George MacDonald, *There and Back,* (Ch. 40)

God, bring to my remembrance this day the Command of Jesus to LOVE you with all my heart, soul, mind, and strength. I do not want to try in vain to love a false image of you that has been perpetuated by theologies I have been taught. Reveal to me the true nature and character of your Fatherhood. Help me know you as you are, so that love for you might flow from within me. Thus, heavenly Father, may I be an instrument in my small corner of the world, by my obedience, for the ultimate salvation of mankind. Amen

4. Love Man

And one of the scribes came and…asked him, "Which commandment is the first of all?" Jesus answered, "The first is, 'Hear, O Israel: The Lord our God, the Lord is one; and you shall love the Lord your God with all your heart, and with all your soul, and with all your mind, and with all your strength.' The second is this, 'You shall love your neighbor as yourself.' There is no other commandment greater than these." (Mark 12:28-31)

The first three gospels all report variations of the incident in which Jesus is asked what is the greatest commandment. If we were truly obedient sons and daughters of God, there would be no need for anything else to be said. We would have no need for the other more specific commandments. *Love God and love man* sums up everything.

The difficulty is obviously in the details. We don't know *how* to love God and love man very well in the moment-by-moment minutes and hours of life. That's why Jesus gave us the rest of the Commands. They are nothing more than the specific ways and means and methods of carrying out these two greatest Commands which include all the rest within them. The two "greatest" commandments—LOVE GOD, LOVE MAN—represent the overarching blueprint for life…for *eternal* life. The rest of the Commands tell us how practically to live the days of our lives according to that blueprint.

The trouble is, most of us don't want to live by God's unambiguous blueprint as much as we think we do. Like the lawyer of Luke 10, we seek with analysis, intellectualization, and justification to identify limits to God's expectations. We do so not to obey *more*, but hoping to find ways to obey *less*. We are just like the lawyer when he asked, "Who is my neighbor?" Between the lines, what he was *really* asking was, "Who *isn't* my neighbor? Whom am I *excused* from loving? Whom *don't* I have to love?"

That's probably the reaction you and I will have time and again as we come face to face with the Commands. "What!" we will say to ourselves. "Jesus expects me to do *that*? How far does it have to go? What are the limits? At what point am I let off the hook? In what circumstances *don't* I have to obey? How can I weasel out of the thing? Who *isn't* my neighbor?"

In response to the lawyer's self-justifying, "Who is my neighbor?" Jesus told the powerful parable of the Good Samaritan. Jesus concludes with four of the most powerful words in the New Testament: *Go and do likewise.*

Every time we squirm at the stark reality of the Commands, and glance about for some escape hatch, some *way out*, those same four words will be staring us in the face. *Go and do likewise.*

> The whole...of human society exists for the express end...of teaching the two truths by which man lives, Love to God and Love to Man...the throbbing of the heart of the great brotherhood [which] could come only from the eternal Father...
>
> And who is [my neighbor]? Everyone with whom I come in contact. He or she with whom I have...any human dealings whatever...Not only the man or woman I love...My neighbor is also the person who makes my clothes, the one who prints my books, the one who drives me in his cab, the one who begs from me in the street...the woman I meet in the market, and even the man who condescends to me. With all such, and hundreds more I pass through the course of a day, there is a chance of doing the part of a neighbor, if in no other way, at least by speaking truly, acting justly, and thinking kindly...
>
> George MacDonald, *Knowing the Heart of God*, ed. Michael Phillips (pp. 329-331)

God, bring to my remembrance this day the Command of Jesus to LOVE MAN. *Remind me that in visibly and practically loving those around me, I show the world your character, your nature...who you are. Though no one around me may recognize its full implications, when I obey the Commands to* LOVE GOD *and* LOVE MAN, *I am doing my small part to fulfill your purpose for your entire creation. Therefore, give me opportunities to love you and to love those about me. Send Samaritan moments into my life, opportunities to do good to my neighbor, which is all men and women whom I pass during the day. Send arrows of clarity into my heart, stabbing me with compassion for my fellows. Instill within me the compassion to* LOVE MAN *as Jesus loved you, his Father, and loved all those he met. Thus, heavenly Father, may I be an instrument in my small corner of the world, by my obedience, for the ultimate salvation of mankind. Amen*

5. Love the Brethren

"By this all men will know that you are my disciples, if you have love for one another….I do not pray for these only, but also for those who are to believe in me through their word, that they may all be one, even as thou, Father, art in me, and I in thee, that they also may be in us, so that the world may believe that thou hast sent me." (John 13:35, 17:20-21)

Jesus makes two of the most shocking statements of his ministry on the night before his death. They are recounted only by the Gospelist John. Though Matthew was also there that evening, it clearly took not only an eyewitness, but one like John with particular insight into the Lord's heart, to capture the powerful essence of this pivotal message that Jesus wanted to leave with his disciples on his last night with them.

Christians tend to think of the "Great Commission" at the end of Matthew's gospel as the Lord's singular evangelistic mandate. But though the challenge to make disciples of all nations was his final recorded charge, it was not his most important. A more significant challenge came in the upper room. During their final hours together Jesus told the twelve the precise basis upon which people would respond to their message, and how the world would be able to tell that they were his disciples. And then, in a mighty prayer to his Father which he allowed them to hear, he illuminated yet further how the world would come to know that he came from the Father and was himself the Son of God.

He did not base the world's response on their preaching, teaching, or persuasive arguments. Neither was it based on their doctrine or theology. His "final apologetic" was far simpler. Jesus said the world would know they were his disciples, and know that he came from the Father, on the basis of their love for and unity with one another.

Whenever we hear two Christians arguing over a point of theology or church practice, the words of Jesus' prayer ought to sting our hearts with grief. When either a lack of love or a breakdown of unity exists between true Christians, whether two individuals or two groups or churches or denominations or movements, the world has the right to conclude that Christianity is not true.

> How, then, is the dying culture going to consider us? Jesus says, "By this shall all men know that ye are my disciples, if ye have love one to another." In… the midst of our present culture, Jesus…gives the world the right to judge whether you and I are born-again Christians on the basis of our observable love toward all Christians…
>
> Jesus turns to the world and says, "I've something to say to you. On the basis of My authority, I give you a right: you may judge whether or not an individual is a Christian on the basis of the love he shows to all Christians." In other words, if people come up to us and cast in our teeth the judgment that we are not Christians because we have not shown love toward other Christians, we must understand that they are

only exercising a prerogative which Jesus gave them.

And we must not get angry. If people say, "You don't love other Christians," we must go home, get down on our knees, and ask God whether or not what they say is true…

But there is something even more sober. And to understand it we must look at John 17:21…Here Jesus is stating something else which is much more cutting, much more profound: we cannot expect the world to believe that the Father sent the Son, that Jesus' claims are true, and that Christianity is true, unless the world sees some reality of the oneness of true Christians.

Francis Schaeffer, *The Mark of the Christian*

God, bring to my remembrance this day the Command of Jesus to LOVE THE BRETHREN. Remind me that in doing so, I demonstrate to the world that I am your disciple. Remind me that when I fail to LOVE THE BRETHREN, by disputation, by criticism, by judgment, by sectarianism, the world has the right to conclude that I am not a Christian at all. Give me opportunities to practice such love by demonstrating visible unity with other Christians who believe differently than I do. Remind me that the world will come to know that Jesus came from the Father, not from my proclamations but by observing my oneness with other Christians. Give me opportunities to learn that Christians of differing perspectives and outlooks are all required to LOVE THE BRETHREN in unity. Thus, heavenly Father, by my demonstrable love for other Christians, may I be an instrument in my small corner of the world for the ultimate salvation of mankind. Amen.

6. Pray

"When you pray, go into your room and shut the door and pray to your Father who is in secret…And in praying do not heap up empty phrases…for your Father knows what you need before you ask him. Pray then like this: Our Father who art in heaven, Hallowed be thy name. Thy kingdom come, Thy will be done, On earth as it is in heaven. Give us this day our daily bread; And forgive us our debts, As we also have forgiven our debtors; And lead us not into temptation, But deliver us from evil." (Matthew 6:6-7, 9-13)

It may be that the injunction toward prayer is the single Command of Jesus we most readily witness throughout the earth. Christians pray, Jews pray, Muslims pray. Even many who profess no religion yet claim to pray. It is an astonishing fact to contemplate that more than half of mankind probably *prays* regularly in some fashion. It is surely no exaggeration to say that prayer is being lifted to the heavens every second round the clock.

Mankind is a praying species. This earth is a praying world.

If prayer is so widespread, so unceasing, so universal, why do we not observe its results? Why is mankind so fragmented and alienated from itself and from God?

Because most of this global prayer is not the kind of prayer Jesus was talking about. It matters *who* we are praying to. It matters *how* we pray. And it matters *what* we pray.

Jesus commanded us to pray to his *Father*. Sad to say much of the Christian world, is not praying to the Father of Jesus Christ, but to an imaginary creation of religious tradition. Most of the rest of the world is praying to a silent and unresponsive idol, not the eternal I AM whom Jesus came to reveal. Our God is a good and loving Father, our *Abba*. He knows our needs, we don't need to set them before him like a shopping list. Prayer with our *Abba* is ongoing communion, a way of life, an ordering of outlook and perspective through his eyes. Prayer, in this sense, is nothing more than life as Jesus lived it.

Then Jesus told us *how* to pray. When we pray, he said not to heap up empty phrases (RSV) and vain repetitions (KJV). Yet how much of the world's prayer is precisely that—memorized cliché, rote formula, and spiritual jargon? Such is not the reality of prayer Jesus taught. That reality is not comprised of *words*. Prayer is the dynamic oxygen of relationship between Creator and created.

And Jesus told us *what* to pray. We are to relinquish our wills into the will of the Father. *Thy will be done* is the essence, not only of what we call the Lord's prayer, but of *all* prayer. Those four words undergird the essence of who Jesus was and is. They define the attitude and outlook he lays upon those who follow him, a continual uplifting of consciousness that says, *Thy will be done.*

> The prayer of Christlikeness truly represents the ultimate road less traveled...It is a quiet prayer, a personal prayer, a humbling prayer, an invisible prayer. It can be a lonely prayer...a painful prayer...a sacrificial prayer. One cannot pray this prayer anywhere but at the altar...
>
> Dedicating oneself to the prayer of Christlikeness begins a lifetime of growth...Every motive is now imbued with new significance, new perspective, new imperative. To respond as Jesus responded suddenly floods into being as the illuminating purpose that gives everything in life definition and meaning...
>
> From the prayer of Christlikeness, therefore, the very practical question immediately arises: How is it to be done, this high and holy thing? How do we, how *can* we possibly appropriate the Christlike life for ourselves?...We can be like him in that most important of ways in which his own Sonship was lived out. As he did, we can turn our hearts to the Father. With Jesus we can say, *Father, what would you have me do?* With that chosen subservience, the prayer of childship, we indeed make ourselves one with Christ.
>
> Michael Phillips, *Make Me Like Jesus* (pp. 21-37)

God, bring to my remembrance this day the Command of Jesus to PRAY. *Infuse within me an inner prayer-focus toward you. Give me the courage to* PRAY *the prayer of Christlikeness: Make me like Jesus. Give me the wisdom to* PRAY *as Jesus prayed, the humility to* PRAY *as Jesus prayed, the selflessness to* PRAY *as Jesus prayed, and the compassion to* PRAY *as Jesus prayed. I yield my will into yours. May the very prayer of my being be that of Jesus in the garden, Not my will, but your will be done. Thus, heavenly Father, may I be an instrument in my small corner of the world for the ultimate salvation of mankind. Amen.*

7. Be Careful and Watchful

"Watch out and beware of the leaven of the Pharisees and Sadducees." (Matthew 16:6, NAS)
"Keep watching and praying that you may not enter into temptation." (Matthew 26:41, NAS)

A serious examination of the Gospels reveals three surprising combinations of injunctions emerging as the most frequently given Commands of Jesus. One would assume, from their prevalence, that these three groups would form the bedrock of Christian teaching, that we would hear them from the pulpits of our churches week after week, that they would form the basis of most dialog and discussion between Christians. If Jesus emphasized them most, would it not be logical to assume that we would too?

But it is not so.

Remarkably, one of the three is almost *never* taught and preached. The other two are considered mere sidelights to the more spiritual, doctrinal, and experiential components of faith. However, here they stand in the Gospels, all three commanded upon us by Jesus *more* often than the Commands to love, pray, believe, trust, or have faith. Jesus speaks but *once* about the necessity of being born again. But these three groups of Commands (toward *watchfulness, fearlessness,* and *mental diligence*) are urged upon the disciples a combined *seventy* times! Yet an entire theology of salvation has grown up around Jesus' conversation with Nicodemus in the third chapter of John, while these far more frequently given Commands lay beside the road virtually unnoticed.

What are these overlooked Commands?

The first is a group of Commands, which we consider here as two, urging watchfulness: *Be careful and watchful,* and *Remain alert and on guard.* These can be seen as a single related group of Commands because they point to a similar mindset and outlook. In many different circumstances, prompted by a multitude of specific situations, Jesus commanded *watchfulness* upon his disciples. We might consider it the opposite of mental sloth and laziness.

Jesus urges watchfulness so often because spiritual health *requires* it.

Attentiveness is no optional element of spirituality but is intrinsic to the "good soil" that produces growth and fruitfulness. There can be no lasting spiritual growth without such mental and spiritual diligence. Absent watchfulness, faith becomes fat, lazy, unthinking, too easily accepting of dogma, dependent on formula and jargon rather than personal spiritual mettle, unaware of danger, oblivious to the enemy's intrusions into one's life.

When one's eyes are opened to this most frequently given of all the Commands, we begin to notice it wherever we turn in our Bible reading. The specific words may vary, but it is the same charge. It is a call to *attentiveness* in all aspects of life—to pay attention, to consider implications and consequences, to keep the heart and brain awake and alert, to examine heart and motives, to be observant and shrewd, insightful and wise, vigilant in matters both internal and external, within oneself and in the world.

> We must avoid the dangers to which this world exposes us. As many as are the dangers...to which your position exposes you, so much the more should you beware of them. Such a state of awareness means turning more readily to God, keeping Him ever before one's eyes, withdrawing into oneself, bearing oneself with propriety in company, devoting oneself as far as is possible to solitude, the reading of good books and prayer and, as the Psalmist says, pouring out one's heart before God: finding Him within oneself, seeking after Him with eagerness, loving Him above all things and doing nothing to displease Him. So much virtue...is to be found in all walks of life.
>
> *Fénelon: The Letters of Fénelon*, letter of June 17, 1691, translated by John McEwen

God, bring to my remembrance this day the Command of Jesus to BE CAREFUL AND WATCHFUL. Remind me that being CAREFUL AND WATCHFUL in matters of faith is no mere option for the Lord's followers—it represents one of his most frequently given Commands. I <u>must</u> be CAREFUL AND WATCHFUL to keep my discipleship vigorous and growing. Keep my mind sharp and awake, attuned to spiritual dangers around me, aware of spiritual laziness within my own heart. Thus, heavenly Father, by my attentiveness, may I be an instrument in my small corner of the world for the ultimate salvation of mankind. Amen.

8. Remain Alert and On Guard

"Be careful lest the light in you be darkness...Beware of the leaven of...hypocrisy." (Luke 11:35; 12:1) "Be on the alert...be on the alert." (Matthew 24: 42; 25:13, NAS) "Take heed to yourselves." (Luke 17:3)

The Command to watchfulness has deep but often overlooked consequences. Counterfeits creep in to distract us when we let our spiritual guards down. The moment attentiveness wanes, our eyes drift off the bull's eye of God's purpose. We observe this pattern with the twelve. Every time they became distracted by peripheral concerns, Jesus brought them back to foundational priorities with one or another variation of, "You lost your focus…now pay attention."

Some read these Commands as urging preparedness for the Lord's second coming. This is indeed one context in which Jesus spoke, "Keep watch, for you know neither the day nor the hour." A fixation on such one-dimensional "preparedness," however, leads many to *obsess* on prophecy, poring over Scripture's details while missing its message, interpreting current events through a prophetic microscope yet overlooking the more personal attentiveness God desires. This is a counterfeit interpretation. Prophetic watchfulness, though it plays a role in spirituality, represents but a small aspect of a larger perspective.

Likewise, others feel called to exercise watchfulness in the political arena, keeping a "watch" on government so that rights are not infringed upon and spiritual values are not trampled. This represents another counterfeit to the true intent of the Commands. Jesus did not command us to beware of the leaven of Caesar, but of the Pharisees and Sadducees. He was not speaking of political or national watchfulness, but *spiritual* watchfulness. The true enemy lies closer at hand than ancient Rome or modern London and Washington D.C.

Jesus said, *Beware of the leaven of the Pharisees and Sadducees.* Luke adds the words, *which is hypocrisy.* (Luke 12:1) *This* is the leaven Jesus warns against. Hypocrisy always creeps in unseen. The hypocrite is blind to his own hypocrisy. To keep hypocrisy at bay requires constant self-examination and prayerful watchfulness. Prophetic obsession and political activity cannot deter hypocrisy. Indeed, they often invite it.

Hypocrisy is Satan's subtlest and most sinister tool to invalidate the Gospel. It does so by destroying my witness to the non-Christians who are watching me every day. They are watching *me.* They don't care about my politics or my prophetic outlook. They are watching to see if my *do* lines up with my *say.* When they don't, red lights go off and sirens blare: *Christianity is a sham.*

It is little wonder that Jesus commands spiritual watchfulness against the leaven of the Pharisees. The truth of the Gospel is at stake.

Jesus points to the same truth in Luke 11:35: *Be careful lest what you think is light within you is actually darkness.* This is the classic definition of spiritual blindness, thinking you are what you are not, thinking you know what you do not know, thinking you are spiritual when self-righteousness is festering within you, thinking you are full of light when your motives and attitudes are a breeding ground for seeds of hypocrisy.

Jesus encapsulates this pivotal requirement of attentive watchfulness in

Luke 17:3—*Take heed to yourselves.*

> The first requirement is that you must not look at the mirror and inspect the mirror but see yourself in the mirror…The witness of truth warns against the error of coming to inspect the mirror instead of to see oneself in the mirror…God's Word is the mirror. By reading or hearing it I shall see myself in the mirror.
> Soren Kierkegaard, *For Self-Examination*

God, bring to my remembrance this day the Command of Jesus to REMAIN ALERT AND ON GUARD. *Keep me diligently awake to the leaven of hypocrisy where the enemy tries to drive a wedge between my say and my do. Keep my eyes* ALERT AND ON GUARD *and focused on the bull's eye of your purpose. Remind me that the world is watching. May I be humbly worthy of being called a disciple of Jesus Christ. Thus, heavenly Father, may I be an instrument in my small corner of the world for the ultimate salvation of mankind. Amen.*

9. Take Heart, Take Courage

"Take heart, my son." (Matthew 9:2)
"Take heart, it is I; have no fear." (Mark 6:50)
"Take courage, I have overcome the world." (John 16:33, NAS)

Another group of the most frequently given but often overlooked Commands of Jesus might be summarized in many ways—bravery, stout-heartedness, courage, valor, fearlessness, boldness. They are here gathered together as two, which we consider as *Take heart, take courage*, and simply *Do not be afraid.*

Like the many exhortations to watchfulness and attentiveness, Jesus urges this group of related Commands upon his listeners more than two dozen times in the Gospels. He emphasizes courage, pluck, and fearlessness more often than any other single Command except watchfulness—more than any of the more seemingly "spiritual" Commands. Once again Jesus shatters our illusions of spirituality with down-to-earth practicality. These are Commands from *Jesus*, not suggestions from one's pastor.

What kind of courage and stout-heartedness is it that is commanded of you and me this day as we go out into the world as Christ's followers?

Is it courage to contend for truth, to speak up vocally against the secularism of our day?

Is it boldness to bear witness, telling others what we believe and why, then urging belief upon them?

Is it fearlessness to fight for Christian values in the social, cultural, and spiritual arenas?

Many of course feel that such is their calling. But a careful reading of the Gospels reveals without much doubt that Jesus was urging none of these upon his disciples with the words *Take heart, take courage.* No tough guy bravado, no brash boldness to get in people's faces, identifies the disciple of Jesus Christ with the uniqueness that will change the world. Rather it is an internal and deep personal boldness in the spiritual realm to stand, not against mortal enemies, but our invisible enemy. Jesus' words in John 16:33 are often translated, *Be of good cheer.* This charge presents no image of outspoken bravado, but of invisible fortitude, of inner strength of character—an outlook of optimism and valor.

Be strong of character. Take heart when the arrows of Satan attack you. Bravely gird up your loins and take heart to believe. Take courage to believe *truly* about God.

It takes courage to ask God to transform us into the image of his Son, and then to live in the reality of allowing him to answer that prayer. Anyone who thinks otherwise has never made the attempt and has no idea of the high personal cost involved. The prayer, *Make me like Jesus,* is a prayer reserved for the most courageous men and women on the planet.

What will change the world is the quiet, unassuming *courage of Christlikeness.*

> Good souls many will one day be horrified at the things they now believe of God. If they have not thought about them, but given themselves to obedience, they may not have done them much harm as yet; but they can make little progress in the knowledge of God, while, if but passively, holding evil things true of him. If, on the other hand, they do think about them, and find in them no obstruction, they must indeed be far from anything to be called a true knowledge of God. But there are those who find them a terrible obstruction, and yet imagine, or at least fear them true: such must take courage to forsake the false in *any* shape...and follow Jesus, not as he is presented in the tradition of the elders, but as he is presented by himself, his apostles, and the spirit of truth. There are "traditions of men" after Christ as well as before him.
>
> George MacDonald, *Unspoken Sermons, Second Series,* "Self Denial"

God, bring to my remembrance this day the Command of Jesus to TAKE HEART, TAKE COURAGE. *Give me the courage to pray to be Christlike, and to ask you to conform me to the image of your Son. Give me courage to be of good cheer in the midst of a hostile world. Banish my natural timidity and give me a stout heart to be your son, your daughter. Give me courage, not always outwardly but within my own heart, to stand against untruth, false priorities, temptations, and all the wiles of the enemy. Especially give me the courage to believe boldly. Thus, heavenly Father, by my courage of character, may I be an instrument in my small corner of the world for the ultimate salvation of mankind. Amen.*

10. Don't Be Afraid

"Why are you afraid, have you no faith?" (Mark 4:40)
"Do not be afraid." (Matthew 17:8, NAS)
"Do not fear, only believe." (Mark 5:36)

What more practical and revealing window exists into the human soul than *fear*? At root we are weak and timid creatures, full of many fears. Fear of death probably tops the list. It is a universal fear shared by our entire race. And individually we each harbor multitudes of our own private fears. All these Jesus sweeps away, saying, "Believe in me and you need fear *nothing*!"

Obviously it's easier said than done. Many of our fears are irrational. We are afraid of things that aren't there. We are afraid of the unknown. We are afraid of what we know to be illusions. We tell ourselves there is nothing to fear. We are afraid anyway. We can't help it.

Much of the fear that surrounded Jesus was the natural awe people in the first century felt simply being in his presence. It was the awe of the unknown. When the disciples were laboring on the Sea of Galilee, they were not nearly as afraid of the storm as to suddenly see Jesus walking toward them. Mark says, "But when they saw him walking on the sea, they…cried out…and were terrified." (Mark 6:49) Their fear had a simple explanation—they thought they were seeing a ghost. They didn't recognize him. *They didn't know who Jesus was.* Storms they understood. But not men who walked on water!

As simple as their fear is to explain, it has an equally simple remedy—*knowing* who Jesus is. On the night before his death, when telling the disciples of the tribulations that would come upon them, he ends with the words, "But be of good cheer. I have overcome the world." (John 16:33). In other words: Believe in who I am and you have nothing to fear.

Jesus doesn't just say, *Don't be afraid*, and leave it at that. He tells us how to obey the Command. Nearly always the Command against fear is linked in the Gospels with *faith* and *belief.* Faith is the antidote to fear. "Why are you afraid," he asks the disciples in Mark 4. "Have you no faith?" Thus we often hear Jesus speaking some variation of, *Do not fear, only believe.* Faith evaporates fear. The opposite of fear isn't unfear—the opposite of fear is *faith*! Believing in who Jesus is for *me*, for *you*, enables us to say to our fears, "Begone! Jesus is beside me and I know who he is. I *believe* in him!"

We might paraphrase what Jesus meant into this: *Have courage to believe in who I am, in what I represent, in the truth that I bring, in what I can be in your life. Don't cower or shrink back. Believe that I will do my very best for you. Do not fear...only believe.*

It is *hard* to exercise faith in the presence of our human fears. The Command, *Don't be afraid,* while seemingly one of the simplest, is also one of the most difficult.

> Even more easily than they believed the first lie, Adam and Eve swallowed the second...They abandoned childness...They attempted to hide from God, cowering in this newfound sensation called fear. Foolish children! Did you truly sin? Then perhaps your Father will have to punish you in order to train you. But He is still your Father...There is but one course open to you.
>
> Run *to* Him, not away from Him!...He is your refuge against these lies...Throw yourselves into the embrace of your Father! Tearfully confess to Him your foolishness. Step back again into the childness in which you were created to live. *Become again His children!*...But none of this was to be. The lie of fear had gained a foothold...And that lie that our Father is to be feared persists today, still poisoning our capacity to correctly discern God's Fatherhood, preventing us from looking into His face, barring the way to intimacy.
>
> Michael Phillips, *God, A Good Father,* "The Second Lie of Genesis 3"

God, bring to my remembrance this day the Command of Jesus DON'T BE AFRAID. *All around me are potential fears—real and imaginary. In your presence I can look my fears squarely in the eye. When you come walking on the water, may I embrace your presence amid my fears, and believe in you. Give me faith to not fear. Remind me of David's words, Even though I walk through the valley of death, I will fear no evil. I do believe, Lord, but help my human unbelief. I am so small, and yes, I am sometimes afraid. I know that you do not mind my being small and timid, only you want me to believe. Help me in my fears, to not fear. Thus, heavenly Father, may I be an instrument in my small corner of the world for the ultimate salvation of mankind. Amen.*

Series Two

"The James Commands"

Purity

The Distinguishing Mark of God's Kingdom

James and John, sons of Zebedee and Salome of Galilee, were, with Peter, the three disciples closest to Jesus. We would call them the "inner circle." It was these three who were often present with Jesus, even singled out by him to share in momentous events—the raising of Jairus' daughter (Mark 5:37), the transfiguration (Mark 9:2), even to accompany him into the innermost depths of Gethsemane (Mark 14:33).

The family of Zebedee was reasonably prosperous and owned a fishing business that employed several hired hands. They may have been in partnership with Peter and Andrew as well. In all likelihood, Salome was the sister of Mary of Nazareth, making James, John, and Jesus cousins. The close friendship and spiritual affiliation was a natural outgrowth of a lifetime's acquaintance.

James had to learn purity and humility the hard way.

Whether or not they inherited the nickname from their father's fiery disposition, Jesus called James and John the "Sons of Thunder." Apparently they possessed the temper and zeal to match the epithet. When a village in Samaria did not receive them, the two brothers were ready to call down upon it fire from heaven. Perhaps their economic status in the community had infected the family with a pride of position, for in Mark 10:35, spurred on by their mother, James and John went to Jesus to request that they be given the most exalted positions in his kingdom.

Yet Jesus loved his two cousins. He felt closer to them, as *friends*, during his life on earth than any others besides Peter and his parents. Though purity, humility, and selflessness did not come easily to these two brothers, Jesus *believed* in them.

John became the Apostle of Love. And James was indeed granted his wish to be the most exalted of the disciples, and to drink the same cup as his Lord and Master.

"Are you able to drink the cup that I drink, or to be baptized with the baptism with which I am baptized?" And they said to him, "We are able." And Jesus said to them, "The cup that I drink you will drink; and with the baptism with which I am baptized you will be baptized...for the Son of man also came not to be served but to serve, and to give his live as a ransom for many." (Mark 10: 38-39, 45)

James was exalted by being the first of the Twelve to be martyred for his faith, a singular honor in the kingdom. He was murdered by King Herod Agrippa I around the year 44 A.D. He was thus the first of the apostles to enter into the fullness of the purity to which he was called.

About that time Herod the king laid violent hands upon some who belonged to the church. He killed James the brother of John with the sword. (Acts 12:1-2)

καθαρός: KATHAROS—*Pure*

Three words in the New Testament are translated "pure." αγνος (HAGNOS) means pure and uncontaminated from any defilement and derives from the same root (HAGIOS) as the word "holy." ειλικρινης (EILIKRINES) was used of unalloyed, unmixed "pure" substances. It is usually used in the New Testament of ethical and moral purity. καθαρός (KATHAROS), however, the word Jesus employed in Matthew 5:8—"Blessed are the pure in heart"—was used for those who have been cleansed and thus have *become* pure. James was willing to have his ambition and temperament cleansed and *made* pure and holy by Jesus, and no longer contaminated by selfish ambition and pride.

Purity is the distinguishing mark of God's kingdom.

Series Two

The Distinguishing Mark of God's Kingdom

11. Be pure.
12. Guard against ambition.
13. Commit no sexual sins.
14. Be patient, enduring, persevering.
15. Repent.
16. Listen.
17. Listen Carefully.
18. Be clear-minded, thoughtful, mentally diligent.
19. Apply yourself to think, learn, understand.
20. Think no impure thought.

11. Be Pure

"Blessed are the pure in heart, for they shall see God." (Matthew 5:8)

Many Christians long for the heavenly day when they will meet Jesus and his Father face to face, when they will actually *see* them. Perhaps the Lord's words in the Beatitudes, however, were not intended as a promise of *future* intimacy, but a recognition of *present* vision.

Might we more deeply apprehend Jesus' meaning, and take the liberty of temporarily adding a single word to the text: Blessed are the pure in heart, for they shall see *like* God? Only purity produces God-like vision. Only the pure in heart are capable of perceiving life and the world and the people around them as God perceives them. Purity gives God-eyes. And only God-eyes, vision pure as God's vision is pure, makes it possible to see God as he truly is.

Seeing *like* God enables us to see God *himself.*

Purity in all aspects of life, therefore—in attitude *and* behavior—has monstrous consequences for the Christian. The hidden sin, sketchy business deal, flirtatious glance, or off-color comment...the semi-truth, the fudging of an application, the stretching of accuracy, the exaggeration to put oneself in a favorable light...a lust indulged, a suggestive laugh, an ethical boundary pushed to the limit, a whispered curse, an immodest neckline...the grudge nursed, the lurking unforgiveness, the outburst of temper, the inattention to influences of unedifying music and film, the justified untruth—mostly unseen by any other human eye...these all build up like scales over spiritual eyesight, dulling true vision, preventing the development of God-eyes.

Yet how easily even Christians justify such violations of purity, thinking their impact negligible on character. How much more lethal to vision capable of seeing God are the gross sins against purity: Lying, cheating, sexual promiscuity, lewdness, and the many moral sins now normalized by our culture. We live in an era that is quick to excuse even these sins of the flesh. But for the Christian who wants to see like God, and thus see God, there is no justification. *All* impurity dulls and blurs the vision—from the dirty joke to the clandestine affair.

Nor must we forget that Jesus condemns impurity of mind, motive, and heart no less than the impurity that leads to visible sin. Impure motives produce what the New Testament's other James (brother of Jesus) calls "a double-minded man"—one who isn't yet quite sure whether he *wants* to obey the Commands of Jesus in all things. *Impurity of motive*—a sort of halfway house of discipleship, where one is able to keep all options on the table in the event selfishness or loose ethics or moral slippage become expedient—will never produce Christlikeness nor reveal the Father of Jesus to the world.

We all come into this life as innocent, spotless babes not only of our earthly parents, but children of the God in whose mind and heart we were created to be the individuals we are. Over the years, the sin of life and the world, and the sin of our own wavering motives of self, corrupts the purity into which we were born. Jesus calls us to become again the children of purity we once were, and to live as his pure-seeing sons and daughters.

Scarce wonder that Jesus says that we must become as children to enter the kingdom. Purity is the heart orientation and spiritual outlook of the childlike.

> I choose to look at people through God, using God as my glasses, colored with His love for them.
>
> Frank Laubauch, *Letters By A Modern Mystic,* Sept 28, 1931

God, bring to my remembrance this day the Command of Jesus to BE PURE. Remind me that by PURITY is my spiritual eyesight developed to see like God, and thus to see God as he is. Keep me from the distraction of the eternal, thinking that in some distant day I will see God. Remind me that by being PURE now, I am enabled to see God and see like him in the now of my moment-by-moment life. Thus, heavenly Father, by the way I live visibly distinct from the world's values, may I be an instrument in my small corner of the world for the ultimate salvation of mankind. Amen.

12. Guard Against Ambition

"You know that those who are supposed to rule over the Gentiles lord it over them, and their great men exercise authority over them. But it shall not be so among you; but whoever would be great among you must be your servant, and whoever would be first among you must be slave of all." (Mark 10:42-44)

We all face personally unique challenges to purity of motive, outlook, attitude, and behavior. For some, sexual purity is life's most difficult arena of temptation. Others are scarcely lured by sexual sin. But deep inside, every one of us has something the enemy will try to use—subtly, invisibly, persuasively, seductively, below the radar of our awareness—to turn our eyes off the bull's eye of the Commands.

Our greatest challenge as Christians is to discover with discerning eyes what is that personal "something" working 24/7 to keep us seeing with self-eyes instead of God-eyes. Where are the hidden corners of impure motive within my heart and mind and soul? To answer that question is life's most significant challenge.

The internal quest is illusive and lifelong. The serious disciple is never allowed to coast. It is too costly a luxury. Even as the illuminating light of the Holy Spirit leads into an awareness of some particular impure motive which must be submitted to the Not my will altar of relinquishment, another will have begun to operate unseen in some other region of the soul. The enemy's tactics are devious, slippery, and remain invisible without the most determined scrutiny. Ambition infiltrates motive in the last place we are looking for it.

We noted earlier that the Apostle James had to learn purity the hard way. The besetting impurity of motive that ensnared him and his brother John was ambition. They wanted to rise high. They wanted to be above the rest of mortal humanity.

Ambition snuck up where they least expected it—in their friendship with Jesus. That's why they never saw it coming. They were Jesus' cousins. They were, with Peter, among his closest friends. They were the first among the disciples. The request they made no doubt seemed perfectly fitting and natural. Thus the subtle impurity of motive crept in—the desire to rule, to occupy a higher status, to be recognized as more important than their fellows.

Ambition is one of the most difficult motives to assess. It is not, in itself, a sin as is lying or adultery. Properly focused and humbly executed, God uses ambition to accomplish his purposes. Ambitious men and women have been at the forefront of God's work throughout history. Paul was a supremely ambitious man. Accomplishment and achievement are essentially good things. Hard work and vision are expected of us, and are rewarded. The parable of the talents, in one sense, is the story of two men—one with God-focused ambition, and the other who was too lazy to have any ambition at all.

Thus, the Command is not "Don't be ambitious"...but Guard against ambition. Watch your motives. Make sure your ambition is that of the servant who makes good use of his talents, not the selfish ambition of James and John. Is your ambition to accomplish for God and for others and to be a good steward over what you have been given? Or is it to rise high, to be above, to accumulate, to be great, to be praised, and to rule?

It shall not be so among you...whoever would be great among you must be your servant.

Some people spend their time dreaming of greatness, envisioning theaters full of people applauding them, imagining themselves giving engaging speeches, fantasizing about having great wealth. All of this is nothing but the fumes of pride, exposing their heart's true wishes.

Jeremy Taylor, *The Rules and Exercises of Holy Living* (From *Devotional Classics,*

p. 271)

God, bring to my remembrance this day the Command of Jesus to GUARD AGAINST AMBITION. Open my eyes to the devious attempts of the enemy to lull me to sleep and infect me with impure motive. Keep my mind and heart awake to the hidden corners of pride lurking in the shadows of my being. Shine your light upon them. Give me the will to place them on the altar to be burned by your consuming fire that will one day burn all sin from the universe. Burn my motives with the purifying fire of your refiner's furnace, that I might be pure in all ways as you are pure. Thus, heavenly Father, may I be an instrument in my small corner of the world for the ultimate salvation of mankind. Amen.

13. Commit No Sexual Sins

"You shall not commit adultery." (Matthew 19:18, NAS)
'Everyone who divorces his wife and marries another commits adultery." (Luke 16:18, NAS)
"Whoever marries a divorced woman commits adultery." (Matthew 5:32, NAS)

Surely the Command against sexual sin is one of the most straightforward in the Gospels.

To love, forgive, return good for evil—these are high things, not always easy to know how to obey. But sexual sin is unambiguous. To put it in contemporary terms, sexual sin is binary. There are only two options—sin or not sin…commit adultery or don't commit adultery…sex outside marriage or no sex outside marriage…marry for life or don't marry for life. No parallel exists with ambition, which has a Godly side and a dark side. There is *no* positive side to adultery. ALL adultery under ALL circumstances is a sin in God's eyes. There are no exceptions. The same is true of ALL sexual sin and every form of sexual perversion. They are *sins*. There is no middle ground.

Some of the Commands of Jesus are vague. This one is not. It is black and white. We either obey it, or we don't. We *choose* to obey it or not. No one accidentally sins the sins of the flesh. A moment comes when sin is willfully chosen. That being the case, this is also a Command that can be obeyed to perfection. Such can be said about very few of the Lord's Commands. But it is possible to *perfectly* avoid all sexual sins and unscriptural sexual activity.

Of course there are many defenses offered to justify wiggling out of the exactitude of the Command. It is not difficult to find a plausible excuse why, in *this* circumstance or that, adultery or divorce or sex outside marriage aren't *really* "sins" but "lifestyle choices."

But the facts are set down on the pages of the Gospel in black and white. We can pretend. But we can't hide.

The stark reality is that our disobedience has consequences. In the midst of its rampant sexual laxity, were the world to observe the church of Jesus Christ boasting a 0% rate of sex before marriage, a 0% promiscuity rate outside Christian marriage, and a 1%-2% Christian divorce rate to account for legitimate causes of divorce...people would stand up and take notice. But this is *not* what the world observes. It observes rates scarcely lower than those of society at large.

What, then, is the observable difference, in social and sexual morality, between Christianity and the world's culture? On what basis can we claim to be following a distinctive lifestyle? On what basis can we claim discipleship to One who said that sexual sin, adultery, and divorce were abominations to God? We can hardly expect the world to listen to the Gospel when as a church we so flagrantly and visibly trample this clear Command of Jesus underfoot before a watching world.

"If you love me, you will keep my Commands...by *this* will all men know that you are my disciples—*commit no sexual sins.*"

> Chastity is the most unpopular of the Christian virtues. There is no getting away from it: the old Christian rule is, "Either marriage, with complete faithfulness to your partner, or else total abstinence." Now this is so difficult and so contrary to our instincts, that obviously either Christianity is wrong or our sexual instinct, as it now is, has gone wrong. One or the other. Of course, being a Christian, I think it is the instinct which has gone wrong.
>
> C.S. Lewis, Mere Christianity, "Sexual Morality"

God, when moral slippage lures my soul, bring to my remembrance the Command of Jesus to COMMIT NO SEXUAL SINS. Keep me from temptation, but more importantly fill me with the will to resist it and walk in purity. You are watching because you are with me every moment. May I be worthy to be called your disciple. Keep me from false justification or excuse in ethical and sexual matters. Protect me from temptation to impure thoughts, motives, and actions. Give me the will to fight the world's immorality and sexual laxity with the determination of a warrior in battle. Thus, heavenly Father, may I be an instrument in my small corner of the world for the ultimate salvation of mankind. Amen.

14. Be Patient, Enduring, Persevering

"He who endures to the end will be saved." (Matthew 10:22)

When Paul enumerates the characteristics of love in 1 Corinthians 13, the familiarity of his words obscures what an astonishing attribute he begins with: Love is *patient.*

When we stop to consider it, this is truly a remarkable thing. Patience is so…mundane, so unspiritual, so down-to-earth. It takes no heightened wisdom or maturity or spiritual insight to be patient. Atheists and heathens can be patient just as well as Christians. And yet Paul considers it *first* among the virtues of love.

Consider further. If God's essence is LOVE, and if patience is the first of love's attributes, it follows that one of God's first characteristics must also be patience. When we exercise patience, we are reflecting the very nature of God!

It takes but a moment to see what a huge and wonderful truth this is. God did not create the world in a moment. He took his time about it…aeons of creating "days." He was in no rush to deliver the Israelites from their bondage. People died during those 400 years. But God's purposes span centuries, even millennia. The world needed redeeming no less in the days of Noah than in the first century. But God waited thousands of years before sending his Son.

His purposes are never rushed. God is never in a hurry.

Thus when Jesus commands patience, he is commanding nothing more nor less than for us to be like God, to *wait* with a graceful heart…to cheerfully *endure* suffering, heartache, pain, grief, disappointment…to *persevere* under hardship.

The impatience of modern Christendom must be heartbreaking to God. Everywhere there is rush, hurry, and freneticism. We are in a hurry for our prayers to be answered, in a hurry to do and become all we want to do and be, in a hurry to serve God, in a hurry to save the world. We are impatient in traffic, frustrated in lines, importune in conversation, demanding in business, more intent to be heard than to listen…eager, interrupting, pushy, vocal, hasty, impulsive, insistent.

Yet in every such instance in which we express frustration or impatience, when our impatience is noticed perhaps even by one we don't know or have no idea is watching, we are proclaiming to the world: I am not reflecting the character of God. Therefore, I must not be a disciple of Jesus Christ.

Slow down. Be calm. Relax. Wait. Take the eternal perspective. Display God's nature to the world.

"By *this* will all men know that you are my disciples, if you keep my Commands. God is patient. If you would be my disciple, therefore, be patient, enduring, persevering."

Love is *Patience.* This is the normal attitude of Love; Love passive, Love waiting to begin; not in a hurry; calm; ready to do its work when the summons comes, but meantime wearing the ornament of a meek and quiet spirit. Love suffers long;

beareth all things; believeth all things; hopeth all things. For Love understands, and therefore waits.

Henry Drummond, *The Greatest Thing in the World*

God, bring to my remembrance this day the Command of Jesus to BE PATIENT, ENDURING, PERSEVERING. Help me, Lord, to go slow—to realize that the grace to wait, as Drummond says is "the ornament of a meek and quiet spirit." Help me not merely to exercise patience, but to be a person of ENDURING, PERSEVERING PATIENCE. When hardship, suffering, confusion, frustration, and pressure come to my life, give me grace to endure and to persevere with a smile. May patience, and the graciousness and calm that accompanies it, become an adornment of character that those around me visibly observe in my outlook and demeanor. Thus, heavenly Father, by my patient and unhurried demeanor, may I be an instrument in my small corner of the world for the ultimate salvation of mankind. Amen.

15. Repent

"The time is fulfilled, and the kingdom of God is at hand; repent, and believe in the Gospel." (Mark 1:15)

The Gospel does not come to us one-dimensionally. The teachings of Jesus, while epitomizing simplicity itself, are also intriguingly complex. The intertwining mix of "spiritual" and "temporal" Commands is constantly in play. The moment we get too spiritual, Jesus hits us with the parable of the Good Samaritan, urging us simply to be good and take care of people. Not a word in the story about getting the man saved or taking him to church…just *Go and do the same.* Yet the moment we begin thinking that kindness toward our fellow man is enough, there is Jesus telling Nicodemus he must be "born again."

This highlights the fact that the Lord's teachings primarily comprise a *spiritual* gospel. Jesus came to inaugurate, not mere goodness or caring for humanity's needs, but a deeply *spiritual* enterprise. Its foundation was a reordering of outlook based on a revolutionary new relationship between man and his Creator, the God whom Jesus called his Father and our Father. It is only after that spiritual foundation is in place that the temporal Commands toward kindness and goodness are drawn up into the grand whole of the Gospel.

That spiritual reordering begins with the recognition that we are *not* kind and good. We are independently minded beings intent on doing things our own way. Worse, we have alienated ourselves from our Creator. Each of us contributes our own share to humanity's universal pride. God gave us life. We have not reciprocated by being his obedient children.

Obedience to the Commands of Jesus thus begins at the point of our independence, our alienation, our rebellion, our self-centeredness, the wrong-going of our natures. It is called sin. In its simplest terms, sin is often defined as "separation from God." It is separation from God and his ways that produces the actions, attitudes, and behavior of *sin* in our lives. Modernism may cringe at the terminology, but we are *sinners* every one.

For that reason Jesus began his ministry on earth with a single, pointed, stark, glaring, and unambiguous Command. It is found in his first eighteen word, four-point sermon in Mark 1:15. It is the one-word Command: *Repent.*

Repentance is the point where a lifetime of obedience to the Commands begins. Repentance is defined in various ways. Literally the word means "change," first of mind, then of direction, to "turn around" and begin moving on a new course. It begins with a recognition of what we are—that we are not what we could be, not the kind of people we are *supposed* to be. Jesus then quickly adds the solution to the dilemma of our wrong-going. Turn around from your sin and...*Follow me.* It is an ongoing, moment-by-moment, two-phase programme for the healing and making right of the human soul: *Repent* and *Follow.*

> Let me say something concerning the word here and everywhere translated repentance...The Greek word...is made up of two words, the conjoint meaning of which is, a change of mind or thought. There is in it no intent of, or hint at sorrow or shame...it is a sending away of sins...Both God and man send away sins, but in the one case God sends away the sins of the man, and in the other the man sends away his own sins...The change must be one of will and conduct—a radical change of life on the part of the man: he must repent—that is, change his mind—not to a different opinion, not even to a mere betterment of his conduct—not to anything less than a sending away of his sins...Some of us...who have already repented, who have long ago begun to send away our sins, need fresh repentance every day...We are so ready to get upon some path that seems to run parallel with the narrow way, and then take no note of its divergence! What is there for us when we discover that we are out of the way, but to bethink ourselves and turn?
>
> George MacDonald, *The Hope of the Gospel,* "The Remission of Sins"

God, bring to my remembrance this day the Command of Jesus to REPENT. *Protect me from the fatal snare of independence, the notion that I am sufficient in myself. I* REPENT *for what I am and for what I do. I recognize that repentance is no one-time act but an ongoing life-outlook. I am weak. My responses so easily become selfish. Over and over, I must ask you to reorient me toward your outlook. Help me always to follow Jesus after repentance, follow him in obedience, that I might be his disciple, and your child. Thus, heavenly Father, may I be an instrument in my small corner of the world for the ultimate salvation of mankind. Amen.*

16. Listen

It is now time to consider the third most frequently given group of Commands that Jesus gave behind Watchfulness and Courage which were considered earlier. That is a group of related exhortations that might be summed up as: *Listen with understanding and discerning insight.* These we will consider as four related Commands: *Listen, Listen carefully, Be clear-minded, thoughtful, mentally diligent,* and *Apply yourself to think, learn, understand.*

Jesus tells his hearers to listen in several ways. The first is simply: *Listen.*

Essentially he is saying, "Close your mouth and hear what I have to say." Later he will add the above admonitions toward careful and attentive listening. But the first Command is just to listen.

Why is listening in itself so imperative to a growing Christian life? Because of the natural human tendency to blab first and ask questions later. Whenever we're confronted with a new idea, a new experience, a new insight, we immediately start talking about it. Yet this is probably the time we should *not* be talking, but rather quietly trying to absorb what this new truth has to teach us in the depths of our beings. Reflection, not endless prattle, is the mark of a heart learning and growing in wisdom.

Christians *talk* far more than they listen. How much foolishness has been spread abroad in the church by the teachings and proclamations and prophecies of the spiritually immature? The first thing a new Christian does is begin proclaiming everything that comes into his head about his new faith to anyone who will listen. A newly married couple begins immediately teaching classes on marriage. Who are the most vocal in nearly any Bible study or discussion group? Usually the most immature.

But it's all backwards. The *first* thing, according to Jesus, is to listen. The wise man and woman know that wisdom comes, not from spouting off with opinions at the drop of a hat...but from a quiet and listening spirit.

The Proverbs echo this imperative over and over. James commands: *Be quick to hear, slow to speak* (1:19). How does Paul indicate that faith is grown in us? *Faith comes from hearing, and hearing from the Word of God.* (Romans 10:17)

The wisdom of Christlikeness is grown in us by attentively absorbing the Lord's teachings and putting them into practice. We must *absorb* and *receive* truth before attempting to proclaim it.

When...we learn to listen, our lives become obedient lives. The word *obedient* comes from the Latin word *audire,* which means "listening." A spiritual discipline is necessary in order to move slowly from an absurd to an obedient life, from a life filled with noisy worries to a life in which there is some free inner space where we can listen to our God and follow his guidance.

Jesus' life was a life of obedience. He was always listening to the Father, always attentive to his voice, always alert for his directions. Jesus was "all ear." That is true prayer; being all ear for God. The core of all prayer is indeed listening, obediently standing in the presence of God.

Henri J. M. Nouwen, *Making All Things New* (From *Devotional Classics,* Richard Foster, ed., p. 95)

God, bring to my remembrance this day the Command of Jesus to LISTEN. In the fullest and deepest sense, give me ears to hear, and then to hear what you want me to hear. Give me not only listening ears and an understanding mind, give me a listening and hearing heart. Remind me that wisdom is slow to speak. Above all things I desire to know your heart that I might hear your gentle breathings into my life. Keep me from the lethal desire to speak all I think I know. Make me an absorber of truth first of all, that my faith may grow by hearing. Thus, heavenly Father, by the example of my quiet and listening spirit, may I be an instrument in my small corner of the world for the ultimate salvation of mankind. Amen.

17. Listen Carefully

"He who has ears to hear, let him hear." (Mark 4:3, 9)
"Take heed then how you hear." (Luke 8:18)
"Consider carefully how you listen." (Luke 8:18, NIV)

There may be those who wonder when reading some of the Commands: *When did Jesus ever say that? I don't remember reading those words in the New Testament.*

We are trying to read the Gospels implicationally, for the big picture, for the spirit not the letter. We are trying to discover what Jesus *meant,* what he expected from his listeners, from his disciples, and from us. We have to dig beneath the surface to find his *implied* Commands as well as his direct Commands.

Why are we so highly emphasizing such a broad range of "listening" and "understanding" Commands? Because they all point to a single mindset, an outlook, a perspective that Jesus wants in his followers—a mindset of mental diligence, of paying attention, of being willing to work hard to understand what he says rather than merely examining the surface of spiritual truth.

In Mark 7, Jesus contrasts the so-called spirituality of the Pharisees, with their love of externals—washing pots and bowls and scrupulously keeping the rituals of their tradition—with *true* spirituality. It is the contrast between the surface and the depths. He is speaking about an outlook of mental diligence at the deep levels, of taking care how we listen and hear and understand. The Pharisees were surface listeners. Their seeming spirituality was completely superficial. Jesus regularly contrasted such external and legalistic spirituality with *deep and understanding* spirituality. Thus he constantly reminded his disciples to listen intently and carefully, and to work to *understand.*

Dare we take these exhortations lightly because they do not address such high concerns as worship, holiness, prayer, salvation? Is *listening carefully* really more important than worship?

According to the emphasis Jesus placed upon it, surprisingly the answer may be yes.

These exhortations in one sense lie at the core of all spirituality—they define how one approaches life with God and one's entire outlook on truth. Our worship and prayer, our seeking after righteousness, our very salvation itself, are all defined, given meaning, and lifted into the presence of God by how we *listen* to him, how we hear him, and whether we *understand* him aright.

In dozens of ways Jesus thus exhorted his disciples—*Be clear minded, think with care. Come on, guys—listen and understand!*

> Often overlooked in the Gospels is the frequency with which Jesus exhorts his disciples and listeners (more than mere "exhortation," indeed, *commanding* it of them) with some form of: *Listen, listen carefully, be clear-minded, apply yourself to think, learn, and understand...* Jesus knew that his disciples had to learn to *think* with clarity and wisdom. His oft-used "Behold" indicates far more than seeing with the eyes but always implies "inner vision"—look earnestly, contemplate, regard, perceive, observe, understand, apprehend. Passive, unthinking, unperceiving, lazy non-thinking discipleship does not exist in the New Testament. Thus the clear frustration with his disciples evident in Jesus' tone in Matthew 16: "Do you not yet νοεω (perceive)? How is it that you fail to νοεω (perceive)? He *expected* them to think. Wise thinking was part of the package.
>
> Michael Phillips, *Bold Thinking Christianity*, Chapter 2

God, bring to my remembrance this day the Command of Jesus to LISTEN CAREFULLY. Grow within me the qualities of a careful and attentive listener. May I also LISTEN CAREFULLY to the needs and concerns of those around me. Make me a CAREFUL LISTENER, to all the wondrous whispers of life—from your Spirit, from the heart of humanity, and from the glories of your creation. Thus, heavenly Father, may I be an instrument in my small corner of the world for the ultimate salvation of mankind. Amen.

18. Be Clear-minded, Thoughtful, Mentally Diligent

"Hear and understand." (Matthew 15:10)
"Hear me, all of you, and understand." (Mark 7:14)
"Listen to me, everyone, and understand." (Mark 7:14, NIV)

Ours is a lethally superficial age. In an era of superhuman technological achievement, the facility to *think* judiciously is on the endangered skills list. Our computerized culture has rendered us dependent on machines to do our thinking for us. All the data anyone could ever want is instantly accessible. No need to engage the mind to figure things out, weigh ideas, and arrive at conclusions. Raw knowledge has replaced introspection. Our culture has made a god of this tidal wave of information. People don't even *try* to think anymore. They don't have to. We are losing our little gray cells from atrophy.

We don't recognize the trap for what it is. The onslaught of information and technology breeds a subtle masquerade of intellectualism. Everyone thinks we are becoming smarter when actually the reality is precisely the opposite.

The result is extreme, and invisibly ruinous to Christianity's witness. Behind a facade of prosperity and political clout, Christians, too, have lost the Gospel imperative to *think*. Add water and you don't even have to stir. Just consult the formula. *Christianity Lite.*

The mindset caused by modernity's worship of knowledge, formula, easy answers, and add-water-and-stir religion has created a generation of Christians content to accept what they are told with the same mentality they bring to their computers—mindlessly absorbing input from others without considering where *truth* is represented and where it is not. Spirituality is no longer viewed as an energetic life of *growth* of heart and mind.

We have changed Jesus' words to the synagogue ruler in Mark 5 from, "Don't fear, only believe," to, *Don't think...only believe.*

In the midst of this drift toward mental laziness in our culture, what do we make of Jesus' repeated exhortations to *Listen carefully*, *Take heed how you hear*, and *Hear and understand?* In a computer age, do they no longer apply to us?

The world recognizes this atrophy of intellectual muscle, even if we do not. The world is full of intelligent people, gifted people, knowledgeable people. The world even contains a surprising number of compassionate people. But the desperate need of our time is for *deep* people. The world is hungry for vitality and reality. It wants to see spirituality harmonized with life. The world is hungry for *real* people, *changed* people, *thinking* people.

In his Commands, Jesus offers us the handbook by which such people live. One of the foundation stones of such an energetically thinking walk with God is his implied Command: *Be clear-minded, thoughtful, mentally diligent.*

> "Bold thinking Christianity" brings to daily faith a vigorous courage to search for spiritual truth, and to probe the depths of God's purpose, outside the box of learned dogma, cliché, and doctrinal formula. The bold thinking Christian…does not live by pat answers or proof-texts but by practical reality that engages heart and brain in a harmony of obedience to the instructions of Jesus. The desire of the bold thinking Christian is not to devise an intellectual framework by which to analyze God and man, but to prayerfully probe the Scriptures and the mind of God himself in order that his nature, character, and eternal purposes are more clearly illuminated. Such a bold thinking disciple will thus be enabled to understand, obey, and fall in with God's purpose in a more dynamic and practical way.
>
> Michael Phillips, *Bold Thinking Christianity,* Chapter 4

God, bring to my remembrance this day the Command of Jesus to BE CLEAR MINDED, THOUGHTFUL, AND MENTALLY DILIGENT. Help me resist the cultural pressure for computers, pastors, and books to do my thinking for me. Rescue me from the drift toward mental sloth. Awake in me the desire to be a thinking disciple of Jesus whose brain is awake and focused. Stimulate me this day to mental action. Prick my brain with disquieting barbs when I need to think with greater acumen about some aspect of my faith. Thus, heavenly Father, by the example of my mental diligence, may I be an instrument in my small corner of the world for the ultimate salvation of mankind. Amen.

19. Apply Yourself to Think, Learn, Understand

"Do you not understand this parable?
How then will you understand all the parables?" (Mark 4:13)
"Understand what I say." (John 8:43)
"Are you so lacking in understanding?" (Mark 7:18, NAS)

One of the fascinating exchanges in the New Testament is recounted in the eighth chapter of Mark's gospel. In it we get a picture of Jesus' frustration with the disciples for not applying themselves to understand. To grasp it, we have to remember the storm at sea that took place after the feeding of the five thousand. Matthew's version, written after twenty or thirty years when the halo mentality surrounding the disciples had set in, reads:

"When the disciples saw him walking on the sea, they were terrified, saying, 'It is a ghost!' And they cried out for fear...And when they got into the boat, the wind ceased. And those in the boat worshipped him, saying, 'Truly you are the Son of God.'" (Matthew 14:26-33)

Mark, however, writing closer in time to the event and seen through Peter's more realistic eyes, tells the story differently. Here the disciples are terrified, confused, and clueless.

"When they saw him walking on the sea they thought it was a ghost, and cried out; for they all saw him and were terrified...And he got into the boat with them and the wind ceased. And they were utterly astounded, for they did not understand about the loaves, but their hearts were hardened." (Mark 6:49-52)

Matthew portrays a company of worshiping disciples who completely understand the divinity of Jesus. Mark tells the tale of a band of dull-witted fishermen with unwilling minds and hard hearts.

A short time later, after more teaching, several more miracles, and again out on the lake, the disciples' preoccupation with externals and unimportant peripherals finally results in a blistering rebuke. *Watch out,* Jesus says. *Why do you discuss having no bread...don't you see, don't you understand? Are your hearts hardened? Don't you hear...don't you remember? DO YOU NOT YET UNDERSTAND?*

How else can we read these words but that Jesus is utterly exasperated, wondering what could be done with this motley crew? The disciples *should* understand. But they had not *applied themselves to understand.* They were not *thinking.* They had not *learned* what they should have learned.

Jesus expects us as his followers to learn this lesson of the disciples' mental laziness. A deep and true understanding of Scripture cannot be gained by cliché, nor by being spoon-fed doctrines of tradition. As it was for the disciples in the first century, some of the doctrines we have been taught may be wrong. We have to apply ourselves individually to *think, learn, and understand* truth as God intends us to understand it.

> Many Christians have the idea that, provided you are "good," it does not matter being a fool. But...Christ never meant that we were to remain children in intelligence...He wants a child's heart, but a grown-up's head. He wants us to be simple, single-minded, affectionate, and teachable, as good children are; but He also wants every bit of intelligence we have to be alert at its job, and in first-class fighting trim.
>
> C.S. Lewis, *Mere Christianity*, "The 'Cardinal Virtues'"

God, bring to my remembrance this day the Command of Jesus to APPLY MYSELF TO THINK, LEARN, AND UNDERSTAND. *Wake me from mental lethargy about my faith. Do not let me be satisfied with learned jargon and rote explanations of your ways that do not square with your Fatherhood as Jesus taught us of you. As Jesus challenged his disciples to think so that they would recognize him for who he was, stimulate my thoughts and prayers to THINK, LEARN, AND UNDERSTAND so that I will know you as the true Father of Jesus Christ. Thus, heavenly Father, may I be an instrument in my small corner of the world for the ultimate salvation of mankind. Amen.*

20. Think No Impure Thought

"You have heard that it was said to the men of old, 'You shall not kill…' But I say to you that every one who is angry with his brother shall be liable to judgment…
You have heard that it was said, 'You shall not commit adultery.' But I say to you that every one who looks at a woman lustfully has already committed adultery with her in his heart."
(Matthew 5:21-22; 27-28)

The Sermon on the Mount is astonishing on many levels. In three succinct chapters, Jesus outlined a revolutionarily new morality which was henceforth intended to visibly characterize the life lived and the attitudes held by those who would call themselves his followers.

Among his most shocking statements must surely be the verses found in Matthew 5:22 and 5:28 in which Jesus seems to say that to *think* a sin is to commit the sin.

Obviously it is not as bad to lust as to actually engage in sex outside marriage, nor is anger to be equated with murder. A careful reading shows that Jesus did not intend to draw an exact parallel between the thought and the deed. But Jesus often speaks with a certain degree of hyperbole to get his point across. The verse concerning lust is followed immediately by the passage telling us to pluck out the eye and cut off the hand that leads us into sin.

Jesus used such emphatic language to leave no mistake in our minds about what his teaching entails. He is calling his followers to a revolutionary lifestyle—where thoughts and attitudes, priorities and motives, are no less scrutinized by the illumination of the Holy Spirit's lantern of truth than actions. He is deadly serious about the kind of outlook and behavior that will change the world. No mediocre goodness will do. Jesus wants us to understand the level of commitment required by this new lifestyle which we now call Christianity. He doesn't even want us *thinking* impure thoughts.

Realistically none of us can ever measure up to this standard. We will never attain to the perfection to which Jesus points in the last verse of this same chapter. However, this is no excuse to ignore the Command, or take it less seriously than Jesus intended. Rather it helps continually to jolt us awake to the challenge of what Jesus demands. Therefore when we do think impure thoughts, our response must be to obey another of the Commands considered a short while ago: *Repent.*

That complete obedience is impossible does not excuse the sin.

This Command brings again into focus the moment-by-moment *work* of discipleship. It is not a lazy life to which we are called. Half-hearted commitment won't get the job done. We've got to remain attentive to what is happening in our hearts every moment, continually asking God for help to do the impossible—live the life of Christ in the shells of our weak, broken, fallen, struggling, self-centered humanity.

Our motives can at least be pure, even when our thoughts may stray, and this is a help the Spirit of God is eager to give.

> God inflames the soul with a burning craving for absolute purity...No man can look on God and live, live in his own faults, live in the shadow of the least self-deceit...The blinding purity of God in Christ, how captivating, how alluring, how compelling it is! The pure in heart shall see God? More, they who see God shall cry out to become pure in heart, even as He is pure, with all the energy of their souls...
>
> No average goodness will do, no measuring of our lives by our fellows, but only a relentless, inexorable divine standard. No relatives suffice; only absolutes satisfy the soul committed to holy obedience. Absolute honesty, absolute gentleness, absolute self-control, unwearied patience and thoughtfulness in the midst of the raveling friction of home and office and school and shop.
>
> Thomas Kelly, *A Testament of Devotion,* "Holy Obedience"

God, bring to my remembrance this day the Command of Jesus to THINK NO IMPURE THOUGHT. *I recognize my human weakness and thus ask for your Spirit's help in thinking purely. You have promised to transform my inner being, and nowhere do I need your divine help more than in the transformation of my thought life. Give me the mind of Christ. Even when my thoughts stray, help purify my motives so that I am not tempted to follow sinful thoughts. Thus, heavenly Father, may I be an instrument in my small corner of the world for the ultimate salvation of mankind. Amen.*

Series Three

"The Peter Commands"

Humility

The Fragrance of Christ

From the very beginning of the Gospel, Peter is bigger than life. It must have been so in the first century as well. He clearly had a reputation. Jesus no doubt knew of him even before they met. As cousin of James and John, it is possible that Jesus was acquainted with their fishermen friend before this time. According to John 1:43, however, this is their first meeting. Andrew had already spent enough time with Jesus to be convinced he was the Messiah. His first order of business was to go find Peter so that he could meet him too.

We almost see a subtle smile creeping over Jesus' face as Andrew approaches with his brother in tow.

"So," said Jesus, "*you* are Simon son of John?"

Immediately Peter became the dominant disciple among the Twelve. If we can phrase it thus, he was Jesus' *best friend.* Obviously Jesus saw Peter's potential from the very start. He began building into him the qualities of character that would make him capable of being the leader of the Christian movement after he himself was gone.

But it was not easy. Peter had both the positive and the negative qualities of a born leader. He was outspoken and volatile. Some commentators call him a hothead. His emotional personality caused anger to erupt, as well as lapses in judgment. All these we see on the pages of the Gospels—enthusiasm, eagerness, stupidity, mistakes, tearful repentance. But through it all...we observe *growth.* One can chart Peter's ups and downs through the Gospels and mark a steady upward progression toward the character that Jesus was persistently infusing into him. After every momentary triumph ("You are the Christ, the Son of the Living God") seems to follow another blunder ("Get behind me, Satan.") But through his blunders, Peter keeps moving steadily on the upward path of growth.

Peter grew toward Christlikeness because above all, he was a *humble* man. He was willing to admit his mistakes, to appear a fool, willing to repent, and to *keep* repenting for his short-sightedness and blindness. He never gave up. After every failure, he returned with tears in his eyes to say to Jesus, "I have failed again...but don't give up on me. Make me into your man."

And Jesus did. Thus it is to Peter, at the very end, that Jesus says, "Feed my sheep."

One of the most fascinating of many between-the-lines stories in the New Testament concerns the dispute several years later between Peter and Paul as recounted in Galatians 2 when Paul publicly rebuked Peter for, as he saw it, Peter's inconsistency on the Judaizing issue. So intent was Paul to justify what he had done that he writes about it years after the fact, and sends his condemnation of Peter out in a letter that was read throughout the entire church.

But does the church ever hear a word about it from Peter? Are we ever told Peter's side? Does Peter defend himself?

Not a word. Paul had spoken about Peter in less than gracious terms. How did Peter respond? The only words we have from Peter about Paul, found in 2 Peter 3:15, are very different. Peter returns the rebuke, not with defense, but with gracious words about Paul's wisdom, and praise of the one he called "our beloved brother Paul." Peter *lived* humility.

The Lord had indeed accomplished his work in the humble giant. Peter had learned to walk the low road. And thus the big fisherman was adorned by the fragrance of Christ.

ταπεινοφροσύνη: TAPEINOPHROSUNĒ—*Humility*

TAPEINOPHROSUNĒ comes from TAPEINOS, low-lying, and means lowliness of mind, the opposite of pride and arrogance. In other words, "lowness" in personal outlook (in a good and positive sense), taking the low position, meek but neither servile nor lacking in confidence or leadership.

Humility is the fragrance of Christ.

Series Three

The Fragrance of Christ

21. Be humble.
22. Give when asked and do more than required.
23. Follow me.
24. Care for the suffering.
25. Give to the poor.
26. Believe.
27. Believe in God.
28. Believe in me.
29. Don't be anxious.
30. Believe that you will receive what you pray for.

21. Be Humble

"Blessed are the meek, for they shall inherit the earth." (Matthew 5:5)

Humility in our day has fallen on hard times. Such can be said for most of the attributes of Christlikeness. But humility is especially embattled. The contrast between the world's perspective and that of Jesus is drawn with yet starker clarity when we substitute the word Jesus used to describe humility—meekness.

The world *hates* the idea of meekness. The very concept scratches like fingernails on a blackboard of the world's sensibilities. Yet Jesus tells us that when all the world's macho posturing, all our strutting to show ourselves better than others, all our pride and independence, all self-sufficiencies, all hinted boasts, all subtle attempts to look important...when all such petty machinations are gone, only *character* will remain. It is the *meek* who will inherit eternity.

What is this meekness, this humility that the Lord commands of us? Is it the wimpy, hanging head, a fearful crouching servility, the sackcloth and ashes of the lowly worm who considers himself unworthy to look another in the eye? Such attributes hardly describe the apostle Peter. Nor do they describe Jesus himself. How do *boldness* and *meekness* intertwine in the character of Christlikeness?

We must therefore look deeper into the thing than what the world considers groveling submissiveness. 1 Corinthians 13 clarifies that love is not puffed up. Humility is simply the opposite of pride. Pride vaunts itself, humility *empties* itself.

Humility seeks not the spotlight. Attention to itself makes meekness shrink back. Sooner would it shine the light of its love in the direction of others. Humility is not anxious to speak out of the storehouse of its own ideas. Humility listens and absorbs. The meek are wise enough to recognize the worthlessness of opinion, yet are willing to speak the gracious word in season. The manners of humility are soft, gentle, courteous. From boastfulness it turns with a sad heart.

Humility walks the quiet, not the talkative road. Humility seeks stillness of character both in itself and in those around it. Humility does not fear life's peaceful and unhurried moments, for it relishes in solitude.

Humility hangs back, defers to others, yet is able to lead when such is required of it. The leadership of humility is soft-spoken, for it is the leadership of character and example not noise and force. The humility of Christlikeness is thus the ultimate true authority in a world full of counterfeit authorities.

Humility always seeks the means and opportunity to serve, while keeping the spotlight off itself. Humility is grace embodied in gentle kindness.

Humility counts others as better than itself, not necessarily because they *are* better, but because humility chooses to treat them as if they are better. Thus humility raises both itself and others into higher realms of being.

> And then, after having learned all that, you have to learn this further thing, Humility—to put a seal upon your lips and forget what you have done. After you have been kind, after Love has stolen forth into the world and done its beautiful work, go back into the shade again and say nothing about it. Love hides even from itself. Love waives even self-satisfaction. "Love vaunteth not itself, is not puffed up."
>
> Henry Drummond, *The Greatest Thing In the World*

God, bring to my remembrance this day the Command of Jesus to BE HUMBLE. *Turn my eyes away from my self that I might be sensitive, aware, tender, listening, and full of grace toward those around me. Open my eyes to opportunities to serve them, counting their needs above my own. May I walk through life wearing the quiet countenance of humble Christlikeness. Thus, heavenly Father, as your humble disciple, may I be an instrument in my small corner of the world for the ultimate salvation of mankind. Amen.*

22. Give When Asked and Do More Than Required

"If any one strikes you on the right cheek, turn to him the other also; and if any one would sue you and take your coat, let him have your cloak as well; and if any one forces you to go one mile, go with him two miles. Give to him who begs from you, and do not refuse him who would borrow from you." (Matthew 5:39-42)

Most are familiar with the tradition behind Jesus' words in the above passage. Many sermon illustrations have explained the right of Roman soldiers in Palestine to compel any citizen to carry their equipment for a mile. To enforce the practicality of the life he would have his hearers lead, Jesus said to carry the burden two miles instead.

Yet most of us have not been struck on the cheek or been sued for our coats. When was the last time a soldier stopped you and commanded you to carry his gun and pack? Therefore, we don't usually pause to consider where obedience might be required of *us*. Jesus' Commands have to be "translated" into our daily lives. We have to find ways to *do* these things. Nobody can tell you or me the specifics. We have to discover how they are to be obeyed...now, today.

Jesus is not merely saying to turn the other cheek, he is speaking of a larger principle—Do more than is expected of you...in *all* things...in *all* circumstances. When you are asked, *give*...and do *more* than is required.

Nor is he speaking merely of our response to the homeless man holding a cardboard sign at the intersection. This Command lies closer than that. It's relatively easy to hand a five dollar bill through the car window and not come within miles of what Jesus meant.

How do we reply when a neighbor or friend or father or mother asks, "Hey, got a minute…?" or "Can you give me a hand?" or "Could I borrow your pickup for an hour?" or "Could you loan me ten dollars?"

How practical do we intend to make the Commands? Will we do *more* than is asked?

Sure. Actually, I've got two minutes and two hands. How can I help? Take my truck for the whole afternoon. And here's twenty dollars for gas.

How should finances function in this upside-down realm called the kingdom of God?

"How much do you want for that desk you're selling?"

"I was thinking a hundred and twenty-five."

"Sounds like a fair price. I'll give you a hundred and thirty."

Absurd! Preposterous! cries the world.

If the rest punch out at 5:00, anxious to work not a minute more than their allotted eight hours, is the Christian giving a hard *extra* ten minutes, ever mindful to provide his or her employer *more* than is required and expecting nothing in return?

How else will the world be changed but by our visible citizenship to a kingdom whose rules are inverted from that in which we are at present pilgrims and sojourners?

This world says: *Do as little as you can get away with. Look out for number one. Get all you can.* The King of our kingdom says: *Look first for the interests of others. Give no thought for yourself. Give when asked, and do more than required.*

> The Christian thinks not of his rights but of his duties; not of his privileges, but of his responsibilities. The Christian is a man who has forgotten that he has any rights at all…What Jesus is saying is: "Don't be…thinking of your liberty to do as you like; be always thinking of your duty and privilege to be of service to others…" There are…two ways of doing things. A man can do the irreducible minimum and not a stroke more…in such a way that he makes it clear that he hates the whole thing…or he can do it with a smile, with a gracious courtesy, with a determination, not only to do this thing, but to do it well and graciously…it is Jesus' demand that we should give to all who ask and never turn away from him who wishes to borrow.
>
> William Barclay, *The Gospel of Matthew, Vol. 1*, pp.165-167

God, bring to my remembrance this day the Command of Jesus to GIVE WHEN ASKED AND DO MORE THAN REQUIRED. Awaken my mind with reminders of your word to go the extra mile in all things asked of me. Give me opportunities to do more than required, not merely with money or possessions…but with my time, with my energies, with myself. Give me a heart not merely of service, but of extra service.

Thus, heavenly Father, may I be an instrument in my small corner of the world for the ultimate salvation of mankind. Amen.

23. Follow Me

"Follow me and I will make you become fishers of men…Follow me." (Mark 1:17; 2:14)
"What is that to you? You follow me." (John 21:22, NAS)

The first Command Jesus issued specifically to his disciples is found in a simple but life-altering challenge: *Follow Me.*

The two words are radical, foundational, imperative. Jesus was not merely saying to Andrew, Peter, James, John, and the others, "Hey, I'm going over to Capernaum…come along and we'll hang out together." He was issuing a sweeping summons: "I want you to leave everything of your past behind—how you thought, how you behaved, what you believed. I want you to come with me forever. I want you to learn to follow me in *all* ways. You will become different men, because, in following me, you will become *like* me."

We have therefore arrived at the *first* Command among the Commands, the Command that draws all others up into it. It is nothing more nor less than the Command to model our lives after that of Jesus. Our response highlights life's singular turning point.

Christianity is not a belief system one drifts into, that one assents to as a mere series of ideas. Certainly discipleship contains progressivity. Grasping the full scope of discipleship did not come all at once for the disciples any more than it does for us. The decisiveness of the Command thus arrives by degrees. We *grow* into a deepening totality of commitment as Christ's disciples. But make no mistake, however it comes in each individual life, "Follow Me" is the defining essence of what is meant by the Christian faith.

There are hosts of so-called "Christians" who adopt any number of counterfeit validating definitions of faith in their own minds. But the word has a precise meaning: A *Christ-ian* is literally a "follower of Christ." There is nothing else it *does* mean, nothing else it *can* mean.

We cannot face forward and backward at the same time. To call oneself a disciple is to turn one's back on the world's outlook and the perspective of its entire system of values. If one is following Jesus, the world will be at his back. There can be no discipleship of co-existence.

The world is full of people pretending to be Christians, those who are drawn to the concept of "Christianity" and link themselves to it in name but who have never made themselves true *Christians.* They are trying to keep one foot in both camps. The world is not nearly so full of serious men and women who have left the nets of past priorities, and are attempting to model their lives after that of Jesus. For it is a moment-by-moment Command. *Follow Me* is no Command to salvation, it is a Command to *live*.

What does it mean to follow Jesus...to be a *Christ-ian*?

Quite simply: To obey what he tells us to do, to do what he says, to think as he thinks, to respond as he responds, to love as he loves, to see people as he sees them, to see God as he sees him, to pray as he prayed, to lay down self-will as he laid down self-will, to take his example into every decision, every response, every attitude, every conversation.

> Everyone first encounters Jesus more or less as a stranger...That moment of...*heart* contact—when He turns and isolates us in the crowd and speaks to our heart and says, "Come...I want you to follow Me," happens before we really know who He is. It is a crossroads moment of life. Though Jesus phrases it as a command, He is really asking a question. "Are you willing to come along...to take a chance...to follow a man you don't know much about?"
> Michael Phillips, *Jesus An Obedient Son,* p. 99

God, bring to my remembrance this day the Command of Jesus to FOLLOW him. Though it may be a fearsome prayer to pray, I ask you, Holy Spirit, to illumine into my mind and heart with vivid clarity those areas where I am still facing in the direction of the world, where the world's priorities and points of view still cling to my outlook. If there are areas where I am playing with discipleship, wake me to the moment-by-moment imperative that to truly FOLLOW Jesus means turning my back on the world's ways of looking at things. Turn my face toward the perspectives of eternity. Make me strong to FOLLOW Jesus Christ in all ways. Thus, heavenly Father, may I be an instrument in my small corner of the world for the ultimate salvation of mankind. Amen.

24. Care for the Suffering

"For I was hungry and you gave me food, I was thirsty and you gave me drink, I was a stranger and you welcomed me, I was naked and you clothed me, I was sick and you visited me, I was in prison and you came to me...Truly I say to you, as you did it to one of the least of these my brethren, you did it to me." (Matthew 25:35-36, 40)

Imbalance has always been the Achilles heel of Christianity. It might truly be said that imbalance in following the Commands of Jesus is responsible for the greater share of the unbelief in the world. Does anyone doubt that if every Command of Jesus had been sacrificially lived by his followers, not only would the world have been largely converted to Christianity, life would be a good and pleasant thing for most of its inhabitants. There is enough food, enough water, enough provision, enough happiness, enough love for all.

But heaven has not come to earth. Strife, greed, and cruelty continue rampant on the earth, and the imbalance of Christians perpetuate them. We especially witness it in our response to what might be called the "spiritual" vs. the "practical" Commands. All Christians, it seems, emphasize one side of that equation more than the other.

This dichotomy has no simple solution. Jesus commands us compassionately to care for those less fortunate than ourselves and those oppressed by life's circumstances. His Command stands without need of comment or explanation. As his followers, we are required simply to do what he tells us.

Does caring for the suffering mean getting them saved, handing out money, giving them food, volunteering in a hospital, inviting them to church, opening our homes, listening to their fears? No one-dimensional solutions exist to life's sufferings. Caring for the suffering may mean all these applied with loving Christlike balance. But it will also contain singularly unique and personal applications for *you* and *me* as we involve ourselves in the pains and sufferings of those God sends *our* way.

None of us have the potential to alleviate the "world's suffering." We may support efforts toward that end. Most Christians give financially to help from a distance in what ways are possible. But the Command *Care for the suffering* strikes much closer to home. There are suffering men and women close beside us. They may be suffering from inner demons and invisible miseries as much as from hunger and poverty. Perhaps the deepest pains are caused by the agonizing ache of loneliness, discouragement, and despair. The homeless man holding a cardboard sign may be hurting no more than a wealthy neighbor enduring a lingering terminal illness behind silent walls of isolation. We are not commanded to choose. We are not commanded to make exclusions or excuses. We are not commanded to rank human need. We are commanded to care for the suffering.

All suffering, *all* pain, *all* grief, *all* inner turmoil, *all* loneliness are the mission fields of our obedience.

A man must not choose his neighbor. He must take the neighbor that God sends him. In him, whoever he or she be, lies either hidden or revealed a beautiful brother or sister. The neighbor is just the man or woman or child who is next to you at this very moment...Thus will love spread and spread in wider and stronger pulses till the whole human race will be to you sacredly lovely...

Does the thought of such love make your heart swell? "Ah brother, sister," do you find yourself saying to one you had hardly noticed before, "you have a soul like mine. Sights and sounds and smells visit your heart and brain as they do mine. We are not so different after all! Oh, my brother, my sister, I will love you! I cannot come very near you yet, but I will love you then all the more."

George MacDonald, *Unspoken Sermons, First Series,* "Love Thy Neighbour," *Knowing the Heart of God,* ed. Michael Phillips (pp. 331)

God, bring to my remembrance this day the Command of Jesus to CARE FOR THE SUFFERING. *Open my eyes to perceive the hidden sufferings of those around me—to see behind the eyes into the inner man or woman. Attune my ears to detect the subtle minor chords vibrating from the strings of their hearts that tell what perhaps their words do not. Give me sensitivity and wisdom to know how you would have me move to the point of their suffering with the love of Christ. Thus, heavenly Father, may I be an instrument in my small corner of the world for the ultimate salvation of mankind. Amen.*

25. Give to the Poor

"If you would be perfect, go, sell what you possess and give to the poor, and you will have treasure in heaven; and come, follow me." (Matthew 19:21)

Observe how much of Jesus' time was spent among the infirm, sick, destitute, crippled, blind, and demon-possessed.

If Jesus is our example, then, the poor indeed must occupy a central focus in a life of obedience. Nothing has so distinguished Christianity throughout its history more than its compassionate ministry to the needy, starving, and suffering…to the widow and the orphan. Nor is this Command one to be obeyed only with bills in a collection plate, coins in a tin cup, or a check sent to missions. *Give to the poor* is an individual and personal Command. Into the life of every Christian intent upon obedience will be sent "poor" who are suffering in many forms of poverty. We are not merely called to give money to the financially strapped, but to *give* to any and all of the poor that God sends uniquely into our lives.

For those who read the Gospels primarily through socially conscious eyes, an almost inexplicable dichotomy in a theology of world improvement appears in John 12. Mary anoints Jesus with expensive perfume. Judas complains about the lavish waste, saying that it could have been sold and the money given instead to the poor. Jesus responds with one of the fascinating statements in the New Testament: *You will always have the poor with you.*

What are we to make of such a peculiar statement?

The answer is plain: Important as it is, charity will *not* eliminate the sufferings of the world. Churches are certainly called to alleviate suffering in the neighborhoods, towns, and cities of their influence. You and I, as *individuals,* are likewise called to address suffering existing close beside us.

However, we will never rid the world of poverty. There are other considerations in the life of Christian discipleship that accompany help to the downtrodden. *Spiritual* poverty is equally the Lord's concern. We are not called to eliminate poverty but to give to the poor.

The conclusion is that the Gospel presents no call to right the world's wrongs. The Gospel is not primarily about making the world a better place, it is about making people better people. It will become a better place only when people become better people.

The Gospel offers no social contract. No political blueprint can be founded on the Gospel of Jesus Christ. Those who derive social and political agendas from the Gospels, quite simply, misread the red letters. The Gospel offers a programme for the transformation of individual hearts. It is an agenda to grow men and women into Christlikeness.

That transformation cannot begin when people are hungry, nor when they are sinking in the despair of spiritual poverty. Compassion for temporal need is the hallmark of a balanced Christianity, whose imperative is the whole man.

> Foolish is the man, and there are many such men, who would rid himself or his fellows of discomfort by setting the world right, by waging war on the evils around him, while he neglects that integral part of the world where lies...his first business—namely, his own character and conduct. Were it possible—an absurd supposition—that the world should thus be righted from the outside, it would yet be impossible...ever to enjoy the perfection of the result....The philanthropist who regards the wrong as in the race, forgetting that the race is made up of...individuals, forgets also...that the wrongness exists in the individual...No evil can be cured in the race, except by its being cured in its individuals...
>
> Rightness alone is cure. The return of the organism to its true self, is its only possible ease. To free a man from suffering, he must be set right, put in health...be free... from sin.
>
> George MacDonald, *The Hope of the Gospel,* "Salvation from Sin"

God, bring to my remembrance this day the Command of Jesus to GIVE TO THE POOR. *Open my eyes to the hidden poverty around me. Give me willing hands and an eager heart to give both financially and in other ways. When Jesus tells me to sell all I have and give to the poor, then to follow him, may I greet his word with rejoicing. Then give me the courage to prayerfully discover what he means me to do, not turn away sorrowfully because I have many possessions. Thus, heavenly Father, by my compassion and by my giving, may I be an instrument in my small corner of the world for the ultimate salvation of mankind. Amen.*

26. Believe

"Do not fear, only believe." (Mark 5:36)

From probably the most down-to-earth, if we may even phrase it thus, a most *un*spiritual among Jesus' Commands, we turn to one of the *most* spiritual: Believe.

Belief in matters of faith is singularly and entirely a spiritual exchange. Though we have seen that "giving to the poor" may also involve alleviating spiritual poverty, on the surface of it providing food, clothing, shelter and comfort does not seem a particularly spiritual activity. Atheists give to the poor. Individuals of all faiths give to the poor. One needs no spiritual inclinations to do so. Giving to the poor may embody prayerful spirituality within it, but the transaction itself is between *man and man.*

One cannot exercise "belief" without the full cooperation of brain, heart, and spirit working in threefold harmony. No one can enter the inner sanctum with us where *belief* is born and nurtured. Belief is a transaction between *man and God.* Others may lead us to the door. But we enter that Holy of Holies deep within the human spirit alone. There we meet God.

Considering the two Commands side by side brings into perfect focus the uniqueness of Christianity as demanding the full spectrum of human response—the intellect, the heart, the soul, and the daily actions of hands and feet. Love God with all your heart...Love your neighbor as yourself. *Give to the poor...Believe.*

It is not surprising, then, that both these seemingly opposite yet interwoven Commands emerge out of Jesus' response to the rich young ruler (Matthew 19, Mark 10, Luke 18). The young man came seeking a *spiritual* answer to the question of eternal life. He wanted his spirituality in a vacuum. Jesus says, "What you desire does not exist. Spirituality must engage the whole man. Belief requires all of life. Now go, give to the poor, and follow me."

Notice, too, the context of Jesus' Command in Mark 5 above. He does not tell the synagogue ruler to "believe" in an abstract sense. The man was a faithful leader of the Jewish synagogue. Intellectually and spiritually, he *already* believed. Jesus tells him to actively *exercise* his belief, to trust his belief, to act upon his belief. He tells him not merely to *think* belief, but to DO belief. It is a variation on the same message he gave to the rich young ruler. Belief lived. Belief acted upon.

This is why none of the so-called "spiritual" Commands of Jesus can be considered in a vacuum. Jesus never gives us that luxury. The intertwining strands of *Love God...Love man* continually provide the warp and woof strength upon which the entire fabric of Christianity is woven. *Every* Command is interlaced throughout *both* of the greatest Commandments: Love God and Love man. No division exists between the spiritual and the temporal. As God is one, Christianity is one. Give to the poor *and* Believe.

> I believe in Jesus Christ, the eternal Son of God, my elder brother, my lord and master; I believe...that to obey him is to ascend the pinnacle of my being...I believe that God is just like Jesus, only greater yet, for Jesus said so...
>
> I believe that there is nothing good for me or for any man but God, and more and more of God, and that alone through knowing Christ can we come nigh to him...
>
> I believe that to him who obeys...God gives the spirit of his son, the spirit of himself, to...lead him to the understanding of all truth...I believe that no teacher should strive to make men think as he thinks, but to lead them to the living Truth, to the Master himself, of whom alone they can learn anything, who will make them in themselves know what is true by the very seeing of it...I believe that to be the disciple of Christ is the end of being.
>
> George MacDonald, *Unspoken Sermons, Third Series,* "Justice"

God, bring to my remembrance this day the Command of Jesus to BELIEVE. *Lead me quietly into the Holy of Holies of your presence and reveal to me truth. Nurture, develop, strengthen, and mature my belief, that it might become the vigorous belief that Jesus intends his people to example to the world. Then give me the faith and strength to act on my belief—to believe by doing. Thus, heavenly Father, by my belief, may I be an instrument in my small corner of the world for the ultimate salvation of mankind. Amen.*

27. Believe in God

"Believe in God." (John 14:1)

We find ourselves looking at a series of Commands subject to widely varied interpretation as we attempt to navigate the conundrum between the temporal and spiritual components of the Christian life—Love God, Love man...Give to the poor, Believe.

There will always be those who read the words of Jesus through the lenses of their own biases and preferences. It seems that in the realm of spiritual things, as the saying goes, there are two kinds of people—those with a built-in disposition toward a more spiritual approach to matters of faith, and those with a disposition toward what they would call greater practicality. The former pass out tracts and invite non-Christians to revival services. The latter operate food banks and work in soup kitchens. For the spiritually minded, nothing is more practical and urgent than eternal life. For the temporal minded, what good is salvation if people's needs are not met. Discussions on the relative merits of the two approaches usually end in an impasse.

Jesus doesn't give us the luxury of picking and choosing, of tailor-making the Gospel to suit our own likes and dislikes. The Gospel comes to us whole. If we are serious about understanding what Christianity actually *is*, not what we might like it to be, even what we might rather it was, then *every* Command, and every type of Command, is in play.

When it comes to belief, it is impossible to ignore the deeply "spiritual" necessity involved in the thing. The idea of "belief" in our day is allowed to mean almost anything. But Jesus does not command a lazy or distantly intellectual belief. He commands belief *in God.* And not just any God—not a God of convenience, not a God of our imagining, not a God whose attributes are built upon the framework of our own preferences...but the God who is his Father.

Simply put, Jesus commands belief in the God of Christianity as revealed in the Gospels, in the Creator of the universe and his own personal *Abba*, his Father. No liberal social gospel god...no inclusive all-religions-are-equal god...no pantheistic life-force god... no impersonal "intelligent design" nebulae. Jesus commands belief in the God of Christianity as revealed in the Gospels.

Christianity is the world's most embracing and expansive faith. But in a sense it is exclusivist as well. Jesus commands us to believe properly, to believe accurately. Much lazy belief passes for Christianity. But Christianity founded in obedience to the Commands of Christ forces a diligent, active, determined, growing belief, not in a doctrinal system, not in an idea, not in a political agenda, not in social justice, not in merely meeting temporal needs...but belief in a God who is a personal and active *Father* and savior to every created being in the universe.

To believe, we must discover who that Father of Jesus Christ is, discover what he is like, discover what he expects of us as his sons and daughters...and then, following Jesus' example, make him our *own* personal, moment-by-moment Father, *Abba*, and friend.

That is what Jesus meant when he commanded, *Believe in God.*

> I do not mean you to believe me submissively and without reason; I do not claim to subdue you by tyranny. Nor do I claim to account to you for everything. To reconcile these contradictions I mean to show you clearly, by convincing proofs, marks of divinity within me which will convince you of what I am, and establish my authority by miracles and proofs that you cannot reject so that you will then believe the things I teach.
>
> Blaise Pascal, *Pensées* (From *Devotional Classics,* Richard Foster, ed., p. 174-5)

God, bring to my remembrance this day the Command of Jesus to BELIEVE IN YOU. *As I read the Gospels, open my eyes to see your Fatherhood, and to see what Jesus taught about you. Give me accurate belief in you. Develop within me the same trusting, loving belief that Jesus had. Help me believe in you daily as my own personal Abba, my heavenly Daddy. Thus, heavenly Father, by my right knowing of you, and by my active belief in you, may I be an instrument in my small corner of the world for the ultimate salvation of mankind. Amen.*

28. Believe in Me

"Believe also in me." (John 14:1)

Jesus does not stop with commanding belief in general, not even belief in God. He zeroes in with yet more precision and specificity by also commanding belief in *him*. This further dismisses the notion that Christianity may be equated with being a kind person and trying to do good in the world. Those are good things. But they are not Christianity.

Christianity is founded upon an encounter of the spirit out of which emerges belief in Jesus Christ and his Father. A Christian is commanded to be good. But being good does not make one a Christian. Jesus' discourse with Nicodemus in John 3 clarifies how deeply spiritual this spirit-encounter is. Jesus commands belief that leads to eternal life, belief in him as the savior of mankind sent by his Father to cleanse sin from the universe.

Belief is the starting point of Christianity. Belief, however, is *only* a starting point. As the rich young ruler discovered, to his sorrow, belief means nothing in a vacuum. Belief is validated by practicality. We believe, therefore we obey.

Can one truly "believe" and ignore the Commands? That is a question for the theologians. Our desire is to discover how to obey the Commands not analyze them. Of one thing we can be certain: Whether or not it is possible to *believe* while ignoring the Commands, Jesus makes clear (John 14:15) that no one who ignores them can claim to *love* him. Love for Jesus is expressed in obedience.

We all know only too well how many games are played with the term "Christian" while the Commands of Christ lay neglected at the side of the road. But let it not be so among those who are in earnest about their belief. Let us prove our belief by our obedience.

What does it mean to *believe* in Jesus in this way? Nothing more than trusting him, following his example, doing what he says, obeying his instructions, and in all ways attempting to model one's life after his. This means keeping an equal focus on the things of eternity and the things of the earth. How can we believe in Jesus but by knowing intimately what he taught? Thus, we grow in such belief by immersing ourselves in the Gospels.

Notice—doctrines and theories and theologies *about* Jesus, about his work, about salvation and the cross and heaven and hell and sin and the atonement and the church and all the rest...these are all secondary. They are not *foundational* components of belief. When Jesus said to his disciples in the upper room, *Believe in God, believe also in me,* he uttered not a word of doctrine. It wasn't a theological Command. Christians are almost desperate to tell others *what* to believe. But not Jesus. He *doesn't* tell the disciples what to believe. He simply says: *Believe in God, believe also in me.* Belief is validated by obedience to the Commands, not by adherence to any theology.

Believe...Believe in God...Believe in me.

> We must learn to obey him in everything, and so must begin somewhere: let it be at once, and in the very next thing that lies at the door of our conscience! Oh fools and slow of heart, if you...do not set yourselves to do his words! you but build your houses on the sand. What have such teachers not to answer for who have turned your regard away from the direct words of the Lord himself...to contemplate plans of salvation tortured out of the words of his apostles...There is but one plan of salvation, and that is to believe in the Lord Jesus Christ; that is, to take him for what he is—our master, and his words as if he meant them...To do his words is to enter into vital relation with him, to obey him is the only way to be one with him. The relation between him and us...can nohow begin to *live* but in obedience: it is obedience.
>
> George MacDonald, *Unspoken Sermons, Series Two,* "The Truth in Jesus"

God, bring to my remembrance this day the Command to BELIEVE IN JESUS. *I thank you, God, for sending your Son for the salvation of mankind. I thank you for his atoning work. I thank you for your provision for sin, and for birthing within me the life of your Spirit. Now may I live this new life as your son or daughter by appropriating the Christ-life into my own. May Jesus be my moment-by-moment example in all things. Help me live by belief through my obedience to the Lord's Commands. Thus, heavenly Father, by my belief in Jesus, may I be an instrument in my small corner of the world for the ultimate salvation of mankind. Amen.*

29. Don't Be Anxious

"Do not be anxious about your life, what you shall eat or what you shall drink." (Matthew 6:25)

It is sometimes difficult to know how to live in the practical reality of Jesus' admonition in the latter half of Matthew 6: *Consider the birds of the air and the lilies of the field. They neither sow nor reap, yet your heavenly father cares for them. So don't worry about what you shall eat or drink.* We are all familiar with his words. But do they not often sound just a little *too* idealistic?

In truth, if we take them to mean that we should never give thought for our daily provision, and simply trust that food will be put before us and clothing provided us, then of course they are idealistic. We can't actually *live* like that. We aren't birds or flowers. The whole of Scripture points to the very opposite of a laissez faire attitude to life. The Bible consistently urges diligence and hard work, as well as foresight, planning, and making provision for our families. On the surface of it, Jesus' words almost seem to contradict the overarching message of the book of *Proverbs.*

Therefore, we must dig deeper into this passage to find what it is that Jesus is actually commanding of us. When we do, we see that he is not speaking against hard work or making provision...but against worry and anxiety. He doesn't say, "Don't think about food or clothing," but rather, "Don't be *anxious* about food or clothing." Reading verses 26-32 almost as a parable rather than a literal teaching may help illuminate the Lord's deeper intent. We might combine the message of *Proverbs* with these words of Jesus into something like: Work hard but don't stress. Recognize that life is more than food and clothing, but living righteously in God's kingdom. Make provision but trust God to meet your needs."

At the end of the passage, Jesus adds a curious twist. He almost seems to condone a certain amount of worry...as long as it is about *today's* troubles, not tomorrow's. He admits that every day brings worries and difficulties. That's life. It can't be helped. All right, he says, fair enough. Deal with them. But don't worry about tomorrow until it comes. *Do not be anxious for tomorrow, for tomorrow will have troubles enough of its own.*

Again, then, we lay hold of the power of this Command, not by reading it in an idealistic vacuum, but by incorporating it into a full scriptural lifestyle. Make provision *and* trust God to supply your needs. Work hard today *and* tomorrow, but don't stress about tomorrow's problems before they come. Plan for the future, but don't be *anxious* about the future.

Above all, seek God's kingdom and his righteousness. Everything else is secondary.

> The real problem of the Christian life comes where people do not usually look for it. It comes the very moment you wake up each morning. All your wishes and hopes for the day rush at you like wild animals. And the first job each morning consists simply in shoving them all back; in listening to that other voice, taking that other point of view, letting that other larger, stronger, quieter life come flowing in. And so on, all day. Standing back from all your natural fussings and frettings; coming in out of the wind.
>
> We can only do it for moments at first. But from those moments the new sort of life will be spreading through our system…This is the whole of Christianity. There is nothing else…but to draw men into Christ, to make them little Christs…God became Man for no other purpose.
>
> C.S. Lewis, *Mere Christianity*, Book 4, Ch. 8, "Is Christianity Hard or Easy?"

God, bring to my remembrance this day the Command of Jesus NOT TO BE ANXIOUS. *This is one of the most difficult of the Commands to obey, for anxiety seems such an intrinsic part of my human make-up. I need your help, Lord. Sometimes the urgencies and needs of life are overwhelming. I can't help worrying how I will pay the bills. I feel that the only prayer I am capable of praying is like the man's in Mark 9:24, "I do worry, help me not to worry!" In my weakness I ask for your help. Deepen my trust in you to meet my needs. May I seek your righteousness above all things. Thus, heavenly Father, may I be an instrument in my small corner of the world for the ultimate salvation of mankind. Amen.*

30. Believe That You Will Receive What You Pray For

"Therefore I tell you, whatever you ask in prayer, believe that you receive it, and you will." (Mark 11:24)

There are fewer more perplexing, misunderstood, misappropriated Commands in the Gospel than this. How many disappointments have been based on grandiose prayers for healing, for financial provision, for restored relationships, and for thousands of other good and worthy things, that have not happened? We have all experienced the ache, frustration, and confusion of unanswered prayer.

It is not a dilemma of the Christian life easily dismissed with the words, "Sometimes the answer is no." Neither does, "We may not *see* the answer, but God *is* answering," do much good. These are worthy principles to keep in mind of course. But Jesus' words in three of the four gospels are definite and unambiguous, adding to the above:

"And whatever you ask in prayer, you will receive it, if you have faith." (Matthew 21:22)

"If you ask anything in my name, I will do it." (John 14:14)

What do we do with such promises? In the face of apparent unanswered prayer, we can fall back on the proviso that we *didn't* truly believe, that we *didn't* have sufficient faith, or that we didn't ask in Jesus' name. But these answers don't satisfactorily resolve the conundrum either. There are certainly millions of prayers that have gone up in true and serious and unwavering faith for results that have *not* materialized.

Do we give up praying? Do we ignore this one of Jesus' Commands?

These are no solutions either. We must keep praying because Jesus commands us to pray. We must keep praying and doing our human best to believe, because Jesus commands us to pray in faith.

Then we have to leave the other half of the equation in God's hands. We are merely commanded to pray and believe. Confusing as that may occasionally be, our responsibility is simply to do what Jesus told us to do. It may be that the answering half of the above Command exists on an eternal plane so far beyond our capacity to apprehend God's full response to our prayers that we cannot possibly see the answers while in this life. In the next life, we may indeed see that truly we *did* receive everything we prayed for in faith—received it in the eternal realm where God was working in ways and means we were incapable of apprehending while in the flesh. How foolish we will feel if, not seeing those eternal ways and means, we stopped praying, and thus prevented much in the eternal realm that God wanted to accomplish through our prayers.

Therefore, we are commanded to pray believing, and to keep praying in faith. That is all we are commanded to do. The rest is in God's hands. And there we must leave the results.

As we pray, we may also take comfort in the wonderful prayer of the father of the deaf and dumb boy in Mark 9:24: *I believe, help my unbelief!*

Jesus will never condemn us for our weak humanity. In our weakness, we are yet commanded to be strong. In our unbelief, we are yet commanded to pray...and to believe.

> Here then is a word of the Lord about prayer: it is a comfort that he recognizes difficulty in the matter—sees that we need encouragement to go on praying, that it looks as if we were not heard, that it is no wonder we should be ready to faint and leave off...he recognizes how the thing must look to those whom he would have go on praying. Here as elsewhere he teaches us that we must not go by the look of things, but by the reality behind the look. A truth, a necessity of God's own willed nature, is enough to set up against a whole army of appearances. It looks as if he did not hear you: never mind; he does...you too will be heard.
>
> George MacDonald, *Unspoken Sermons, Second Series*, "The Word of Jesus On Prayer"

God, bring to my remembrance this day the Command of Jesus to BELIEVE THAT I WILL RECEIVE WHAT I PRAY FOR. *I admit my struggle with prayer. So often I see no results. But let me not weary in prayer. Give me faith to believe in Jesus' words though I do not see your half of the eternal transaction. I believe, yet help my unbelief. Thus, heavenly Father, may I be an instrument in my small corner of the world for the ultimate salvation of mankind. Amen.*

Series Four

"The Matthew Commands"

Righteousness

What Separates God's People from the World

At first appearance, Matthew the tax collector, also known as Levi, son of Alphaeus, was singularly unqualified to be one of Jesus' disciples, and especially unqualified to speak to the world about righteousness. He was no mere "sinner," he would have been considered a "chief of sinners." We observe in Mark 2:15-16 that the term *tax collector* was synonymous with sinner. No greater condemnation was leveled against Jesus than that he ate with "sinners and tax collectors." In first century Palestine, they didn't come lower than tax collectors.

Imagine the scandalous paradox of Jesus going about with tax-collectors, prostitutes, and rough-and-tumble fishermen...and teaching about *righteousness*. No wonder the scribes and Pharisees were outraged! Then to take one of them into his inner circle! Matthew was no ordinary sinner. He was a traitor. He had gone into business against his own people. Had it not been for Judas, it might well have been Matthew who was associated with the word betrayal.

Yet Jesus knew Matthew's heart. He saw in him what no one else saw. Therefore, when he said, "Follow me," Matthew left his tax collection booth, left his past life, and followed. But as William Barclay says, he did not leave *everything* behind. Matthew took with him one very important item when he followed Jesus—his pen. And decades later, when he sat down to write an account of Jesus' life, Matthew decided to write specifically to his own, the people he had once betrayed, the nation of Israel. Matthew is the "Jewish gospel," presenting Jesus as the redeemer and Messiah long foretold by Israel's prophets.

All four gospel writers had to choose what material to include, and in what order to present it. In all likelihood, Jesus did not in the first weeks of his ministry walk up a mountain and deliver what we call the "sermon on the mount" fully intact as we have it in Matthew 5-7. Matthew chose to open the teaching portion of his gospel with this material for two reasons. First, he wanted to present a summarized overview of the revolutionary lifestyle to which Jesus was calling his followers. It had taken Matthew and the other disciples a long time to "get" everything he meant when he said, "Follow me." Matthew wanted no one who read his gospel to be in doubt about the totality of commitment required in every corner of life if one intended to call oneself a "Christian."

There is another reason Matthew began as he did. He was aware of his own past. Because of what he had once been—a reviled sinner—the thought of "righteousness" must have been very dear to him. Can there be any doubt that Matthew was speaking of the cry of his own heart when he recounted Jesus' words, "Blessed are those who hunger and thirst for righteousness, for they shall be filled." Matthew's hunger had indeed been satisfied by the love of God, poured into him by Jesus himself. He now longed to share his love of righteousness with all those who, like him, were ready to leave their sin...and follow. The fifth chapter of his gospel could be called the "righteousness chapter," between the lines of which we catch a glimpse of Matthew's own testimony of a life transformed by Jesus.

δικαιοσύνη: DIKAIOSUNĒ—*Righteousness*

Righteousness, δικαιοσύνη, means literally just what it implies: Being right or just, both in attitude and action. It was originally spelled in English "rightwiseness." Jesus elevates righteousness to a much higher level than had ever been heard of in Israel before—not legalistic or what passed for "religious" devotion, but *personal* righteousness. After several examples in the latter portions of Matthew 5 illustrating how this revolutionary new DIKAIOSUNĒ should think and behave, Jesus climaxes with the stunning proclamation (5:48): *You, therefore, must be perfect, as your heavenly Father is perfect.*

Righteousness is what separates God's people from the world.

SERIES FOUR

WHAT SEPARATES GOD'S PEOPLE FROM THE WORLD

31. Be righteous.
32. If part of your body sins, get rid of it.
33. Be at peace, reconciled, and united with others.
34. Deny yourself.
35. Lose your life.
36. Be a servant.
37. Do not defraud.
38. Be a son or daughter of God.
39. Pray, fast, give, and do good in secret.
40. Beware of practicing piety to be noticed.

31. Be Righteous

"Blessed are those who hunger and thirst for righteousness…
You, therefore, must be perfect, as your heavenly Father is perfect." (Matthew 5:6, 48)

The Commands of Jesus seem to come in two broad categories: Those that are straightforward and relatively simple to obey…and those that are *impossible* to obey.

When stuck in traffic or in a line at the bank, when the Command *Be patient* rears its head, do we complain and fret…or take a deep breath and whisper, "This is the opportunity I have prayed for, Lord, to strengthen patience and be an example to the world."

When we find ourselves in a potentially compromising moral dilemma and the Command *Commit no sexual sin* speaks to the conscience, do we obey or give in to the temptation?

When we find ourselves drawn into a contentious debate over doctrine with a Christian brother or sister, and the Command, *Love the brethren* shoots an arrow of light into the brain, do we persist in the argument, or lay it down in love?

These and many of the Commands may not be *easy* to obey, but we know *exactly* what we are supposed to do or not do. It boils down to whether we are willing or not. However, there are other Commands we have no idea how to obey. They are *impossible* Commands!

The sermon on the mount, for which Matthew's gospel is perhaps best known, is full from beginning to end with the call to an uncommon righteousness never before witnessed in the dealings of man with his fellows. Jesus begins by commending those who hunger to be righteous (5:6). He goes on to say that those who are persecuted because they are righteous are blessed (5:10), adding that true righteousness must be greater than that of so-called religious leaders (5:20). Clearly, it is no average morality to which Jesus calls those, like Matthew, who would leave the sin of their former lives and follow as his disciples. It is the very righteousness of God himself.

The *most* impossible of the impossible Commands concludes the righteousness chapter of Matthew 5: *You, therefore, must be perfect, as your heavenly Father is perfect.*

None of us can possibly be perfect…yet Jesus commands exactly that of us. He says we *must* be perfect. It is not even optional.

Again Jesus speaks to motive, priority, life-orientation. I will never *be* perfect, but do I use my imperfection as an excuse to ignore the Command, or do I prayerfully strengthen my resolve to aspire *toward* Christlikeness in all things? Do I let myself off the hook, or do I humbly pray, "Lord, help me…make me like Jesus." When I look myself in the mirror, can I honestly say that I *want* to be made perfect...or do I cherish hidden pockets of Self that I do not want to yield to God's recreating Spirit? These and many more such questions of prayerful self-knowing rise to the surface when we read Matthew 5 with eyes of humble insight. Can I honestly be said to "hunger and thirst for righteousness?" If not, if I don't *want* to be perfect, then something is missing in my walk with God.

Jesus did not call his followers to mediocrity of devotion, but to lives of righteousness.

> The man who exercises [faith in God] may...well be called a righteous man, however far from complete in righteousness...In the Bible men are constantly recognized as righteous men who are far from perfectly righteous. The Bible never deals with impossibilities, never demands of any man at any given moment a righteousness of which at that moment he is incapable; neither does it lay upon any man any other law than that of perfect righteousness. It demands of him righteousness; when he yields that righteousness of which he is capable, content for the moment, it goes on to demand more: the common-sense of the Bible is lovely.
>
> George MacDonald, *Unspoken Sermons, Third Series,* "Righteousness"

God, bring to my remembrance this day the Command of Jesus to BE RIGHTEOUS. *I recognize how unrighteous I am. But it is my desire to be your right-thinking and right-behaving son or daughter. By the miracle of your Spirit, work rightwiseness in me. Deepen my hunger to be righteous. If I cannot be perfect, may the desire of my heart be perfect, which is to grow into Christlikeness. Make my* <u>*motives*</u> *perfect. Thus, heavenly Father, may I be an instrument in my small corner of the world for the ultimate salvation of mankind. Amen.*

32. If Part of Your Body Sins, Get Rid of It

"If your hand causes you to sin, cut it off...and if your foot causes you to sin, cut it off...and if your eye causes you to sin, pluck it out; it is better for you to enter the kingdom of God with one eye than with two eyes to be thrown into hell, where their worm does not die."
(Mark 9:43, 45, 47-48)

It has been mentioned before that Jesus occasionally uses overstatement and exaggeration to get his point across. That is obviously again the case here. No one seriously believes this Command is to be obeyed *literally*. None of Jesus' own disciples, to our knowledge, obeyed this Command as it stands, nor did Jesus expect them to.

The reason is obvious. No hand, foot, or eye actually causes anyone to sin. Sin is born in the mind and heart, then carried out in the will. Motives begin internally, and lead to the attitudes and actions that follow. Jesus makes this clear in Mark's gospel shortly before the above passage: "For from *within*, out of the heart of man, come evil thoughts..." (7:21)

Cutting off a hand or foot, or plucking out an eye, won't prevent sin. The origins of sin lie deeper.

But Jesus wants to leave no doubt how serious sin is. We are called to righteousness, to perfection itself. *All* sin is the enemy of righteousness. Therefore, we must be so in earnest about rooting out sin that we would even be willing to cut off a hand if that would accomplish it. It *won't*...but that's how serious the thing is.

So what is Jesus *really* commanding of us?

Quite simply: If there is sin in your life, anywhere in your life...deal with it. Deal with it ruthlessly. Do not delay—get rid of it.

There is another potential problem here. It is fearfully easy for a Command such as this to be glossed over and ignored. The fact that it is obviously not to be taken literally becomes an excuse for not taking it seriously at all. With that door open, *any* Command one wants to "explain away" is easily enough dispensed with in the same way. It is a lethal pattern, employed by Christians the world over, to render the Commands of Christ meaningless, and thus gut the essential power from Christianity's witness. If we want the world to think that the Christian gospel really doesn't matter, all we have to do is start explaining away this or that Command and our objective will be achieved quickly enough.

All the Commands matter. If certain of Jesus' words are not to be taken literally, then it is incumbent upon us to discern their deeper *spiritual* intent...and then obey them. Only so will the world know that Jesus came from the Father.

If part of your heart is responsible for sin, find it, deal with it, get rid of it.

> There is [an] important misapprehension of the words of the messengers of the good tidings—that they threaten...punishment because of the sins we have committed, whereas their message is of forgiveness, not of vengeance; of deliverance, not of evil to come. Not for anything he has committed do they threaten a man with the outer darkness. Not for any or all of his sins that are past shall a man be condemned; not for the worst of them needs he dread remaining unforgiven. The sin he dwells in, the sin he will not come out of, is the sole ruin of a man. His present, his live sins—those pervading his thoughts and ruling his conduct; the sins he keeps doing, and will not give up; the sins he is called to abandon, and clings to; the same sins which are the cause of his misery, though he may not know it—these are they for which he is even now condemned.
>
> George MacDonald, *The Hope of the Gospel,* "Salvation From Sin"

God, bring to my remembrance this day the Command of Jesus to GET RID OF SIN IN MY LIFE. *Keep me from the fatal error of explaining away any of the Lord's Commands. Give me eyes to see the enormous practicality of this Command to discern where sin originates in my heart, and then deal with it swiftly and ruthlessly. Give me insight and wisdom to see all Jesus' Commands, even those that seem figurative, as intensely practical in my life. Then give me opportunities to obey them.*

Thus, heavenly Father, by my serious attention to the sin in my life, may I be an instrument in my small corner of the world for the ultimate salvation of mankind. Amen.

33. Be at Peace, Reconciled, and United with Others

"First be reconciled with your brother, and then come and offer your gift." (Matthew 5:24)
"Be at peace with one another." (Mark 9:50)
"I…pray…that they may be one even as we are one." (John 17:20, 22)

The enormity of this Command is of such scope and magnitude that it is impossible to overstate. If *Love* is the first Command, this surely represents one of the most important dimensions of Love itself. Indeed, unity with our fellow man is one of Love's significant visible expressions. If we would "Be righteous," this is where it begins.

The point bears repeating: It is upon the basis of visible and practical unity within the body of Christ that Jesus said the world will determine whether or not his claims are true. Unity is thus the basis for all evangelism. Absent visible oneness with other Christians, all our books, tracts, Bible studies, conferences, and church services will accomplish precisely zero toward expanding the kingdom of God. Do you want to share God's love with an acquaintance? Don't invite them to church—instead let them participate in an exchange between Christians of opposing views and observe the love that flows. Seeing Christians loving one another will accomplish more than a hundred church services. Jesus said, "By *this* all men will know that you are my disciples, if you have love for one another."

This unity between the brethren takes many forms, each of which find their way into our lives by obedience. We are commanded to be peacemakers, to be at peace with one another, not to delay but settle disputes promptly. When contentions arise, we remain silent. We lay down opinion for the greater good of peacemaking. When others contend, we gently move into the gap of division with soothing words of unity, reconciliation, and good-will.

We are also commanded to leave spirituality aside whenever a difference exists between ourselves and any other. *Leave your gift at the altar* has a thousand personal imperatives for each one of us. How many "altars" of seeming spirituality do we bow in front of while ignoring the disputes, annoyances, angers, and sour attitudes that lurk unseen in our hearts. While our hearts remain cold toward the brethren or toward any brother or sister of our common humanity, our multitude gifts of worship mean nothing to God.

How many churches are full of distracted minds cherishing animosities, resentments, unforgivenesses. We waste our time pretending to worship God while remaining distant from our brothers and sisters. The world will never listen. God is not listening.

"*First* be reconciled with your brother, and *then* come and offer your gift."

Jesus prayed for us. He prayed that we would be one with the brethren in the same way that he and the Father were one. What a mighty truth—Jesus prayed for you and me!

His prayer can only be answered following our obedience: *Be at peace, reconciled, and united with others.*

> Through the centuries men have displayed many different symbols to show that they are Christians...But there is a much better sign—a mark that...is a universal mark that is to last through all the ages of the church until Jesus comes back.
>
> What is this mark?
>
> At the close of his ministry...Jesus makes clear what will be the distinguishing mark of the Christian...
>
> Love—and the unity it attests to—is the mark Christ gave Christians to wear before the world. Only with this mark may the world know that Christians are...Christians and that Jesus was sent by the father.
>
> Francis Schaeffer, *The Mark of the Christian*

God, bring to my remembrance this day the Command of Jesus to BE AT PEACE, RECONCILED, AND UNITED WITH OTHERS. Sting my heart with the immediacy of reconciliation. May my heart hunger for unity and reconciliation. Let me never try to worship you while ignoring the claim of a brother's love. May I be a reconciler and peacemaker. Root out unforgiveness from within me wherever it hides in the shadows. Let me discover the joy of unity! Thus, heavenly Father, by my visible unity with my brethren, as Jesus said would be the result, may I be an instrument in my small corner of the world for the ultimate salvation of mankind. Amen.

34. Deny Yourself

"If any man would come after me, let him deny himself..." (Mark 8:34)

The great moral teacher interpretation of the life and impact of Jesus Christ is surely one of the most naïve perspectives ever proposed for such an important historical figure. C.S. Lewis has memorably argued that anyone making the claims Jesus did must either be a lunatic, a madman, or what he claimed to be. It is not merely Jesus' claim to be one with God that is astonishing and revolutionary, however, so too is much of the rest of his teaching. Far from being a traditional "moralist," a great deal of what Jesus said turned conventional wisdom upside-down.

Take the simple Command: *Deny yourself.* Everything in life from beginning to end shouts, "Fulfill yourself!" All animal and human instinct is devoted to self preservation, self advancement, self fulfillment. Even much Christian teaching is devoted to pampering, feeding, indulging the self, even promoting the self. Look at *me*, Listen to *me*. Yet Jesus commands his followers to relinquish everything the *self* represents. He says, "I want you to do the very opposite of what life seems to tell you." On its face, it is a patently ridiculous Command. Such the disciples found it—unbelievable, impractical, absurd.

The Gospel story can be divided into two halves. We see the demarcation with particular clarity in Mark's gospel at the halfway point. In the first eight chapters, Jesus attempts to get the disciples to recognize who he is. This process culminates in Mark 8:29 with his momentous question, "Who do you say that I am?" and Peter's breakthrough answer, "You are the Christ."

Immediately thereafter Jesus begins to teach them what that great truth *means*. It means *death*. Death to self. *If any man would come after me, let him deny himself.* It is the first and foremost Command following the revelation of Jesus as Messiah. Self-denial is what "Follow me" means. Henceforth, he says, no decision is to be set before the judgment seat of Self-will for a verdict rendered according to, "What do I want?" Life's moments, rather, are placed before the Throne where the moment-by-moment question becomes, "What does *he* want of me?"

Many complain at the idea of self-denial, thinking that it means a loss of individuality and personhood. In truth, however, as in all aspects of kingdom life, precisely the opposite is actually the case. In *yielding* the Self is the Self *fulfilled*. The loftiest exercise of freedom is to lay down, by the choice of free will, the only thing that is truly our own—the *Self*—and its seat of control in the depths of the soul—the *will*. In using *free* will to abandon *self*-will, in saying, *Not MY will but YOURS be done,* we step into the highest personhood possible for mortal man. Thus we take our Gethsemane-place with Jesus as a son or daughter of God.

> Verily it is not to thwart or tease the poor self Jesus tells us...He tells us we must leave it altogether—yield it, deny it, refuse it, lose it: thus only shall we save it...The self is given to us that we may sacrifice it; it is ours that we like Christ may have somewhat to offer—not that we should torment it, but that we should deny it....that we should abandon it utterly...
>
> It means this:—we must refuse, abandon, deny self altogether as a ruling, or determining, or originating element in us. It is to be no longer the regent of our action. We are no more to think, "What should I like to do?" but "What would the

Living One have me do?"...

"Self, I have not to consult you...You may be my consciousness, but you are not my being... Submit, or I will cast you from me, and pray to have another consciousness given me...

"Good-bye, Self! I deny you, and will do my best every day to leave you behind me."

George MacDonald, *Unspoken Sermons, Second Series,* "Self Denial"

God, bring to my remembrance this day the Command of Jesus to DENY MYSELF. *When decisions come, remind me not to think of my own leanings, but to silently breathe, "What would you have me do?" Lord Jesus, remind me often this day of your mighty Gethsemane prayer. May the orientation of my heart fall in line with this true North of the universe—dying into the will of the Father. May everything within me desire your will above my own. Thus, heavenly Father, may I be an instrument in my small corner of the world for the ultimate salvation of mankind. Amen.*

35. Lose Your Life

"Whoever loses his life for my sake and the Gospel's will save it." (Mark 8:35)

Most of Jesus' Commands are reasonably straightforward, easy enough to understand, uncomplicated, unambiguous. Easy to *obey*—no. Easy to *understand*—yes. It is not usually a question of being confused about what is required. Rather it is a question of how serious we are about *wanting* to obey.

Even though a Command such as *Deny yourself* appears to one unpracticed in the mechanics of self-denial to be less than practical, a little experience quickly brings "self-denial" very close to home. The decision, the weighing of options, the fork in life's road—perhaps momentous, perhaps involving no more than the next ten minutes—changes the choice from, "What do I want to do?" to, "I have made myself Jesus' follower, therefore what does *he* want me to do?" In that moment of decision, my Self has been relegated to the back seat. Jesus is driving now. *He* is in charge. *Self-denial* has become very practical indeed. Out of ceaseless practice, practicality emerges.

Some of the Commands, however, are genuinely elusive in the hubbub and tumult of daily life. High on this list of "elusive Commands," is the one before us now. What does Jesus mean for us to actually *do* that will demonstrate what it means to "lose" our lives for his sake and the Gospel's? Surely he is not speaking of martyrdom. The Commands are always practical in the immediacy of *now,* not the distant future. Most of us don't walk out the doors of our homes and face the likelihood of martyrdom. Something closer at hand must be implied by these words.

Jesus was always practical. Christianity is the most practical faith of all the world's belief systems. Jesus sends his followers into the midst of life—

involved, active, vigorous, energetic. Jesus *engages* life. So what does he mean by calling us to *lose* our lives in the midst of this close encounter with the daily flow of life?

Here we confront a Command pointing toward an outlook, a perspective. Jesus is addressing motive and orientation. Enormous clarity comes into focus by considering that Paul's words in 1 Corinthians 13 may unlock the secret of what is meant by losing one's life for Jesus: *Love…seeks not its own.*

In one sense, my life *is* my own. Yet Paul tells me not to seek it. Jesus tells me to lose it. It may be yours, he says—lay it down anyway. Let *me* manage it, and you will find greater life in the end. *Lose your life,* then, is but another side to the multi-faceted prism of "self-denial" (no mere glass prism; this is the *diamond* of true spirituality)—subserving my will to God's will. *Losing* my life simply means abandoning *my* will into *God's* will.

We should hardly be surprised that the two Commands go hand in hand. Jesus uttered them almost in the same breath: "If any man would come after me, let him deny himself and take up his cross and follow me. For whoever would save his life will lose it; and whosever loses his life for my sake and the Gospel's will save it." (Mark 8:34-35)

> "Love seeketh not her own." Observe: Seeketh not even that which is her own…There come times when a man may exercise even the higher right of giving up his rights. Yet Paul does not summon us to give up our rights. Love strikes much deeper. It would have us not seek them at all, ignore them, eliminate the personal element altogether from our calculations. It is not hard to give up our rights. They are external. The difficult thing is to give up ourselves. The more difficult thing still is not to seek things for ourselves at all…The only greatness is unselfish love.
> Henry Drummond, *The Greatest Thing in the World*

God, bring to my remembrance this day the Command of Jesus to LOSE MY LIFE. *Obedience to these words may take place deep inside my heart unseen, unnoticed by those I meet through the day. Yet when I yield to your outlook above my own, my whole perspective of life will slowly be transformed. I hunger for you to carry out this work within me. I hunger for it with every breath, that I might see and feel and respond as Jesus himself does. I long to lose my life into his. I ask you to carry out this high and holy transformation within me. Thus, heavenly Father, may I be an instrument in my small corner of the world for the ultimate salvation of mankind. Amen.*

36. Be A Servant

"If anyone would be first, he must be last of all and servant of all." (Mark 9:35)
"Whoever would be great among you must be your servant." (Matthew 20:26)

From the elusive Command, *Lose your life,* we now encounter one of the most down-to-earth of all the Commands: *Be a servant.* No mystery exists here. We all know what it means to serve, to put someone else's need ahead of our own…the good deed, the kindness shown, the helping hand, the burden shared, the load lifted, the feet washed, the cup for the thirsty wayfarer. Opportunities for service are presented us every moment of every day.

Though it is the most difficult of training grounds, service begins in the family. If it does not begin here, it will be meaningless elsewhere. We have all witnessed the futility of those so involved in "service" and "ministry" that they have no time to *Be a servant* to those closest to them. Yet God invented the family as a servanthood boot camp. Out of this training ground toward wives, husbands, children, parents, brothers, sisters, aunts, uncles, grandparents, and cousins, servanthood unto Christlikeness emerges. From these beginnings, service spreads like widening ripples out into churches and communities, the leaven of God's love planted into the world and bearing multifold fruit of goodness.

We live in an era where self-reliance is the god of our age. One of the grievous resultant tragedies has been a disappearance of lifelong "honor" to generations that have come before. Servanthood remains deeply ingrained in the hearts of fathers and mothers. But the other half of the equation is fading in our culture as a memory of bygone times. Because this foundation of humble submission of children to parents has been trampled underfoot by modernism, the church itself is rapidly losing the capacity to know what *Be a servant* means.

Practical obedience to Mark 9:35 begins at home. There is no age limit, no matriculation age beyond which one is excused from service to mothers and fathers. This fundamental requirement of life does not end until they are laid to rest to rejoin those who came before, whom they were called to honor and serve throughout *their* lives.

For the Christian, the servanthood imperative within the Command, "Honor your father and mother," carries monumental consequences. For along this path we discover right relationship with God. Obedience to parents trains spiritual muscle to obey Jesus in the trenches of life. Honor of *earthly* fathers instills the wisdom to rightly honor and obey our *heavenly* Father. The one must follow the other. Obedience follows obedience. Honor follows honor. Earthly fatherhood is the necessary and divinely appointed door through which to approach the Fatherhood of God.

Through the familial door of service the whole world opens with opportunities to serve—neighbors, friends, strangers, acquaintances, fellow customers in the grocery store, and legion of life's "passers-by" whom the unthinking never notice but to whom the hand of Jesus would reach out with compassion. To serve is to notice need, and move to fill it.

> Remember…that not in any church is the service done that he requires. He will say to no man, "You never went to church: depart from me; I do not know you;" but, "Inasmuch as you never helped one of my father's children, you have done nothing for me." Church or chapel is not the place for divine service. It is a place of prayer, a place of praise, a place to feed upon good things, a place to learn of God, as what place is not…But the world in which you move, the place of your living and loving and labour, not the church you go to on your holiday, is the place of divine service. Serve your neighbour, and you serve him.
>
> George MacDonald, *Unspoken Sermons, Third Series,* "Righteousness"

God, bring to my remembrance this day the Command of Jesus to BE A SERVANT. As reorienting as it may be to change my thinking, turn my eyes toward the servanthood that is required of me toward my family, especially my parents. Renew within me the heart of a loving servant toward them, and use it to open my eyes to opportunities to serve those around me with cups of kindness-water to ease their life's burdens. Grow within me the heart of a true servant, and a knowledge of what "divine service" means. Thus, heavenly Father, may my servant's heart act as an instrument in my small corner of the world for the ultimate salvation of mankind. Amen.

37. Do Not Defraud

"Do not defraud." (Mark 10:19)

Countless sermons and devotions have been based on Jesus' exchange with the man we know as the "rich young ruler." The first three gospels recount the story using largely identical words and phrases. Indeed, this passage is one of those upon which scholars base their conviction that Matthew and Luke founded their writings upon Mark's gospel.

As the first gospel, *Mark* contains intriguing details that drop out of the longer accounts. Mark was Peter's traveling companion and scribe. He wrote his gospel based on Peter's lifetime of reminiscences. Thus, Mark's gospel is told through Peter's eyes. It is a vivid, raw account. Peter makes no attempt to gloss over his foibles, and Mark preserves this brutally honest perspective. Mark also keeps many obscure details. When Jesus fed the 5,000, though Matthew was presumably there too, only Mark notes that they sat down on the *green* grass. When the storm arose on the Sea of Galilee, only Mark notes the touching detail that Jesus was asleep *on the cushion.* The next time the disciples found themselves on the sea in a violent wind and Jesus came to them on the water, only Mark is candid enough to give the reason for the disciples' terror. He concludes: "They were utterly astounded, for they did not understand about the loaves, but *their hearts were hardened.*" (Mark 6:51-52). It is a blunt and unvarnished account.

In the story of the rich young ruler, we encounter another of those curious disparities in the Gospels. Only Mark notes that Jesus *loved* the young man. And only Mark includes among the injunctions given him, *Do not defraud.* A look at the Ten Commandments, however (Ex. 20, Deut. 5), reveals that these three words are nowhere to be found. Fearing that Jesus had made a mistake, did Matthew and Luke omit them to prevent readers concluding that Jesus didn't know the Ten Commandments? But *did* Jesus make a mistake? Or does the eyewitness account of Peter reveal that Jesus does not want us obeying the mere letter of the law, but its spirit?

Do not defraud is large and sweeping. It draws stealing, coveting, and bearing false witness all up into it. You must not, Jesus says, do your neighbor wrong, play him false, or defraud him in *any* way. It is not enough simply not to steal from him. You must not even defraud his character, his honor, his integrity, his worth as a person. You are to be entirely honest in all your dealings. You are to be above reproach in all ways.

Again, through Mark's intimate account, we see deeper into the exchange. Perhaps we discover another reason than wealth alone that the young man went away sorrowful. Jesus was not merely challenging him to give to the poor, he was challenging him to live the full depth and scope and spirit of the commandments.

What is "fraud" but the opposite of honesty? Turning *Do not defraud* into a positive construction, therefore, we find Jesus commanding: *Be entirely and scrupulously honest...in all ways, all dealings, all thoughts, all actions, with all men.*

> It is unnecessary to inquire precisely what [the youth] meant by *eternal life.* Whatever shape the thing took to him, that shape represented...something which, it was clear to him, could be gained only in some path of good. But he thought to gain a thing by a doing, when the very thing desired was *a being*: he would have that as a possession which must possess him.
>
> The Lord cared neither for isolated truth nor for orphaned deed. It was truth in the inward parts, it was the good heart, the mother of good deeds, he cherished. It was the live, active, knowing, breathing good he came to further. He cared for no speculation in morals or religion. It was good men he cared about, not notions of good things.
>
> George MacDonald, *Unspoken Sermons, Second Series,* "The Way"

God, bring to my remembrance this day the Command of Jesus DO NOT DEFRAUD. *Instill within me a love for the spirit of your commandments. Give me wisdom to see the practicality of* DO NOT DEFRAUD, *and that the Command compels scrupulous honesty in all things. Give me courage to be honest with myself, and to see my heart with the clarity of your vision. Then let me yield the broken places within me to the transformation of your hand. Thus, heavenly Father, may I be an instrument in my small corner of the world for the ultimate salvation of mankind. Amen.*

38. Be a Son or Daughter of God

"...be sons of your Father who is in heaven." (Matthew 5:45)

Created by his hand and in his image, all humanity are God's children. Yet we are put upon this earth to become something more, to become true *sons and daughters* of chosen obedience. Given life and, in time, independence, our destiny is gained by yielding back that independence into the hand of our Creator, and thus, by that relinquishment, discovering eternal childship.

George MacDonald illuminates this pivotal Command to childship by juxtaposing the words *child, son,* and *daughter* for emphasis. Though we *are* God's children, says MacDonald, we have to BE his children. Though we were created as children, we have to BECOME true sons and daughters: "He is our father, but we are not yet his children. Because we are his children, we must become his sons and daughters. Because we are the sons of God, we must become the sons of God." This "becoming" we do in our will, by *choosing* to lay down the independence we have gained in life, and taking the Father's will for our own.

In doing exactly this, exampling it for us, Jesus created in himself, by the free choice of perfect love, a new form of life—the life of laying down his own will and taking upon himself the will of the Father. This is the life in the Son that corresponds to the creating power of the Father. The two forms of love in the Godhead—*creating* love and *self-denying* love—mirror one another yet reveal the same Source of love. The Father's love is outgoing, the Son's love responds to it by deathing his own motives into the love of the Father.

MacDonald adds: "The life of Christ is this—negatively, that he does nothing, cares for nothing for his own sake, and positively, that he cares with his whole soul for the will and pleasure of his father. Because his father is his father, therefore he will be his child."

> [In] This choice of his own being, in the full knowledge of what he did, this active willing to be the Son of the Father, perfect in obedience...Jesus rose...to the height of his being...in the act of subjecting himself to the will of the Father as his only good, the only reason of his existence. When he died on the cross, he did...that which he had done at home in glory and gladness. From the infinite beginning—for here I can speak only by contradictions—he completed and held fast the eternal circle of his

existence in saying, "Thy will, not mine, be done!"

He made himself what he is by deathing himself into the will of the eternal Father...thus plunging into the fountain of his own life, the everlasting Fatherhood, and taking the Godhead of the Son...This life, self-willed in Jesus, is the one thing that makes such life...possible, imperative, essential, to every man, woman, and child. The Father has sent us all into this outer world that we may go back into the inner world of his own heart...There is no life for any man, other than the same kind that Jesus has. His disciple must live by the same...devotion of his will to the Father's...

Because we are come out of the divine nature, which chooses to be divine, we also must choose to be...of God, to be one with God. We must choose to love and live as he loves and lives...Man cannot originate this life. It must be shown him, and he must choose it...

We are not and cannot become true sons without our will willing his will...He was not the son of God because he could not help it, but because he willed to be in himself the son that he was in the divine idea. So with us: We must be the sons and daughters we are...We are sons and daughters in God's claim. Then we must be sons and daughters in our will.

And we can be sons and daughters, saved into the original necessity and bliss of our being, only by choosing God for the Father he is, and doing his will—yielding ourselves as true sons to the absolute Father. Therein lies the only and essential human bliss.

George MacDonald, *Unspoken Sermons,* "The Creation in Christ."

God, bring to my remembrance this day the Command of Jesus to BE A SON OR DAUGHTER OF GOD. *Deepen my awareness of the difference between being a mere child, and choosing by an act of the will to death myself into the will of God, and thereby become a son or daughter of obedience. This childship I must choose moment-by-moment. Help me, Lord Jesus, to choose it, as you chose it. Let me follow your brothering example of sonship throughout this day. Thus, heavenly Father, by my progressive growth into eternal childship, may I be an instrument in my small corner of the world for the ultimate salvation of mankind. Amen.*

39. Pray, Fast, Give, and Do Good in Secret

"When you give alms, do not let your left hand know what your right hand is doing...when you pray, go into your room and shut the door and pray to your Father who is in secret...and when you fast, anoint your head and wash your face, that your fasting may not be seen by men but by your Father who is in secret." (Matthew 6:3, 6, 17-18)

It is fearfully easy to read the *Do not* Commands and assume, "Oh, I would never do *that*." Because the context of examples used by Jesus occasionally seems so ludicrously absurd, we too easily overlook our own glaring presence in the midst of the Gospel pages. Who can imagine a rich man walking along the street, then calling for trumpets to arrest everyone's attention so they will stop what they are doing and watch while the boastful hypocrite drops a coin in a beggar's cup? The very idea is laughable. Maybe the Pharisees actually did that in the first century, but no one would do it now.

So we read the words and gloss over them.

Yet the Command is more subtle and piercing than first meets the eye. For we all have our own kinds of trumpets. They are clever, invisible, sometimes even silent, but we are highly skilled in using them to turn eyes toward us. We've been doing it so long, we don't even realize the dozens of ways we go through the day blowing our horns to turn attention onto ourselves.

How many times have you fasted, and no one from beginning to end knew it? When the fast was over, still you told no one, you hinted nothing. No one ever knew...*ever*. Or, with the little sigh, the weary expression, the comment dropped—by so many tiny notes from the trumpet—did you allow your spiritual discipline to be known, yet still convinced yourself that you were fasting in secret?

Our prayer-trumpets are yet more blaring. Public prayer has been elevated to an art form all its own. Where did it come from? Where do we find public prayer urged upon us in the Gospels? Jesus' words could hardly be more clear: *When you pray, go into your room and shut the door and pray to your Father who is in secret.* How much of our prayer, however, is actually devised to be heard by men? The pastoral prayer from the pulpit, the memorized prayers from the prayer book, the loud exhortations during worship, the round-robin prayers of small group meetings, the chanted prayers between priest and congregation during mass—who are we really kidding...eighty percent of the words of prayer spoken in our places of worship are for the benefit of those listening. Our motives may be good. Yet how is all this different from what Jesus spoke of: *And when you pray, you must not be like the hypocrites; for they love to stand and pray in the synagogues...that they may be seen by men. Truly, I say to you, they have their reward.* (Matthew 6:5)

To be heard by God, Jesus says, pray in secret to *him*, not openly to men.

Do good without anyone knowing it. Smile, clean your face, and look nice when you fast.

Blow no boastful trumpets.

> There is one word...in the authorized version, that used to trouble me, seeming to make its publicity a portion of the reward for doing certain right things in secret: I mean the word *openly*, at the ends of the fourth, the sixth, and the eighteenth verses [of Matthew 6], making the Lord seem to say, "Avoid the praise of men, and thou shalt at length have the praise of men"...Glad was I to find that the word is not in the best manuscripts...
>
> The whole question is of the kind of reward expected...The man, then, who does right, and seeks no praise from men, while he merits nothing, shall be rewarded by his Father, and his reward will be right precious to him.
>
> George MacDonald, *The Hope of the Gospel*, "The Right Hand and the Left"

God, bring to my remembrance this day the Command of Jesus to PRAY, FAST,

GIVE, AND DO GOOD IN SECRET. Alert me to the grating sound of my own personal boastful trumpets. Make me so aware of their screeching noises that I will be appalled when I hear them. Fill me with the joy of solitude in devotion, and the reward of secrecy in well-doing. When I pray, may all my words be directed from my heart to you alone. Thus, heavenly Father, by my unseen well-doing, may I be an instrument in my small corner of the world for the ultimate salvation of mankind. Amen.

40. Beware of Practicing Piety to Be Noticed

"Beware of practicing your righteousness before men to be noticed by them." (Matthew 6:1, NAS)

Righteousness is one of the more curious character qualities of the committed Christian disciple. Jesus tells us to let our light shine before men, but to pray, fast, and do good in secret. If it is visible obedience by Christians that changes the world, why are we also commanded to be *invisibly* righteous?

Righteousness is doubly curious in that it is especially scorned by the world. It is scorned because it is so little understood. The word sounds so *religious*. It annoys modern sensibilities. The mildewed aroma of old churches, boring sermons, dowdy fashions, stale doctrines, dreary conversation, dry clergymen, goody-two-shoes simpletons, and effeminate paintings of Christ all spring to the minds of most people when they hear the word *righteousness*.

How different is this from true righteousness! Who does not honor a man or woman of integrity, virtue, purity, humility, truth, honesty, goodness, courage, and character? *This* is true righteousness—a thoroughly "right" person.

Obviously, such rightness will be seen. In our time, it cannot help but be seen. The contrast between the world's valueless morals on the one side, and goodness, virtue, integrity, and purity on the other is stark and plain for all to observe.

Jesus' Command here is not to try to hide who we are. As is his regular custom, he is speaking to motive. Jesus never commands surface attributes, but attitudes, priorities, and motives that originate in the heart. Do not be good, truthful, honest, and humble *to be noticed*, he says, but rather because you want to be like God. The idea that we would try to be pious to be noticed is an ugly, sickening, disgusting thought. Such a conceited awareness of what others think is Pharisaism. May we cast such self-righteousness from us, and trample it underfoot as the foulest of demons.

Recalling to mind that the verse and chapter notations in our Bibles are a relatively recent addition, the break between chapters 5 and 6 in Matthew's gospel are not found in the original manuscripts. It may be that the two verses should be read as a single seamless progression: *You, therefore, must be perfect, as your heavenly Father is perfect. Beware of practicing your piety before men, in order to be seen by them.*

Righteousness is born in the desire to be like God, not to be seen of men. If men are paying attention, they *will* see goodness, virtue, purity, honesty, and humility. They will see it and take notice. But that is nothing to us. We are simply trying to do what Jesus tells us, which is to be like our Father in heaven. They may notice, but we will not. We do not desire mere rightness, but the perfection which defines the character of God himself.

That we know we will never *be* perfect in this life changes nothing. The desire of our heart, our motive in all things, is to reflect the character of God.

> Let your light out freely, that men may see it, but not that men may see you...The injunction is not to hide what you do from others, but to hide it from yourself. The Master would have you not plume yourself upon it, not cherish the thought that you have done it, or confer with yourself in satisfaction over it...A man must not desire to be satisfied with himself. His right hand must not seek the praise of his left hand. His doing must not invite his after-thinking...[To] imagine any merit...would be to love a lie...Is there anything to be proud of in refusing to worship the devil?...There is no pride so mean...as the pride of being holier than our fellow, except the pride of being holy. Such imagined holiness...is the vermiculate life of a corpse.
>
> George MacDonald, *The Hope of the Gospel*, "The Right Hand and the Left"

God, bring to my remembrance this day the Command of Jesus not to PRACTICE PIETY TO BE NOTICED. Protect me from the cancer of Pharisaism. If I am noticed doing good, may I not notice it. Purify my motives with the humility that shuns the spotlight. Make my heart recoil with disgust at the merest suggestion that I am watching for what others think of my attempts to be virtuous, truthful, and upright. May my only desire be to reflect your nature to the world, yet may I remain completely unconscious of the way you answer this prayer. Thus, heavenly Father, may I be an instrument in my small corner of the world for the ultimate salvation of mankind. Amen.

SERIES FIVE

"THE PHILIP COMMANDS"

Forgiveness

THE RECREATIVE ENERGY OF ETERNITY

Most scholars believe that there were two men by the name of Philip in the New Testament—Philip the apostle, and Philip the deacon chosen in Acts 6 who later spread the Gospel in Samaria and baptized the Ethiopian eunuch. Both men were evangelists.

Though he is listed in the first three gospels, the apostle Philip makes his first appearance in John 1:43. The chronology of Jesus' life is impossible to determine with certainty. Many, however, consider the events of John 1 among the first of Jesus' public ministry. According to John, Philip is the first of the twelve to whom Jesus spoke the words, "Follow me."

This immediately places Philip in a unique position. Though we know little about him, he was obviously close to the inner circle. What was his first act after being called by Jesus? To tell others. Just as Andrew went to Peter, Philip went immediately to his friend Nathaniel, saying, "We have found the one Moses and the prophets wrote about." When questioned, Philip gave the perfect answer to Nathaniel's initial doubt. He didn't argue doctrine. He didn't try to counter his skepticism. He simply said, "Come and see." Andrew and Philip are thus the first two gospel missionaries.

We continue to meet Philip throughout John's gospel. At the feeding of the 5,000, it is to Philip Jesus turns to ask about provision for the multitude. We see him again when certain Greeks wanted to meet Jesus in Jerusalem. They took their request to Philip. Finally we see Philip in the Upper Room, again close at hand and hanging on Jesus' words, making perhaps one of the most important appeals ever put to Jesus: *Lord, show us the Father.*

Jesus' reply is gently tinged with frustration, "Have I been with you so long, Philip, and yet you do not know me?" But how grateful we are for Philip's request. What follows is one of the pivotal exchanges in the Gospel story, illuminating the relationship between the Father, Jesus, and his followers. Philip is thus responsible for providing us one of the clearest images of the Godhead at work: *He who has seen me has seen the Father…The words that I say to you I do not speak on my own authority; but the Father who dwells in me does his works. Believe me that I am in the Father and the Father in me…If a man loves me, he will keep my word, and my Father will love him, and we will come to him and make our home with him.* (John 14:9-11; 23)

ἄφεσις: APHESIS—*Forgiveness*

Though forgiveness sits at the very center of Christian doctrine, it is one of the least understood components of Christianity. This misunderstanding stems from the vicarious sacrifice of the Old Testament, where sins were remitted, passed over, and the debt of punishment cancelled by the death of an innocent. Sadly, this same primitive old covenantal punitive mentality of sin-punishment found its way early into Christian doctrine and persists to this day.

Jesus, however, said that he came to make all things *new*. This includes our understanding of the sacrifice and the nature of God's forgiveness. Jesus did not come to merely *cancel* the debt of sin, while men remained as they were. He came to make men into new men. In the disciples we observe the transforming power of forgiveness. God's forgiveness is no mere passing over of punishment due, while the debtor remains capable of continuing in sin as always. God forgives that we might become like Jesus, sending our own sins away by taking God's will for our own. APHESIS is no longer to be understood by legalities—in the cancellation of penal sentence. It is now transformational. The cross does not merely wipe the slate clean. It has the power to *transform*. This is the eternal ἄφεσις of God for his created universe.

Forgiveness is the recreative energy of eternity.

Series Five

The Recreative Energy of Eternity

41. Forgive.
42. Forgive 70 x 7 times.
43. Do good, be good.
44. Seek first God's kingdom.
45. Store up treasure in heaven.
46. Be kind.
47. Love and pray for your adversaries.
48. Do good to those who hate you.
49. Do not exalt yourself.
50. Honor your father and mother.

41. Forgive

"Forgive and you will be forgiven." (Luke 6:37)

We noted that forgiveness is one of the least understood components of Christian doctrine. Sadly, it is misunderstood by Christians and non-Christians alike. This verse from Luke, and its counterpart in Matthew 6:14-15, conveys the impression that God's forgiveness is conditional: *If you forgive men their trespasses, your heavenly Father also will forgive you; but if you do not forgive men their trespasses, neither will your heavenly Father forgive your trespasses.*

As we have seen, it is dangerous to "explain away" Jesus' words. In this case, however, we are compelled to recognize that his meaning lies deeper than what the words appear to say on the surface. God's forgiveness is *not* conditional. Yet passages such as this, often misinterpreted by well-meaning Christians, contribute to a false image of a capricious God whose forgiveness is doled out to some and withheld from others. Mark 3:29, the well-known verse condemning the unforgivable sin of blasphemy against the Holy Spirit, adds to the misconception that there are limits to God's forgiveness. The erroneous conclusion is that God's forgiveness is finite. Upon this dreadful premise are built all the doctrines of punitive hell, of a predestined elect and an equally predestined damned, and the holiness doctrine that God cannot coexist with sinners.

A careful study of the Greek originals of these texts reveals much light to illuminate the darkness of such doctrines. In Mark 3:29 especially, such study uncovers a great truth—that unforgiveness is not permanent. A *sequence* of heart condition is revealed in the Greek that determines whether or not forgiveness can operate. *As long as* untruth in the heart persists (whether blindness toward the Spirit's work, or unforgiveness against a neighbor), God's forgiveness cannot take root. God does not *withhold* forgiveness. Forgiveness is simply blocked. His heart is infinitely forgiving! The blockage is all on our side. Remove the blockage, and God's forgiveness flows in like a flood! There does not exist such a thing in the universe as an "unforgivable sin." *All* sin is forgivable. Nor does a time limit exist on God's forgiveness. He will continue forgiving eternally. As God is infinite, all his attributes are infinite.

How much better we will understand the above passage if we read it with the meaning Jesus intended to convey: "If you forgive men their trespasses, your heavenly Father will also *be able to* forgive you; but if you do not forgive men their trespasses, your heavenly Father *will not be able* to forgive your trespasses."

It is imperative to grasp this mighty truth in order to unlock forgiveness within our own hearts. Wrongly believing that there are those who may eternally lie outside the scope of God's forgiveness keeps alive the evil fancy that there are those we may not have to forgive either. God *will* forgive…therefore, we *must* forgive.

We thus study and seek to understand more deeply the nature of God's forgiveness for one reason alone, so that *we* will be empowered to forgive. As God's forgiveness is unconditional, so must our forgiveness be unconditional. We have all been hurt, mistreated, lied to, lied about, spoken ill of, cheated, yelled at, mistrusted, and *not* forgiven by others.

Jesus commands simply: *You…forgive.*

> God is forgiving us every day—sending from between him and us our sins and their fogs and darkness…When some sin that we have committed has clouded all our horizon, and hidden him from our eyes, he, forgiving us…sweeps away a path for…his forgiveness to reach our hearts…God's love is ever in front of his forgiveness. God's love is the prime mover, ever seeking to perfect his forgiveness… The love is perfect, working out the forgiveness.
>
> George MacDonald, *Unspoken Sermons, First Series,* "It Shall Not Be Forgiven"

God, bring to my remembrance this day the Command of Jesus to FORGIVE any and all who have in any way hurt, injured, disappointed, or been cruel to me. May I forgive all those who have not forgiven me. Give me love to forgive, humility to forgive, courage to forgive, and patience to forgive. Thus, heavenly Father, through my forgiveness, may I be an instrument in my small corner of the world for the ultimate salvation of mankind. Amen.

42. Forgive 70 x 7 Times

"How often shall…I forgive? As many as seven times?…"
"I do not say to you seven times, but seventy times seven." (Matthew 18:21-22)

If we transplant Peter's question and the Lord's response from Matthew 18 into the sixth chapter where the theme of forgiveness emerges out of the Lord's prayer, we would have the following succinct teaching on prayer, forgiveness, and the reach of forgiveness:

"And forgive us our debts, as we forgive our debtors; and lead us not into temptation, but deliver us from evil. For if you forgive men their trespasses, your heavenly Father also will forgive you; but if you do not forgive men their trespasses, neither will your heavenly Father forgive your trespasses."

Then Peter came up and said to him, "Lord, how often shall my brother sin against me, and I forgive him. As many as seven times?"

Jesus said to him, "I do not say to you seven times, but seventy times seven."

Remember that Jesus' words in Matthew 6 have proceeded out of the astonishing conclusion of Chapter 5: *You, therefore, must be perfect, as your heavenly Father is perfect.* Jesus is not merely spelling out the parameters that are to regulate *our* forgiveness. He is speaking of the scope of *God's* forgiveness. God's forgiveness is *perfect.* Jesus is telling Peter—there are NO limits, either to God's forgiveness or to yours. God's forgiveness never ends. You must be like God. Therefore, your forgiveness must never end.

Though focusing on obedience *to* the Commands rather than doctrine *about* them, we yet find ourselves facing a stunning implication hidden in Jesus' words. He is clearly using the phrase *seventy times seven* as a metaphor for inexhaustibility. God's forgiveness is both perfect and infinite. The view of the afterlife held by many, however, has at its core a doctrine of unending retribution against sin. Though responsibility may rest on the unrepentant sinners themselves, the doctrine yet allows that there will be souls *unforgiven* by God to all eternity. How then can his forgiveness in any sense be considered eternal and limitless...with this glaring *limit* to the reach of his forgiveness as the basis for this doctrine? It may be that the Commands will force a reevaluation of many such doctrines.

You...forgive, and never cease forgiving.

> If I were rendering Mark 3:28-29 interpretively, I would paraphrase it thus: "I tell you the truth, men will be forgiven all their sins, careless words, and thoughtless attitudes. But whoever speaks wrongly of the work of God's Spirit and does not acknowledge that work in his own heart, cannot yet experience forgiveness as long as that blindness persists. He is liable for a sin that prevents him from recognizing the truth. That sin will remain with him for as long an age as he refuses to open the door of his understanding and humbly acknowledge God for who he is."
>
> I would not be supposed to mean that the word "never" should be stricken from the divine lexicon. There are indeed some things that God will *never* do: God will *never* cease the relentless knock of his Fatherly love on the stubborn heart's doors of his wayward children as long as a single one remains lost. God is not even capable of "never" forgiving. To *never forgive* contradicts his very nature!
>
> He is not a God who will arbitrarily and endlessly punish to all eternity, *refusing* to forgive, *will-ing,* choosing "never" to forgive. Rather he is a God who is *anxious* to forgive, and who seeks all opportunities for the entry of his Spirit into the wayward human heart.
>
> Verily, he is not the unforgiving tyrant of erroneous orthodoxies, but he is rather the *always* forgiving, the *ever*-forgiving, the *ceaseless* forgiving God and Father of Jesus Christ!
>
> Michael Phillips, "The Great Sin," Leben 7

God, bring to my remembrance this day the Command of Jesus to FORGIVE 70 X 7 TIMES. *As my eyes are opened to see that you never cease desiring to forgive, even in hell itself, may I have eyes to see the infinite scope of your eternal plan. May the limitlessness of your forgiveness fill my heart and overflow in my own forgiveness for my brothers and sisters of humanity. Give me wisdom to believe infinite things of you, and enlarge my heart to live moment-by-moment in the inexhaustibility of your loving forgiveness. Thus, heavenly Father, may I be an instrument in my small corner of the world for the ultimate salvation of mankind. Amen.*

43. Do Good, Be Good

"If you do good only to those who do good to you, what credit is that to you." (Luke 6:33)
"Love…and do good…expecting nothing in return." (Luke 6:35)

One of the profound mysteries of the Christian church is that human *goodness* has not comprised more focus in its theology. While it is true that greater good has been done throughout history by Christianity than any nation, movement, or creed, one is hard-pressed to find goodness at the center of any doctrinal teaching. How many thousands of volumes have analyzed every theological intricacy of God's nature, which yet gloss over the fundamental resounding reality of the universe: God is good.

Without the centrality of Goodness undergirding the whole, that massive Christian theology degenerates into noisy gongs and clanging symbols of religious gobbledegook. Goodness and love are the character strands upon which the entire tapestry of Christian theology must be woven. Without their interbonding strength, the fabric disintegrates.

So far has Christian theology missed this essential bull's eye, that there is even a teaching prevalent in its more pious forms implying that goodness is a deception. "Ah, don't forget, brother, our goodness is as filthy rags. It won't get you into heaven." The Church of England's Thirty-Nine Articles of Faith of 1571 asserted that good works in the absence of faith "have the nature of sin." Many evangelistic agendas are based upon the perspective that goodness is no virtue. Without salvation, so the teaching goes, goodness is a snare of the enemy.

If ever a preposterous falsehood needed to be trampled underfoot, it is this. In whatever form it manifests itself, goodness is a wonderful and glorious reflection of our Creator. Goodness is a *good* thing! As Christ's followers, goodness is *commanded* of us.

In Mark 10:18, we see why. When the young man asked him about eternal life, Jesus answered by reminding him of this fundamental component of his Father's essential nature—simple goodness. *God is good.*

If we truly laid hold of this single Fact of the universe, so many of the intricacies and conundrums of our theologies would instantly resolve themselves. Doubts would vanish, fears evaporate. The world would be changed because God's people would march forth every day into its highways and byways in the living reality of knowing *who God is.*

Every word of Jesus' teaching is infused with the implication: *Be good.* When Jesus commands goodness upon his followers he is saying nothing more than, "Be like God."

Let us then today, you and I, go out into the world and simply be good people. For this day let us lay aside our multitude of doctrines and theologies. Let us simply discover how we can *do good* and *be good,* and thus reflect God's nature and character to the world.

> In my search for foundations, I often return to the book of Genesis. And there, at the very beginning of all foundations, several years ago I discovered a remarkable truth…the undergirding Truth upon which the entire creation was established.
>
> GOODNESS…The Word of God simply says: *God saw that it was good.* It is repeated six times for each of the six days. And then, the resounding conclusion on the seventh day, the seven of perfection, when the creation was complete—a creation which *included* man…God saw that it was *very good!*
>
> What a triumphant foundation upon which to establish a world—*goodness,* the very goodness of God himself…You and I have goodness within us that bears the imprint of the very nature of God himself…
>
> The universe…was founded and established in goodness. God is good. His creation was good. Mankind was created with goodness in his nature, because his nature possessed God's nature.
>
> Michael Phillips, "Foundations and the Nature of Man," *Leben 4*

God, bring to my remembrance this day the Command of Jesus to DO GOOD AND BE GOOD. Remind me that goodness is of your character, your nature…who you are. When I obey the Command to DO GOOD AND BE GOOD, I visibly fulfill my discipleship as Christ's follower before a watching world. Open my eyes to the imperative that GOODNESS is my calling whenever another of your children crosses my path. Thus, heavenly Father, through simple goodness, may I be an instrument in my small corner of the world for the ultimate salvation of mankind. Amen.

44. Seek First God's Kingdom

"Seek first his kingdom and his righteousness, and all these things shall be yours as well." (Matthew 6:33)

Among the "spiritual" Commands, few are so illusive as this. Jesus concludes his *Do not be anxious about your life* discussion of the birds of the air and lilies of the field in Matthew 6 with the words: *Your heavenly Father knows that you need them all. But seek first his kingdom and his righteousness, and all these things shall be yours as well.*

As noted earlier, Jesus' words cannot be read as condoning laziness, not holding a job, taking no responsibility for life, and simply waiting for God to provide. There are those who read them thus, and they have been a thorn in the side of Christ's church for nearly two thousand years. Who among us have not known certain pious types who, pointing to the above verse, think that the height of spirituality is reached by sitting around and talking about God all day long…but who never put any of their lofty ideals into practice. They are those of whom it is said, *They are too heavenly minded to be of any earthly good.*

Jesus, however, is not promising that God will provide our needs miraculously as manna dropping from heaven. He is pointing to a deeper principle. He is speaking of a mindset, an orientation, a life-focus which recognizes the truth of the old adage that we truly are pilgrims in this world. This is not our final home. This is merely a training ground, our temporary residence where we are schooled and prepared in readiness, where we are made into God's sons and daughters, so that we might be his true sons and daughters to all eternity. At the foundation of that outlook is the Truth of all truths: We have a God who is a true *Father*, who loves us and cares for us and makes provision for us.

Such a focus becomes more natural as one ages. As eternity draws closer with every passing year, the lures of the world lose the grip they once had. This is a perspective one must begin to nurture early. Only a lifetime's obedient practice sends the roots of this eternal perspective into every nook and cranny of being, and bears the fruit of childship in our hearts.

One of these fruits that results from seeking first the kingdom of God is that the cares and anxieties of this world gradually lose their power over us. Our true citizenship lies elsewhere. *Righteousness* is the supremely valued commodity in the kingdom where we live. What do we care for temporal things like food, clothes, money, cars, status, elections, fashions, stock markets? We may be *interested*, as any traveler is interested in a foreign country he is visiting. We have to eat. We must provide for ourselves. We attempt to be good stewards of what we have been provided, as any traveler in a foreign land must. We are legal immigrants to this world. We desire to fit in responsibly with its ways and customs, and are free to enjoy them. But all these things have no power to move our foundations. We are looking toward a different ultimate kingdom, where righteousness is the meat and drink that sustains eternal life.

We may, therefore, read Jesus' Command along these lines: *God's kingdom is your true home. In that kingdom, only righteousness matters. Therefore, keep your eyes focused on the principles that define how things function in God's kingdom and don't worry about what you will eat or what you will wear. Provide for yourselves, but do not worry about these temporal concerns. Live responsibly and they will take care of themselves.*

"This world never did seem my home; I have never felt quite comfortable in it...
"Does the Bible itself not tell us that we are pilgrims and strangers in this world...? It is but a place to which we come to be made ready for another."
George MacDonald, *What's Mine's Mine*, Ch. 32

God, bring to my remembrance this day the Command of Jesus to SEEK FIRST YOUR KINGDOM. Open my inner eyes to this revelation, that throughout my busy day, your kingdom is right beside me, inside me, all around me. In the midst of my work, keep me from anxiety, knowing that the concerns of my life will take care of themselves. Teach me what it means to SEEK FIRST YOUR KINGDOM. Fill my heart with a hunger and thirst for righteousness. Thus, heavenly Father, may I be an instrument in my small corner of the world for the ultimate salvation of mankind. Amen.

45. Store Up Treasure in Heaven

"Do not store up...treasures on earth...but store up for yourselves treasures in heaven."
(Matthew 6:19-20, NIV)

The Command, *Do not store up for yourselves treasures on earth, but store up for yourselves treasures in heaven*, may also seem an illusive one. A moment's reflection, however, reveals this as one of the most down-to-earth of all Jesus' Commands.

There are many kinds of financial accounts: Checking accounts, savings accounts, retirement accounts, stock market portfolios, IRAs, 401-Ks. They all have one thing in common, however. Assets don't appear in these accounts of themselves. The value of the account is based on what has been put *into* it. The total cumulative amount of deposits made, plus interest, determines the final value.

The principle is a simple one. If an individual, starting early in life, puts a dollar a day into an account, the total value with interest at the end of his life will be staggering. If he puts in more, his modest investment may grow into a small fortune. There also exist spiritual accounts. They do not produce a quarterly printout of deposits, withdrawals, and balance. This does not change the fact that they are more real and long-lasting than any bank account on earth.

In Matthew 6, Jesus is speaking of an account in which every one of us is making deposits and withdrawals every moment. It is called our *Character Account.* Every time we humbly and sacrificially obey one of the Commands, every time we are kind to a neighbor, do a good deed, whisper *Not my will,* forgive one who has wronged us, or pray for an adversary...with every turn of the heart in obedience we add a deposit into the Character Account. We are not limited to a dollar a day. We can make twenty deposits a day!

These deposits *change* us. They deepen the character of Christlikeness within us. These changes to our character represent the interest added to our obedience-deposits. All our lives we are invisibly building a spiritual character that defines who we are.

C.S. Lewis explains it this way: "Every time you make a choice you are turning the central part of you...into something a little different from what it was before. And taking your life as a whole, with all your innumerable choices, all your life long you are slowly turning this central thing either into a heavenly creature or into a hellish creature...Good and evil both increase at compound interest. That is why the little decisions you and I make every day are of such infinite importance." (*Mere Christianity*, Book 3, Ch. 4; Ch. 9)

When we are met by Jesus in the next life, and all the investments and savings accounts of this world have become less than a speck of dust, the balance in our Character Account will suddenly be revealed. What were we making of ourselves all along?

"Do you have something for me?" came his words, as I stood on the morning of my waking.

I now noticed that the hand of he who met me in the garden was extended...as if waiting for me to place something into it...

"But I arrived here with nothing. Only myself."

"You speak truly. Your *Self*...was given you spotless, brimming with potential for development. I gave you opportunity to make something of it..."

"But I didn't know I was making my Self into something that...*you* would want to see."

"All things are given for that purpose. Why would it have been given you?...That was the only thing that mattered. In a million ways I told you every day to make your Self into something you could hand me on this day...Now come, my young brother, *what have you made of what you were given?*...Your Self is my Father's...You were given it for a season. The time has now come when you must give it back...The time has come for us to see what you made of that which my Father gave you."

Michael Phillips, *The Garden At the Edge of Beyond,* Chs. 2-3

God, bring to my remembrance this day the Command of Jesus to STORE UP TREASURE IN HEAVEN. Fill every choice, attitude, word, and response with reminders of my heavenly Character Account in which I am making deposits every day. May I thus be prepared on that day when Jesus asks me, "What have you made of what you were given?" Thus, heavenly Father, may I be an instrument in my small corner of the world for the ultimate salvation of mankind. Amen.

46. Be Kind

"...be sons of the Most High; for he is kind..." (Luke 6:35)
"As you did it to one of the least of these my brethren, you did it to me." (Matthew 25:40)

Biblical literalists more eager to find loopholes in the Commands than to obey them will be the first to point out that Jesus never specifically commanded *kindness* upon his disciples. We could find no better example of straining at a gnat to swallow a camel.

To the legalist mind, they would be right. Seen accurately, however, for the big picture, the entire Gospel is infused with kindness from beginning to end. In this larger sense, every word, every gesture, every prayer of Jesus speaks of kindness. Love, kindness, and goodness provide the underlying life-pulsating air of the Gospel. Jesus hardly needed to *say*, "Love, be kind, be good." Every teaching, every parable, every exhortation positively *shouted*, "Love, be kind, be good."

Thus, to understand the Commands of Jesus, and to live them as he expects, requires us to read between the lines, to obey the *implied* Commands as well as the direct Commands. Chief among the implied Commands is: *Be kind.*

It has been said that the teaching of Jesus, in its simplest form, can be expressed as, "Be *nice* and treat people with *kindness*." Such a prescription for the practical and observable Christian life in the midst of a selfish, greedy, corrupt, and sinful world might not be far wrong. Evangelists anxious to "Get people saved" may disagree. But how else can we read Jesus' words in Luke 6:35 than, *Be kind and thus be like God.*

When Paul spelled out the components of love in 1 Corinthians 13, he begins with two towering attributes that ought to be the first character-clothes we put on every morning: *Love is patient and kind.*

We might call them our Discipleship Coat and Christlikeness Cloak.

If God is love, and love is patient and kind, then *God himself* is patient and kind. They are of God's very nature.

Every kindness we show, however large or small—a cup of cold water, a kind word, a smile, a gracious gesture—is a visible expression of the face of God smiling into humanity, the hand of the Creator reaching into his world to touch the brother and sister, made in his image, beside us.

Kindness. Love active. Have you ever noticed how much of Christ's life was spent in doing kind things—in *merely* doing kind things? Run over it with that in view, and you will find that He spent a great proportion of His time simply in making people happy, in doing good turns to people. There is only one thing greater than happiness in the world, and that is holiness; and it is not in our keeping; but what God *has* put in our power is the happiness of those about us, and that is largely to be secured by our being kind to them.

"The greatest thing," says someone, "a man can do for his Heavenly Father is to be kind to some of His other children." I wonder why it is that we are not all kinder than we are. How much the world needs it. How easily it is done. How instantaneously it acts. How infallibly it is remembered. How superabundantly it pays itself back—for there is no debtor in the world so honourable, so superbly honourable, as Love. "Love never faileth." Love is success. Love is happiness. Love is life. "Love, I say," with Browning, "is energy of Life."

Henry Drummond, *The Greatest Thing in the World*

God, bring to my remembrance this day the Command of Jesus to BE KIND. *This day, this very day that I have in front of me, will present me with a dozen or more opportunities simply to* BE KIND *to my brothers and sisters of humanity. Perhaps, were my eyes truly open, ten times that! To walk in the steps of Christlikensss lies at my very door—in the next five minutes...all day long. Therefore, Lord, bring the smile, the gracious word, the helping hand to my eyes, my lips, my gestures without even thinking about it. May your* KINDNESS *radiate from my being. Lord Jesus, remind me how close you are—in the faces and needs and aches and fears of those about me. Give me grace to* BE KIND *in your name, because I am your follower and call myself a Christian. Thus, heavenly Father, through simple human kindness, may I be an instrument in my small corner of the world for the ultimate salvation of mankind. Amen.*

47. Love and Pray for Your Adversaries

"Love your enemies and pray for those who persecute you, so that you may be sons of your Father." (Matthew 5:44-45)

As world changing as would be the influence of Christians taking the words seriously, *Rejoice and be glad when you are reviled and persecuted* (Matthew 5:11-12), Jesus goes on to elevate the relation between Christians and their adversaries to a shockingly ambitious level. "I don't merely want you to rejoice when you are ill-treated," he says, "I want you to *love your enemies*." We are so familiar with the words that their revolutionary power escapes us. This was *an unheard of* teaching. There had *never* been anything like it.

Many in the world look upon Jesus as a "great moral teacher" yet feel no imperative toward serious obedience to his teachings. They regard him with a detached regard that keeps any personal demand of character from touching them practically. Even Islam *claims* to honor Jesus, though the superficiality of the assertion is not difficult to see.

Many skeptics make the point that the teachings of Jesus are not really so unique at all. Truth, kindness, unselfishness, goodness, and love have been universally taught by most of the world's great men. In one teaching, however, Jesus stands alone. In his challenge about treatment of one's adversaries, he obliterated all past and all future notions of what it means to be a person of faith in God. *Love and pray for your enemies* is not merely a revolutionary expectation to place upon his followers, Jesus raises it to the summit of importance among his teachings. By *this*, he says, you will utterly distinguish yourselves from the world...by *this* will you become sons of your Father.

It is true that many pretend to obey the injunction to pray for their enemies while keeping animosity alive: *Lord, convict my enemy of their sin against me*. This may technically be called a "prayer." But it is not a prayer borne out of love.

Some also pray versions of David's prayer: *Lord, punish my enemies...give me victory over them...vindicate me in the sight of my foe.* Others occasionally pray in the tradition of James and John: *Lord, rain down fire from heaven on my enemies.* To all these counterfeit self-motivated prayers Jesus replies, "But it shall not be so among you."

The Command is *LOVE and pray for your adversaries*. Pray for them *in love*. Pray for God's goodness in their lives. That is a more difficult assignment than merely praying for them to be convicted of sin. In this Command Jesus addresses the orientation and attitude of *my* heart, not the sin of my adversaries. *Their* sin is not the point. The attitude of *my* heart is. This prayer is one to be prayed in front of the mirror.

In Jesus' mighty example on the cross, he did not ask God to convict his enemies of their sin. He did not pray for vengeance. He prayed for goodness in their lives. He merely said, *Father, forgive them*.

> Is not this at length *too* much to expect? Will a man ever love his enemies?...When he is the child of his Father in heaven. Then shall he love his neighbour as himself, even if that neighbour be his enemy...
>
> Is it then reasonable to love our enemies? God does; therefore it must be the highest reason. But is it reasonable to expect that man should become capable of doing so? Yes; on one ground: that the divine energy is at work in man... For this our Lord prayed when he said: "That they all may be one, as thou, Father, art in me, and I in thee, that they also may be one in us."...
>
> "Be ye therefore perfect, even as your father which is in heaven is perfect." "Love your enemies, and ye shall be the children of the highest." It is the divine glory to forgive.
>
> George MacDonald, *Unspoken Sermons, First Series*, "Love Thine Enemy"

God, bring to my remembrance this day the Command of Jesus to LOVE AND PRAY FOR MY ADVERSARIES. *There are few Commands so difficult as asking for good in the lives of those who have done me harm. But with all the honesty I can summon, I relinquish my desire to get even, and I ask you to accomplish your purposes in their lives. If those purposes involve me, give me humility to do what you require of me. Root all unforgiveness out of my heart. I do not love them as I know you do. But I ask you to help me love them. Perhaps at first I can only try. But with your help, this I am willing to do. I will try to love. Thus, heavenly Father, may I be an instrument in my small corner of the world for the ultimate salvation of mankind. Amen.*

48. Do Good to Those Who Hate You

"Do good to those who hate you. If you do good to those who do good to you, what credit is that to you?" (Luke 6:27, 33)

Jesus does not even leave it at *Rejoice when you are persecuted* and *Love and pray for your enemies.* He goes further still. The three-tiered progression of response to ill-treatment in Luke 6 is incredible and completely impractical. The programme Jesus outlines is impossible by any earthly standards.

It's not enough, he says, merely to love and pray for your adversaries. That's the easy part. Those you can do privately, without actually having to engage your enemy personally.

Now I want you to take it further. Having rejoiced within yourself, having prayed for him, I want you now to actively engage with him, and find ways to *do good* to the bitterest of your adversaries—to one who actually hates you.

We cannot counterfeit obedience to this most extreme of Jesus' Commands. Here we discover whether we mean business. It is easy enough to gloss over some of the more palatable Commands—*do good, be kind, do unto others, believe in God.* Not that we actually *obey* these Commands perfectly. How many of us would claim to treat others as we would be treated even for an hour a day? *All* Jesus' Commands are impossible. Yet many are tolerable. We don't squawk and squirm at the level of self-denial required.

But *Do good to those who hate you.* The very words are stark, blunt, unyielding, a slap in the face of religious complacency. We are left no place to hide. Jesus intended it so. Throughout this passage he contrasts the world's way with his way. No one in the world would for a moment consider such a crazy thing as doing good to one who hates you. But Jesus says, "If you would follow me...that is exactly what *you* must do."

To consider seeking out such a one, going to him or her with kindness, finding a way to *do good,* without condescension, without judgment, without defense or justification, knowing our actions may be misunderstood, willing to appear the fool, even to be laughed at...the very thought scratches with claws across our souls.

What price are we willing to pay to follow Jesus when he says, "Do as I do."

By this will all men know that you are my disciples—if you do good to those who hate you.

The question must be put to each man by himself, "Is my neighbour indeed my enemy, or am I my neighbour's enemy... For we are accountable for the ill in ourselves, and have to kill it; for the good in our neighbour, and have to cherish it. He only, in the name and power of God, can kill the bad in him; we can cherish the good in him by being good to it across all the evil fog that comes between our love and his good.

Nor ought it to be forgotten that this fog is often the result of misapprehension and mistake, giving rise to all kinds of indignations, resentments, and regrets. Scarce anything about us is just as it seems...O brother, sister, across this weary fog...I call to the divine in thee...not to rebuke thee, not to rouse thee, not to say "Why hatest thou me?" but to say "I love thee; in God's name I love thee."...

In the working of the Divine Love upon the race, my enemy is doomed to cease to be my enemy, and to become my friend. One flash of truth towards me would destroy my enmity at once; one hearty confession of wrong, and our enmity passes away; from each comes forth the brother who was inside the enemy all the time...

George MacDonald, *Unspoken Sermons, First Series*, "Love Thine Enemy"

God, bring to my remembrance this day the Command of Jesus to DO GOOD TO THOSE WHO HATE ME. As distasteful as I find it, I pray that you would present me opportunities to do them good. I will need your help, your wisdom, your encouragement, Lord, because to DO GOOD TO THOSE WHO HATE ME goes against all I am as a fleshly human being. But I desire your will above my own, and I know there is no other path to Christlikeness than this. Thus, heavenly Father, may I be an instrument in my small corner of the world for the ultimate salvation of mankind. Amen.

49. Do Not Exalt Yourself

They had discussed with one another who was the greatest. And he sat down and called the twelve; and he said to them, "If any one would be first, he must be last of all and servant of all." (Mark 9:34-35)

"Do not sit down in a place of honor...go and sit in the lowest place." (Luke 14:8, 10)

After passing through Galilee and returning home to Capernaum, Jesus posed a very pointed question to the disciples: "What were you discussing on the way?" Their response was that of a group of children caught red-handed with their hands in the cookie jar. Mark merely says, "They were silent; for on the way they had discussed with one another who was the greatest." Jesus had nailed them, and they knew it.

Luke's version of the incident is expanded and sheds additional nuance of meaning: *A dispute arose among them, which of them was to be regarded as the greatest. And he said to them, "The kings of the Gentiles exercise lordship over them...But not so with you; rather let the greatest among you become as the youngest, and the leader as one who serves...I am among you as one who serves."* (Luke 22:24-27)

In all ways, the rules of the kingdom in which Jesus desires his followers to live are completely upside-down from those of the world. Being human and living in the world, however, these new and inverted priorities are difficult to get into our heads. They go against everything we have been taught, everything we feel, everything the world proclaims. The Command to be *in* the world but not *of* the world hits us in the face the minute we get out of bed every day, and every time we read a single one of Jesus' Commands.

Everything within us shouts to exalt ourselves, to put ourselves first, to seek the best seat, to go to the front of the line, to be praised and well-thought of, to be in the spotlight. We *want* to be great. Who doesn't? Who wouldn't rather be lauded in front of a crowd than sit ignored in the back row? Who wouldn't rather be on the music team or stand in the pulpit than come into church on Monday to clean the toilets?

George MacDonald explains how inverted this is from God's perspective: "It is a fundamental necessity of the kingdom of heaven, impossible as it must seem to all outside it, that each shall count other[s] better than himself; it is the natural condition of the man God made, in relation to the other men God has made...Man is made, not to contemplate himself, but to behold in others the beauty of the Father." (*Home Again*, Ch. 10)

When Jesus says, *Do not exalt yourself*, he is issuing an intensely practical Command that *can* be obeyed. It is as simple as doing what he says. When you attend a function, he says, don't look around for the best seat—go and sit in the lowest place. If you have a good voice and perfect pitch, maybe the place for you to use your gift is in the congregation not standing in front where you will be seen and praised for your talent. In the workplace, do we try to look better and be seen as "greater" than our co-workers? Do we seek to rise the ladder of authority at every opportunity by raising ourselves in the eyes of our superiors? Do we desire to "rule" and "exercise authority?" In how many ways throughout our lives are we subtly trying to "get ahead" and make ourselves "look good"? How might a politician who is serious about obeying the Commands actually live by *Do not exalt yourself*? That's pretty practical!

> The man who refuses to assert himself, seeking no recognition by men, leaving the care of his life to the Father, and occupying himself with the will of the Father, shall find himself, by and by, at home in his Father's house, with all his Father's property his.

George MacDonald, *The Hope of the Gospel,* "The Heirs of Heaven and Earth"

God, bring to my remembrance this day the Command of Jesus NOT TO EXALT MYSELF. It is almost frightening to pray it for fear of how shocking it may be, but I ask you to open my eyes to see, really SEE the many ways I subtly try to exalt myself every day. Teach me the glorious freedom of counting others as better than myself. Fill me with the joy of walking the low road among my peers, as I seek to serve them not rise above them. Infuse me with the humility of Christ. Thus, heavenly Father, as I learn to cease self-contemplation, may I be an instrument in my small corner of the world for the ultimate salvation of mankind. Amen.

50. Honor Your Father and Mother

"You know the commandments…Honor your father and mother…" (Mark 10:19)

None of the Ten Commandments has been so diminished of its power by our modern culture more than honor to one's parents. Independence is the god of our age. The cancer that has infected our time is not merely anti-family, as serious as that threat is. It goes far deeper. It is the cancer of anti-ANYBODY else. *I-me-mine* is the only voice modernism says I am required to heed.

Naturally, then, that we have been placed on this earth with those *over* us whom we are commanded to *obey* is an absolute anathema to modernism. *Obedience* and *submission* are hateful words. But so too is the notion of honor. SELF is the only being our culture honors.

Thus we are swimming upstream in an attempt to honor, esteem, and revere our parents with the full breadth and scope that we must believe characterized Jesus' feelings toward Mary and Joseph. It is not mere "obedience," for that clearly shifts and changes through the years. A full-grown adult is not responsible for the same level of submission and obedience to his or her parents as he or she is at ten. Yet if anything, the "honor" Jesus speaks of does not diminish but grows and deepens through the years. The obedience of early life is transformed to an eternal perspective of reverential esteem and *honor.*

Of certain children, George MacDonald says, "They were greatly proud of their father…believing him…the best man that ever was in the world;

and to believe so of one's parents is a stronger aid to righteousness than all things else whatever until the day-star of the knowledge of the great Father goes up in the heart." (*Weighed and Wanting*, Ch. 23)

Does this mean we pretend not to notice our parents' failings? Of course not. We are commanded to honor them, not because they have been perfect parents or perfect people, but because they are the men and women God chose as *our* parents.

Discovering God's Fatherhood in my earthly father was not easy...My father was not what would be called an overtly and expressively 'spiritual' man. He did not *teach* me about God...Yet he was *my* father. God gave him to *me* to teach *me* about his infinite and perfect Fatherhood.

The responsibility was thus upon *me* to find that "divine reflection" of the eternal among the human limitations that my dad brought to the relational equation between us as father and son. *All* human fathers bring imperfection to that life-equation. If human fatherhood is a mirror reflecting the image of God, it is a broken one whose reflection is imperfect and distorted. Yet it is the tool God has given us...I have therefore come to view it as entirely *my* responsibility to discover God in my father. It was not *his* responsibility to be anything other than the man he was. It was *my* responsibility to learn to see God in him. The *issues* common to the life-experience of parents and children were *mine* to take accountability for and grow from, not his. The charge given me was to *honor* him, not for being a perfect father, but for being *my* father, for giving me life, and, in a deeply mysterious way, for being God's earthly representative to me of the divine nature...

I firmly believe that this process is the doorway that leads to intimacy with God. We have *issues* with God, too...We have to find his love for us in the midst of humanity's brokenness...

This is the universal human story, though the books being written by each of our lives are unique. Orphans have a particularly difficult time connecting the dots from earthly to heavenly in this process of personal accountability and discovery. Yet there are unique lessons God can nevertheless teach them about himself. Some sons and daughters have cruel fathers, some have wonderfully kind fathers. Children of divorce and separation face much different challenges...But *all* humanity is issued the same challenge—*Discover who God is, discover what Father means.* I happen to believe...that human fatherhood is the preeminent doorway into this discovery.

Michael Phillips, "A Biographical Sketch," From FatherOfTheInklings.com

God, bring to my remembrance this day the Command of Jesus to HONOR MY FATHER AND MOTHER. *Open my eyes to my parents in new ways, no more dwelling on their faults but rather perceiving my responsibility to discover what you have for me to learn through them. Deepen my regard and esteem for them both, even after they are gone. Fill me with reverential honor at every thought of them. I thank you for giving me the mother and father you chose for me. Thus, heavenly Father, may I be an instrument in my small corner of the world for the ultimate salvation of mankind. Amen.*

Series Six

"The Judas Commands"

Hypocrisy

Why the World Hates Religiosity

One of the theological conundrums of all times is: Did Jesus know Judas would betray him when he called him as one of the twelve? The variety of potential answers depends on the theological leanings of those trying to solve the riddle more than upon any information or evidence that is given in Scripture. We do not know the answer.

It seems unlikely he did. If Jesus *knew* of the betrayal that would take place on the last week of his earthly life, for him to choose Judas *knowing* that "it would be worse for him than had he never been born," what can we call it but an act of cruel treachery? The possibility that Jesus *didn't* know, and thus did not see the future with perfect clarity, may to some indicate a limitation on his divinity. On the other hand, we are told that, except for sin, Jesus experienced the fullness of our human nature just as we do. *Doubt* about the future is so systemic to our humanity, it seems he must have experienced it. Indeed, his prayer in the garden on the night before his death, asking God to remove the cup of impending death, seems to confirm that, in Jesus' mind, the future contained uncertainty, and some degree of doubt about its final outcome.

One thing we can be sure of—Judas did not begin his life of discipleship as a betrayer. Like the others, he began heeding the summons, *Follow me.* He heard the teaching. He was sent out as an Apostle. With the other eleven, he returned exultant at having healed and cast out demons. Think of it—Judas performed miracles in Jesus' name.

Therefore, it is obvious that Judas *changed.* When, and why—we will never know. The first hint of it comes in Matthew 26 and John 12 when Judas complains about Mary's anointing Jesus' feet with expensive perfume. His motives seem noble—saying that the money could have been used for the poor. John adds, however, that it was not so much concern for the poor that was on Judas' mind, but keeping the money box full because he was a thief and was in the habit of stealing from it.

Then a few days later Judas made his fateful bargain with the Jewish leaders for thirty pieces of silver, for which he agreed to betray Jesus into their hands.

Was he moved by money? Or was he trying to force Jesus to declare himself openly as the Messiah, seize power in Israel, and lead an insurrection to cast off Roman rule?

The character of Judas is filled with questions. We know but two things for certain. We know that Judas changed. Men and women can obey the initial *Follow me,* full of vitality and enthusiasm and commitment...and yet in time fall away. They may still call themselves Christians. But obedience to the Commands ceases to be the motivating force in their lives. The example of Judas is played out in every church in the land. People *change*, lose their fire, and grow lukewarm in their obedience. No one is immune from the danger. It is *hard* to obey over a lifetime. The other thing we know about Judas, if we are to take John's words as written, is that he pretended to be more spiritual than he was. He made pretense of caring for the poor. But what he really wanted was the money. We can read the scene in John 12 as a clever bit of play-acting on his part. This is hypocrisy—pretending to be what we're not. No Christian is immune from the danger of hypocrisy either.

And it gives off a stench that is foul to a watching world.

ὑπόκρισις : HUPOKRISIS—*Hypocrisy*

The word "hypocrisy" derives from the Greek verb "to answer." It was used for masked stage actors who spoke in dialogue, "answering" back and forth to one another. It thus came to mean pretence, play-acting, adopting a role. Most of the New Testament uses of *hypocrisy* and *hypocrite* are found in Matthew and nearly all are aimed at the Pharisees. Jesus' meaning is clear: They are those who make a pretense of religiosity, who pretend to be what they are not.

Series Six

Why the World Hates Religiosity

51. Guard against hypocrisy.
52. Let your light shine before men.
53. If someone takes from you, do not demand back what you have given.
54. Seek no spiritual signs.
55. Be born again.
56. Do not justify or worry how to defend yourself.
57. Learn of me.
58. Receive the kingdom of God like a child.
59. Have salt in yourselves.
60. Be a good steward over what God has given you.

51. Guard Against Hypocrisy

"Woe to you, scribes and Pharisees, hypocrites! for you are like whitewashed tombs, which outwardly appear beautiful, but within they are full of dead men's bones and all uncleanness. So you also outwardly appear righteous to men, but within you are full of hypocrisy and iniquity." (Matthew 23:27-28)

"Beware of the leaven of the Pharisees, which is hypocrisy." (Luke 12:1)

Note that Jesus does not directly command *Don't be a hypocrite.* Is the reason perhaps because, in truth, to a degree we cannot help being hypocrites. We are all sinners, and thus hypocrites, together. It is part of the human condition.

He tells his disciples to *beware* of hypocrisy. It is a word full of meaning. It calls to mind yet again his repeated injunctions to *Remain alert and on guard.* Be especially on guard when standing in front of the mirror, for that is where the deception will take place.

Hypocrisy, otherwise known as self-righteousness, is, along with pride, the most subtle of sins. It slips in unseen. Without unceasing vigilance against our slippery self, we almost cannot help trying to put on a front of pretending to be better than we are. This doesn't mean we should go around telling every negative thought that pops into our minds, and confessing every five minutes how terrible we are. Obedience to this Command has less to do with open confession of our sins as it does the private dialog that takes place in our prayer closets. If we aren't playing games with God, it is unlikely we will play games with people either. The scribes and Pharisees, whom Jesus rebuked with such scorching language in Matthew 23, were play-acting with God. This was the root of their hypocrisy.

When we are alone with God, gazing into the mirror of our own souls, this is the time to heed Jesus' words: *Beware of the self-righteous leaven of the Pharisees, pretending to be better than you are...which is hypocrisy.*

God is not a God that hides, but a God that reveals. His whole work in relation to the creatures he has made...is revelation—the giving them truth, the showing of himself to them, that they may know him, and come nearer…to him…That we are in the dark about anything is never because he hides it, but because we are not yet such that he is able to reveal that thing to us…

God [can sometimes] not do [a] thing at once which he takes time to do…His will cannot finally be thwarted; where it is thwarted for a time, the very thwarting subserves the working out of a higher part of his will. He gave man the power to thwart his will, that, by means of that same power, he might come at last to do his will in a higher kind and way than would otherwise have been possible…God sacrifices his will to man that man may become such as himself…he makes man able to do wrong, that he may choose and love righteousness…

In whatever mode the Lord may intend that it shall be wrought out, he gives us to understand…that all such things as the unrighteous desire to conceal, and such things as it is a pain to the righteous to have concealed, shall come out into the light.

"Beware of hypocrisy," the Lord says, "for there is nothing covered, that shall not be revealed, neither hid, that shall not be known." What is hypocrisy? The desire to look better than you are; the hiding of things you do, because you would not be supposed to do them, because you would be ashamed to have them known…The doing of them is foul; the hiding of them, in order to appear better than you are, is fouler still. The man who does not live in his own consciousness as in the open heavens, is a hypocrite—and for most of us the question is, are we growing less or more of such hypocrites? Are we ashamed of not having been open and clear? Are we fighting the evil thing which is our temptation to hypocrisy? The Lord has not a thought in him to be ashamed of before God and his universe, and he will not be content until he has us in the same liberty. For our encouragement to fight on, he tells us that those that hunger and thirst after righteousness shall be filled, that they shall become as righteous as the spirit of the Father and the Son in them can make them desire.

George MacDonald, *Unspoken Sermons, Third Series,* "The Final Unmasking"

God, bring to my remembrance this day the Command of Jesus to GUARD AGAINST HYPOCRISY. *Remind me that life is neither a play nor a game. As I cannot hide my true self from God by putting on a mask of self-righteousness, neither should I try to deceive those around me by pretending to be other than I am, which is a sinner trying to follow Jesus and become your son or daughter. Keep me from Pharisaism. Thus, heavenly Father, may I be an instrument in my small corner of the world for the ultimate salvation of mankind. Amen.*

52. Let Your Light Shine Before Men

"Let your light so shine before men, that they may see your good works and give glory to your Father who is in heaven." (Matthew 5:16)

We continue to encounter the strange dichotomy in the Lord's words between public and private righteousness. How do we balance, *Beware of practicing your piety before men,* with, *Let your light so shine before men?* The two Commands appear less than a chapter apart in the Sermon on the Mount, yet seem to instruct us in completely opposite directions.

This Command seems more simple than it is. The complexity of letting one's light shine exists on a higher plane than being "a sunbeam for Jesus."

In fact, this is one of the most difficult of all the Commands, both to understand and to obey. It is difficult because of what lurks around its edges. If we think wrongly about this one Command, disobedience to another dozen may indeed put a bushel over the light and extinguish it. Extraordinary maturity is required to walk the tightrope between letting one's light shine, while avoiding hypocrisy, self-righteousness, and trying to be noticed. It will not be accomplished by Sunday school songs. This is graduate level spirituality.

The key is found in the first word of the Command. Jesus does not say to *Shine* your light before men. In the effort to make one's *own* light shine is self-righteousness born. We have no light of ourselves. We cannot originate light on our own. We are created spiritual moons. We can only reflect the light of God's Sun. That light has been birthed within us, but *we* did not birth it. The light comes, not from us, but from God's goodness working in us. Therefore, Jesus says, *Let* the light of your good works shine…*Allow* your light to shine. Get out of the way, that God may shine *his* light, reflecting from our obedience, into the world. Jesus is the Light of the World. By our obedience to his Commands, that light is shed abroad into humanity around us.

What does Jesus mean by our "good works?" Nothing more nor less than obeying his Commands. Doing what he says. The most brilliant, visible, world transforming such "good work" of all is Love. *By this will all men know that you are my disciples, if you have love for one another.* This is the light that the world is hungry to see, that it wants to see, and that will convince the world that Jesus came from the Father.

Do not practice your piety to be seen…do good in secret…and *Let God's light within you shine before men.*

Let us…inquire how we are to let our light shine.

To the man who does not try to order his thoughts and feelings and judgments after the will of the Father, I have nothing to say; he can have no light to let shine. For to let our light shine is to see that in every, even the smallest thing, our lives and actions correspond to what we know of God; that, as the true children of our father in heaven, we do everything as he would have us do it. Need I say that to let our light shine is to be just, honourable, true, courteous, more careful over the claim of our neighbour than our own, as knowing ourselves in danger of overlooking it…

The outshining of any human light must be obedience to truth…our first show of light as the Lord's disciples must be in doing the things he tells us. Naturally thus we declare him our master, the ruler of our conduct, the enlightener of our souls; and while in the doing of his will a man is learning the loveliness of righteousness, he can hardly fail to let some light shine across the dust of his failures…Thus will his disciples shine as lights in the world…

To shine, we must keep in his light, sunning our souls in it by thinking of what he said and did, and would have us think and do. So shall we drink the light like some diamonds, keep it, and shine in the dark. Doing his will, men will see in us that we count the world his, hold that his will and not ours must be done in it. Our very faces will then shine with the hope of seeing him, and being taken home where he is. Only let us remember that trying to look what we ought to be, is the beginning of hypocrisy.

George MacDonald, *The Hope of the Gospel,* "The Salt and the Light of the World"

God, bring to my remembrance this day the Command of Jesus to LET MY LIGHT SHINE BEFORE MEN. *Let me reflect your light by my obedience, never thinking of myself, not trying to be a light myself, only thinking to do as Jesus tells me. Thus, heavenly Father, may my reflection of your light be an instrument in my small corner of the world for the ultimate salvation of mankind. Amen.*

53. If Someone Takes from You, Do Not Demand Back What You Have Given

"Give to every one who asks of you; and if anyone takes what belongs to you, do not demand it back…But love…and do good, and lend, expecting nothing in return."
(Luke 6:30 [NIV], 35 [RSV])

There are a variety of Commands that all point in the same direction: Give and expect nothing in return. Some emphasize giving more than has been requested: Go two miles instead of one, when asked for your coat give your cloak as well. The Command before us from Luke 6 contains three messages. One, give when you are asked. Two, if someone takes from you, don't demand back what you have given. Three, give and lend without expecting a return. The language here is ambiguous. The RSV has verse 30, *Give to every one who* BEGS *from you,* though that meaning is not found in every translation. Is Jesus speaking of the beggar on the street, or the neighbor who asks to borrow your car? Perhaps both.

However, if he is speaking of lending your car, he is obviously not saying to *give* your neighbor your car just because he has asked to borrow it. So we come up against another ambiguity: By "taking what belongs to you," is Jesus referring to what you have willingly loaned or given to a friend, or something of yours that has been stolen? When he commands us to "lend, expecting nothing *in return*," is he speaking of *interest*, or of not expecting ever to see *any* of the money again. If so, then why does he use the word *lend* rather than calling it a *gift*?

These questions may seem like splitting hairs. But they are important to consider for two reasons. One, they remind us again how easy it is to legalize the Scriptures through overmuch analysis, and thus rob them of their life. But two, and most importantly, they remind us that obedience to the Commands is not one-dimensional. Jesus never simply gives us a list of do's and dont's. He always speaks of large eternal principles.

Obedience to this Command, therefore, cannot be universalized to apply in exactly the same way in every situation. We simply have to pray to be given wisdom how to apply the large principle in the varying specific circumstances in which our *giving* places us.

This entire range of Commands, even in their ambiguity, point toward a giving, servant's heart. They are summed up a few verses later, when Jesus makes the sweeping Command and promise: *Give, and it will be given to you; good measure, pressed down, shaken together, running over, will be put into your lap. For the measure you give will be the measure you get back.* (Luke 6:38)

What are we for but to do our duty? We must do it and think nothing of ourselves...

"No man can do right for the sake of reward. A man may do a thing indifferent, he may do a thing wrong, for the sake of reward; but a thing in itself right, done for reward, would, in the very doing, cease to be right." At the same time, if a man does right, he cannot escape being rewarded for it...The whole question is of the kind of reward expected. What first reward for doing well, may I look for? To grow purer in heart, and stronger in the hope of at length seeing God...

"Creator," the childlike heart might cry, "give me all the wages, all the reward thy perfect father-heart can give thy unmeriting child. My fit wages may be pain, sorrow, humiliation of soul: I stretch out my hands to receive them. Thy reward will be to lift me out of the mire of self-love, and bring me nearer to thyself and thy children...Thy highest reward is thy purest gift; thou didst make me for it from the first; thou, the eternal life, hast been labouring still to fit me for receiving it—the vision, the knowledge, the possession of thyself. I can seek but what thou waitest and watchest to give: I would be such into whom thy love can flow."

George MacDonald, *The Hope of the Gospel,* "The Right Hand and the Left"

God, bring to my remembrance this day the Command of Jesus to GIVE AND NOT DEMAND BACK *WHAT I HAVE GIVEN. Whether I am loaning money or possessions, or giving them, may I not be possessive of what I give. I came into the world with nothing, I will leave it with nothing. Let me therefore use what you give me to spread your goodness, thinking of no return that will come to me as a result. Perhaps in some situations I may ask for the return of what I have given, but may I not demand it. May I give as freely as I have received from you. Thus, heavenly Father, may I be an instrument in my small corner of the world for the ultimate salvation of mankind. Amen.*

54. Seek No Spiritual Signs

"Why does this generation seek a sign? Truly, I say to you,
no sign shall be given to this generation." (Mark 8:12)
"This generation is an evil generation; it seeks a sign." (Luke 11:29)

One of the curious anomalies to arise out of the Evangelical and Pentecostal renewal of the late 20th century has been an inordinate obsession with spiritual "signs and wonders" as validating the work of the Holy Spirit. Entire churches, ministries, evangelistic movements, and schools have devoted themselves to the miraculous, and the encouragement of its manifestations to the exclusion of many other aspects of a rounded Christian life of obedience.

Have those many thousands swept up in this *What-miracle-will-God-perform-next* frenzy never read what Jesus says of sign-seekers? His words could hardly be more unambiguous: It is evil to seek signs from heaven to validate that God is at work on earth.

God *does* perform miracles. Jesus healed the sick, raised the dead, and rose on the third day. Yet he says not to *seek* signs. He may perform one in our midst. We can receive it with rejoicing. But do not seek them.

The *Miracle-of-the-Day-Club* is no place to hone obedience. The world will not be brought to Christ by outpourings and manifestations, but by doing what Jesus said. Do you want to be part of a temporal movement within Christendom that *cannot* change the world for Christ? Or do you want to participate in the eternal work of revealing God's being to a watching world through the *only* means by which Jesus said that revelation will occur?

Why does Jesus speak so strongly against seeking spiritual signs? Because signs will not convince the world of truth. He said that even if one were to come back from the dead for all to see, the world would still not believe. He *did* come back from the dead, and the world does not believe. Signs, wonders, manifestations, and miracles do not produce faith.

There is another serious danger inherent in sign-seeking. When one is *looking* for signs, and *expecting* miracles around every corner, it becomes fearfully easy to imbue commonplace events with a false glow of the supernatural. The parking place in the midst of busy traffic is thus interpreted as a "miracle" and an "answer to prayer," when in reality it is nothing more nor less than what it appears—a parking place and a nice bit of good luck. God does not perform as many miracles as sign-seekers give him credit for. Jesus commands us to rejoice in our circumstances and sufferings, not pray that the Holy Spirit would walk through life a step ahead of us smoothing the way. Jesus called the Holy Spirit the Spirit of Truth and our Comforter, not a Miracle Working Sorcerer.

This is a blunt word. Obedience to this Command may for some be the stumbling-block upon which the true Gospel taught by Jesus stands or falls. But there is no way to escape his words: *An evil and adulterous generation seeks for a sign.* (Matthew 16:4)

> If he came to reveal his Father in miniature, as it were...to tone down his great voice, which, too loud for men to hear it aright, could but sound to them as an inarticulate thundering, into such a still small voice as might enter their human ears in welcome human speech, then the works that his Father does so widely, so grandly that they transcend the vision of men, the Son must do briefly and sharply before their very eyes...
>
> What in the hands of the Father are the mighty motions and progresses and conquests of life, in the hands of the Son are miracles. I do not myself believe that he valued the working of these miracles as he valued the utterance of the truth in words; but all that he did had the one root, *obedience*...And what is the highest obedience? Simply a following of the Father—a doing of what the Father does. Every true father wills that his child should be as he is in his deepest love, in his highest hope. All that Jesus does is of his Father. What we see in the Son is of the Father.
>
> George MacDonald, *The Miracles of Our Lord*, "Introduction"

God, bring to my remembrance this day the Command of Jesus to SEEK NO SIGNS. *Give me discerning eyes to perceive the occasional miracles that fall from your hand, while not seeking signs and wonders in everything that happens. Let me rejoice no less in coincidence than in miracle, for both are opportunities to be thankful. May my faith be based on obedience not signs. Thus, heavenly Father, may I be an instrument in my small corner of the world for the ultimate salvation of mankind. Amen.*

55. Be Born Again

"You must be born again." (John 3:7, NIV)

With so much emphasis in Christendom through the centuries on salvation, it is remarkable that Jesus did not spell out in more detail exactly what salvation is. In his conversation with Nicodemus, in which he said that one must be "born again" to see the kingdom of God, in the single most well-known verse of the Bible, he connects being born again with "belief": *For God so loved the world that he gave his only Son, that whoever believes in him should not perish but have eternal life.* (John 3:16)

Yet Jesus does not explain what it means to be *born again* into such belief. He gives no formula. Therefore men, in their desire to codify large spiritual principles into doctrines small enough for their legalizing minds to grasp, have taken it upon themselves to shape and mold Jesus' words to fit formulas of their own devising. These many recipes and rituals of salvation they have pressed upon their hearers with all the authority of Scripture itself.

The fact remains, however, that there is no prescription for salvation or being born again in the Bible. As far as we know, not a single person in all the Gospels ever prayed what we commonly call a "sinner's prayer." Jesus gave no altar call at the conclusion of the Sermon on the Mount. No one went forward. None of the disciples "invited Jesus into their hearts." Jesus held no catechism classes where he taught the correct doctrines of belief. He told no one to join a church, gave no lists of scriptures to memorize, distributed no tracts.

That he did not spell out the process, however, does not lessen the importance of this Command. Jesus said that we *must* be born again. Yet he doesn't tell us how it is to be done. The conclusion seems inescapable that the process is a private one that takes place in the depths of each human heart, between every individual and his Maker. In that solitary chamber of prayer, the language spoken is one of deepest intimacy between Creator and created, between Father and child. There are no formulas.

If "belief" emerges out of that holy exchange, Jesus *does* tell us what it means to *believe* in him. No salvation prayers, ideas, doctrines, church affiliations, or spiritual revelations define or produce belief. Belief in Jesus means doing what he said.

We must recognize, then, that being born again incorporates into it the changed perspective that obedience to the Commands produces. It is an ongoing birth into the citizenship of a new kingdom whose rules are upside-down from those of the world—where servants rule, where the last are first, where evil is returned by good, and where one loves rather than hates his enemies. We are being born into a new form of childship, a *chosen* childship in which we yield—through obedience—to being made into God's sons and daughters.

To be a child is not necessarily to be a son or daughter. The childship is the lower condition of the upward process towards the sonship, the soil out of which the true sonship shall grow...God can no more than an earthly parent be content to have only children: he must have sons and daughters— children of his soul, of his spirit, of his love...For this...he dies to give them himself, thereby to raise his own to his heart; he gives them a birth from above; they are born again out of himself and into himself...His children are not his real, true sons and daughters until they think like him, feel with him, judge as he judges, are at home with him...because he and they mean the same thing, love the same things, seek the same ends. For this are we created; it is the one end of our being...He is our father all the time, for he is true;

but until we respond with the truth of children, he cannot let all the father out to us; there is no place for the dove of his tenderness to alight. He is our father, but we are not his children. Because we are his children, we must become his sons and daughters.

George MacDonald, *Unspoken Sermons, Second Series,* "Abba Father"

God, bring to my remembrance this day the Command of Jesus to BE BORN AGAIN. Free me from the bondage of formulas and clichés. Liberate me to be born from above into the childship of the kingdom. May I desire to be nothing more nor less than your obedient son or daughter. By my obedience, may I live in moment-by-moment born again belief in your Son. Thus, heavenly Father, may I be an instrument in my small corner of the world for the ultimate salvation of mankind. Amen.

56. Do Not Justify or Worry How to Defend Yourself

"Do not be anxious how or what you are to answer or what you are to say." (Luke 12:11)

Self-defense is one of the most automatic of human responses. When challenged, threatened, contradicted, or accused, we blurt out a defense before the voice of criticism has even died away. Often we do not wait so long as that to defend ourselves, but interrupt to counter the word against us before it is even finished. Our justifications are passionate. We are self-defensive about everything! The closer to home the threatening verbal arrow strikes, the more clamorous, with counter accusation, is our defense.

Yet witness Jesus before the Sanhedrin:

And the high priest stood up and said, "Have you no answer to make? What is it that these men testify against you?" But Jesus was silent. (Matthew 26:62-63)

And before Pilate:

Then Pilate said to him, "Do you not hear how many things they testify against you?" But he gave him no answer, not even to a single charge. (Matthew 27:13-14)

It is one of the most difficult things we face in life, simply to be silent in the face of accusation. Again we must ask, who is our role model?

Now it can be argued that Jesus was speaking specifically about self-defense when his followers are put on trial for their beliefs. The context of the above and similar verses reveals further that Jesus does not enjoin us to absolute silence. He simply says that the Holy Spirit will give us the words we are to speak. Since most of us do not find ourselves on trial for our beliefs, do we then ignore this word? Or do we discover within it a larger implied principle that is illuminated further by his words to the Pharisees in Luke 16:14: *You are those who justify yourselves before men.* Jesus' example of silence would certainly seem to indicate that we have much to learn in our daily exchanges and conversations. A lifetime spent allowing defensiveness to erupt at the drop of a hat ill-prepares us to follow Jesus' example when crisis comes. It seems, therefore, that God would have us widen the context of Jesus' words to include the deeper problem of justification and defensiveness in general.

Some may object to reading this Command interpretively. But we are trying to model our lives after Jesus, to truly be his "followers" in every sense of the word. Should we not seek every opportunity and means of doing so, rather than explaining why, because of a strict literal interpretation, in this case we do *not* have to follow his example?

Notwithstanding such arguments on both sides of a complex question, a practical reason exists why it is prudent *not* to defend oneself. Curiously, the stronger the attempted defense the more likely it is that the accusation or challenge or threat is accurate. Shakespeare's famous line, "Methinks he doth protest too much," offers remarkable insight into human nature. It is the innocent who are usually confident enough to be silent. The guilty are nearly always defensive.

The next time you are tempted to gush in self-defense, try instead curbing your tongue. You may discover the silence of being quick to hear and slow to speak liberating. "If any man thinks he is religious, and does not bridle his tongue…this man's religion is vain." (James 1:26)

> The meek are those that do not assert themselves, do not defend themselves, never dream of avenging themselves, or of returning aught but good for evil. They do not imagine it their business to take care of themselves…Self shall be no umpire in affair of his…the meek man's self always vanishes in the light of a real presence…No bristling importance, no vain attendance of fancied rights and wrongs, guards his door, or crowds the passages of his house; they are for the angels to come and go.
>
> George MacDonald, *The Hope of the Gospel,* "The Heirs of Heaven and Earth"

God, bring to my remembrance this day the Command of Jesus NOT TO JUSTIFY OR WORRY HOW TO DEFEND MYSELF. *However you meant it for your disciples, I take it as a word to me to not justify myself, or react in defensiveness, in any situation. May I discover freedom in following Jesus' example, not just when I am on trial for my faith, but always. Thus, heavenly Father, may I be an instrument in my small corner of the world for the ultimate salvation of mankind. Amen.*

57. Learn of Me

"Take my yoke upon you, and learn of me; for I am meek and lowly in heart: and ye shall find rest for your souls." (Matthew 11:29, KJV)

We continually find that the familiarity of certain of Jesus' words often obscures their astonishing meaning. Here, for example, many images of what it means to take upon oneself the Lord's "yoke" spring to mind, along with his oft-quoted words of comfort, *You shall find rest for your souls.*

But the Command, *Learn of me*, is usually overlooked as an intrinsic component of this passage. In truth, to take his yoke upon ourselves requires that we know him well enough to know what direction he is going. Again we discover the perhaps surprising fact that discipleship requires mental work. How can we learn of him without reading, poring over the Gospels, listening to his parables, Commands, teachings, insights, and observations over and over until our hearts and minds are full of them? What does "learning of him" mean if not imbuing our thoughts, attitudes, responses, perspective, and worldview, with *his* way of seeing and responding to everything in life? This is precisely why we are reading, reflecting, and praying about his Commands. We are attempting to obey this all-important Command: *Learn of Me*

Some translations have it, "Learn *from* me," which may be the more accurate rendering of the Greek original. We learn *from* Jesus, to learn *of* him—to learn what manner of man he was. He is our master. Therefore, we listen to his words, we let them sink into the deep places within us. We ponder his parables and teachings. We pray over them. We absorb and *digest* them into our spiritual marrow. We allow them to nourish our souls and minds and hearts. We learn *from* him, that we might learn *of* him…and thus *know* him as he truly is.

The words, teachings, and Commands of Jesus, are our lifeline, our life's Instruction Manual. The writings of the other Apostles are subordinate in every way to the red letters in the daily ordering of our steps as followers of Jesus. He said, *Learn from me, learn of me.* One thing he did not say was, "Learn *about* me." Though the Bible is often used for that purpose, we are not trying to devise theologies about Christ and his work. We are trying to do what Jesus said. Therefore, theories and doctrines and speculations *about* that work must always subserve the high calling of obedience to the Commands. A careful reading of the words of Peter, James, John, and Paul reveals that such was precisely the objective of their writings as well—pointing their hearers back toward the Foundation-Stone of Jesus' own teachings and Commands.

"The one use of the Bible is to make us look at Jesus, that through him we might know his Father and our Father, his God and our God. Till we thus know Him, let us hold the Bible dear as the moon of our darkness, by which we travel towards the east; not dear as the sun whence her light cometh, and towards which we haste, that, walking in the sun himself, we may no more need the mirror that reflected his absent brightness." (George MacDonald, *Unspoken Sermons, Series One,* "The Higher Faith")

"Your business…is to make yourself acquainted with that man: he will be to you nobody save in revealing, through knowledge of his inmost heart, the Father to you. Take then your New Testament as if you had never seen it before, and read—to find out…Till then, this point remains: there was a man who said he knew him, and that if you would give heed to him, you too should know him. The record left of him is indeed scanty, yet enough to disclose what manner of man he was—his principles, his ways of looking at things, his thoughts of his Father and his brethren and the relations between them, of man's business in life, his destiny, and his hopes…."
George MacDonald, *Thomas Wingfold, Curate,* Ch. 19

God, bring to my remembrance this day the Command of Jesus to LEARN OF HIM. *Give me fresh insight to see myself in the Gospels among Jesus' hearers, watching him, listening to him, absorbing his words, observing his example, and thus both learning from him and learning of him. May Jesus be my example in all my ways, in thought and deed, in outlook and response. Imbue my being with the daily practicality of the red letters. Thus, heavenly Father, by my true knowledge of Jesus, may I be an instrument in my small corner of the world for the ultimate salvation of mankind. Amen.*

58. Receive the Kingdom of God Like a Child

"Let the children come to me, do not hinder them; for to such belongs the kingdom of God. Truly, I say to you, whoever does not receive the kingdom of God like a child shall not enter it." (Mark 10: 14-15)

At first I wrote *Bring children to me* in order to more directly represent Jesus' words. Then I realized that Jesus was addressing a larger principle: The childlikeness required to receive the principles of God's kingdom. There are several huge implications involved.

One, children take what is offered them without question, as gifts to be received and treasured. This does not mean that children are gullible, but that they are *trusting*. In a sense, life in God's kingdom is a *gift* to us. We might say that the Commands of Jesus are likewise a gift. Can we receive them with that same childlike trust…and then, treasuring the gift, obey the Commands?

Children also receive what is given them without intellectual dissection. The kingdom of God is thus not entered into by doctrine, theology, or spiritual analysis, but again with the *trust* of a childlike heart. We have already seen that Jesus repeatedly commands mental and intellectual acuity. Christianity's deepest precepts, however, are not apprehended by analysis, logic, or doctrinalism. Neither are they apprehended by rote acceptance of a set of beliefs, undergoing any ritual of conversion, or joining a church. But children *grow.* With a trusting heart, Jesus commands us to *think* and *understand.* Grasping the character of God initially through obedience to the Commands, the muscles of our faith are strengthened to probe deeper realms of truth by applying all the powers of the brain he has provided us. The child of trust grows into the manhood or womanhood of intellectually rigorous faith.

There exists a third mystery hidden in the words of this Command. This mystery is illuminated with clarity and brilliance in George MacDonald's sermon, "The Child in the Midst." MacDonald makes the astonishing claim that Jesus uses a child as a "type" of the kingdom, not primarily because of the qualities *of the child,* but because his childlikeness is a reflection of *God himself.* In saying we must become like children, Jesus is commanding us to become like God. "Our Lord," MacDonald says, "was, is, and ever shall be divinely childlike." It is a revolutionary way of seeing God. Yet what else could be the intrinsic personality of the kingdom of God (childlikeness) but a reflection of the personality of God himself? The truth of MacDonald's assertion is as obvious as it is powerful.

> Childhood belongs to the divine nature... In this, then, is God like the child: that he is simply and altogether our friend, our father—our more than friend, father, and mother...He is utterly true and good to us, nor shall anything withstand his will.
>
> How terribly, then, have the theologians misrepresented God...Nearly all of them represent him as a great King on a grand throne, thinking how grand he is, and making it the business of his being and the end of his universe to keep up his glory, wielding the bolts of a Jupiter against them that take his name in vain...Brothers, have you found our king? There he is, kissing little children and saying they are like God. There he is at table with the head of a fisherman lying on his bosom, and somewhat heavy at heart that even he, the beloved disciple, cannot yet understand him well. The simplest peasant who loves his children and his sheep were...a true type of our God beside that monstrosity of a monarch.
>
> The God who is ever uttering himself in the changeful profusions of nature; who takes millions of years to form a soul that shall understand him and be blessed...this God is the God of little children...Therefore, with angels and with archangels, with the spirits of the just made perfect, with the little children of the kingdom, yea, with the Lord himself, and for all them that know him not, we praise and magnify and laud his name in itself, saying *Our Father*...For it is his childlikeness that makes him our God and Father.
>
> George MacDonald, *Unspoken Sermons, First Series,* "The Child in the Midst"

God, bring to my remembrance this day the Command of Jesus to RECEIVE THE KINGDOM OF GOD LIKE A CHILD. *May I see the astonishing truth that your divine nature is childlike. This is why childlikeness is required to enter your kingdom. Purge from me the false images of your fearsome aloofness that I have been taught. May I receive your childlikeness into my soul, and thus become like a child myself as I continue to learn to live in your kingdom. Thus, heavenly Father, may I be an instrument in my small corner of the world for the ultimate salvation of mankind. Amen.*

59. Have Salt in Yourselves

"You are the salt of the earth; but if salt has lost its taste, how shall its saltness be restored?" (Matthew 5:13)

"For every one will be salted with fire. Salt is good; but if the salt has lost its saltness, how will you season it? Have salt in yourselves, and be at peace with one another." (Mark 9:49-50)

New Testament scholar William Barclay says plainly about Mark 9:48-50, "These three verses are amongst the most difficult in the New Testament to interpret." (*The Gospel of Mark*, p. 241) He goes on to explain that in all likelihood these pithy statements by Jesus were simply placed together as Mark compiled his gospel because they stuck in his mind, or Peter's, in this order. Though they all had to do with fire and salt, however, originally they were disconnected sayings that had little to do with each other.

The purpose of salt was for both *purification* and *seasoning*. Salt on the altar "purified" and "seasoned" the sacrifice. Leviticus 2:13 commands, "You shall season all your cereal offerings with salt; you shall not let the salt of the covenant with your God be lacking…with all your offerings you shall offer salt." Jesus' words, *Every one will be salted with fire* thus calls to mind the final chapters of the Old Testament, in which the prophet Malachi describes the purification by fire that will come to Israel, perhaps prophesying as well concerning the purifying purpose of hell to rid the universe of sin. Salt's preservative properties with food are also well known. In climates where ice was not abundant, salt was indeed the only substance that made it possible to keep certain foods from spoiling.

All three of these uses combined in the ancient world to make salt, like fire, a symbol of *purity*. It was said that no substance was purer than salt, for it came from the sun and the sea, it was white, and it seasoned, preserved, and purified everything it touched.

We begin, then, in the midst of these perhaps unrelated statements about fire and salt, to gain a picture of what Jesus is commanding of us. We are reminded, too, of Jesus' statement in Matthew's gospel following the Beatitudes: *You are the salt of the earth.*

Jesus is commanding us to be a people set apart, a people who flavor and season the world around us by being pure and above reproach, purified and cleansed within by the work of God's Spirit and by our own obedience. There is also a warning attached. Salt can *lose* its saltness, as Mark says. In that case, Jesus says, it is good for nothing. The Greek of Matthew 5:13 contains a different shade of meaning. Matthew's original reads, "but if the salt has become tainted."

Jesus' words, then, specifically remind us to "take heed unto ourselves." He does not say, *Go out and BE the salt of the earth,* he says, *Keep your own heart and motives and attitudes pure and you WILL be the salt of the earth.* When we are thinking about the influence of our own righteousness, pride taints the saltness. Self-righteousness is indeed good for nothing except to be trampled underfoot. Instead, says Jesus, keep your eyes on your own need to be continually cleansed. Purify yourselves on the altar of sacrifice with the fire of purification. Salt yourselves with fire. Have salt in yourselves.

> The Lord knew these men...They were in danger, it is true, of pluming themselves on what he had said of them, of taking their importance to their credit. Yet the Lord does not hesitate to call his few humble disciples the salt of the earth; and every century since has borne witness that such indeed they were...Where would the world be now but for their salt and their light!...No sooner has he used the symbol of the salt, than the Lord proceeds to supplement its incompleteness. They were salt which must remember that it is salt; which must live salt, and choose salt, and be salt. For the whole worth of salt lies in its being salt; and all the saltness of the moral salt lies in the will to be salt.
>
> George MacDonald, *The Hope of the Gospel,* "The Salt and the Light of the World"

God, bring to my remembrance this day the Command of Jesus to HAVE SALT IN MYSELF. *Let me never forget that this is another Command to be prayerfully heeded in front of the mirror, where the searchlight of your Spirit illuminates the dark places within me and reveals where my saltness is becoming tainted with self-righteousness. Purify me with your cleansing fire, now and in eternity, that I might become your pure son or daughter. Thus, heavenly Father, may I be an instrument in my small corner of the world for the ultimate salvation of mankind. Amen.*

60. Be a Good Steward Over What God Has Given You

"Well done, good and faithful servant; you have been faithful over a little, I will set you over much; enter into the joy of your master." (Matthew 25:21)

It is unfortunate, in one sense, that the Lord's parable of the talents is about money and the return gained from its use. This has led to the false idea that God cares about the world of finance. The misappropriation of the truth of this parable has contributed to many foolish prosperity doctrines that are an embarrassment to the church. Because of its deeper meaning in the parable, however, the first century unit of money-weight Jesus spoke of actually became our English word for "talent," which certainly brings us much closer to Jesus' intent.

Jesus is not talking about money at all, but about the full scope of gifts, intelligence, insights, personality, and opportunities with which we have been blessed in life. This is a parable about stewardship over *everything* we have been given to make use of—time, energy, and our wills most of all—the choices we make. Money is the last thing on Jesus' mind, but the full created individual you are, the entire man I am, both of us brimming with potential to do good, to grow, to become more than we are, to put others first, to obey Jesus, to feed the hungry, to love mercy and do justly and walk humbly with our God.

With the master of the parable distributing five talents to one, two to another, and one to the third, we tend to misinterpret another aspect of this teaching. It is not only the wealthy, the clever, the skillful, or those with winning personalities who have great things to offer God. We are *all* five-talent people! By outward appearance, some may seem to possess greater gifts. Opportunities fall more favorably to some. But Jesus makes no such comparisons except to drive home his point: God has given *you* a range of "talents." They may be invisible to anyone else. You may all your life be in such dire financial straits that you never have money to use for God. You may be a deaf mute. You will never sway crowds with your oratory. But *whatever* are the internal characteristics of personhood that you possess—those are *your* unique five talents. No one else in all creation possesses exactly the same combination of unique "talents." You have been given stewardship over them. And a day will come when Jesus will hold out his hand and say, "What have you made of what you were given?" He will not be asking for a list of temporal accomplishments. The return he will be seeking lies in the eternal realm.

As God's sons and daughters we are to make something of our lives, something lasting and of eternal value in the kingdom of God. This involves principally two regions of endeavor. One, what are we making of *ourselves*? Are we using our gifts and the circumstances of life to grow into God's obedient sons and daughters who reflect the Christlikeness of Jesus? An old saying pinpoints this ultimate priority in life: *God is not so much concerned with what we do, but with what we are.* Then secondly, how are we using the time, energies, and opportunities given us, and the choices that accompany them, to build into the lives of others? Our "talents" and opportunities are not given us in a vacuum. They are given us to *use*, and to spread God's love and goodness into lives all around us.

I saw that to every man, every woman, every child, are given abilities and capacities...along with strengths and weaknesses of personality...I perceived...that the circumstances presented to every man and woman vary...through life...In spite of the infinite gradations of advantage and possibility, I saw that all share one thing in common—the *potential* to make something more of themselves...I saw that such *opportunity of character* is independent of external events or advantage and laid equally before all. In the reality of eternity...all possess *equal* capacity to give their Maker back a worthy return.

Michael Phillips, *The Garden at the Edge of Beyond,* Ch. 12

God, bring to my remembrance this day the Command of Jesus to BE A GOOD STEWARD OVER WHAT GOD HAS GIVEN ME. *Keep me from comparing my "talents" with others, or from envying another's gifts or opportunities. Fill my heart with thankfulness for the uniquenesses you chose to give me. No one else in all the world possesses exactly those same uniquenesses. May I use them to the full, and be a good steward, and give you a full return by growing into a son or daughter of whom you can be proud. Thus, heavenly Father, may I be an instrument in my small corner of the world for the ultimate salvation of mankind. Amen.*

Series Seven

"The Bartholomew Commands"

Trust

The Brain of a Man, the Heart of a Child

Bartholomew has always been perhaps the most enigmatic of all the disciples, though we really know nothing about many of the twelve. The confusion of names in the Gospel lists of the twelve offers fruitful basis for all manner of speculation.

It has been conjectured that Nathaniel and Bartholomew are the same man, as both are always mentioned in association with Philip. "Bar" means "son of" and thus the name would likely be a surname. He could therefore be "Nathaniel son of Tolmai." The reference in John 21:2 to Nathaniel as one of the disciples seems to make this likely. *If* Bartholomew and Nathaniel are the same man, what high praise he received from Jesus to be called a man without guile. It is hard to imagine a higher compliment of character.

Even if Bartholomew is not Nathaniel, however, maybe we know enough about him. For we know that when Jesus said, "Follow me," he was a man with faith enough and wisdom enough and trust enough to obey that summons. He was willing to truly be "the least of these" among the twelve. Others put themselves forward, asked questions, tried to cluster near the front, and shared the limelight. But Bartholomew was always in the background. Not only is he the unknown disciple, he was the quiet disciple. We know of no words that passed his lips other than (potentially) Nathaniel's brief exchange with Philip in John 1.

We can almost hear him saying:

My name will go down as one of the great curiosities of history. No one will know about me for certain. But I believe in your purpose for me. I will trust you in the midst of anonymity. I put my faith in you, not my reputation. I will become as nothing to be your disciple. I will leave but one legacy behind: My posterity will know that I put my faith in you, and I followed you.

Thus, in Bartholomew's very inscrutability, we discover a rudimentary and profound lesson about faith.

πίστις: PISTIS—*Faith*

It is not often in Scripture that we are blessed with *definitions* of spiritual truths. The Bible is frustratingly indistinct. For reasons that are unclear, God has desired for us to search diligently to find his truths, which are often hidden like mysteries that man is required to discover.

We are, however, fortunate in two instances. We have John's toweringly simple definition of God's character: *God is love.* And we have the introductory verse to the Bible's "chapter of faith." But though it comes in the form of a definition, the writer of Hebrews does not mirror John's simplicity. Indeed, Hebrews 11:1 stands as one of the Bible's most sophisticated verses: "Now faith [PISTIS] is the substance [*assurance*] of things hoped for, the evidence [*conviction*] of things not seen." (KJV, italics RSV) The writer then goes on to use PISTIS twenty-four times in the examples that follow.

Faith (PISTIS) and trust (PEITHO) derive from the same essential root. Faith means exactly what it implies—*trust,* being assured of reliability, to "believe" in with absolute confidence. Clearly faith in the truths of God (which are *invisible*) is essentially distinct from trust in *visible* laws and principles. Thus *spiritual* faith implies being able to trust in what is *unseen.* Such is the basis for Hebrews 11:1. We also observe in the gallery of Hebrews 11 the faith not only to believe big things *of* God, but also faith to believe big things *about* God, his purposes, and the eternal reach of his love. It takes πίστις to believe in a truly infinite God.

Series Seven

The Brain of a Man, the Heart of a Child

61. Trust and have faith in God.

62. Do not be called teacher or leader.

63. Do not be diverted by externals, traditions, and doctrines, but look to the heart.

64. Don't fret about trifles.

65. Do not show goodness and hospitality only to those who are kind to you.

66. Worship the Lord and serve him only.

67. Do not desire more than God gives you.

68. Do not pray ostentatiously and with empty phrases.

69. Remain gratefully aware of your spiritual need.

70. Take up your cross.

61. Trust and Have Faith in God

"Have faith in God!" (Mark 11:22)
"Do not be faithless, but believing." (John 20:27)

Faith is truly one of the most complex attributes of spirituality. It is a word bandied about easily and casually by the unbelieving world as readily as it is used in the believing world. Whereas a term like "righteousness" is ridiculed by the world, *faith* is widely considered a virtue. The world is on good and pleasant terms with faith.

Or so it would like to think. But everything depends on what is the basis for the so-called "faith" the world pretends to honor. Is it having "faith in your star," having "faith in your guardian angel?" Is it a nebulous feeling about life in general and the belief that everything will somehow turn out okay?

These are not what Jesus meant. Jesus commands us, "Have faith *in God*."

Faith *in God* carries monstrous implications. Such faith is obviously founded on knowing who God is. How can we trust him if we are clueless about his essential character, and how he works and what are his purposes? Trust implies falling in with those purposes, aligning ourselves with the direction God is going, and the direction he wants *us* to go. All this is implied by Jesus' words. And since the way we get to know God is from what Jesus told us about him, and from the astounding fact that Jesus said that God the Father was just like him, only greater, then faith in God also implies trust *in Jesus*. The two trusts (in *Jesus* and in *God*) are inseparable because the Father and Son are inseparable.

The complexity of faith is heightened yet more in that its two intrinsic components are seeming opposites. Trust requires the *brain* of a man, and the *heart* of a child.

It has often been said that Christianity is a thinking man's religion. That does not make it primarily an "intellectual" religion. Its truths cannot be apprehended by the intellect alone. But intellectual rigor is the all-important first half of the equation. Jesus repeatedly emphasizes the necessity of hard thought, of applying oneself to understand, of being mentally engaged with the principles of truth.

Yet hydrogen alone cannot sustain temporal life any more than intellectualism can lead to eternal life. Oxygen is required in the spirit world as well, to energize hydrogen's life-giving properties—the spirit-oxygen of childlike trust. Combine the two elements—the *brain of a man* and the *heart of a child*—and a miracle of eternal life is born.

It is the miracle of *faith*.

I know the words "leave it to God" can be misunderstood, but they must stay for the moment. The sense in which a Christian leaves it to God is that he puts all his trust in Christ: trusts that Christ will somehow share with him the perfect human obedience which He carried out from His birth to His crucifixion: that Christ will make the man more like Himself...To trust Him means, of course, trying to do all that He says. There would be no sense in saying you trusted a person if you would not take his advice. Thus if you have really handed yourself over to Him, it must follow that you are trying to obey Him...

Christians have often disputed as to whether what leads the Christian home is good actions, or Faith in Christ...The answer to that nonsense is that, if what you call your "faith" in Christ does not involve taking the slightest notice of what He says, then it is not Faith at all—not faith or trust in Him, but only intellectual acceptance of some theory about him.

The Bible really seems to clinch the matter when it puts the two things together in one amazing sentence. The first half is, "Work out your own salvation with fear and trembling"—which looks as if everything depended on us and our good actions; but the second half goes on, "For it is God who worketh in you"—which looks as if God did everything and we nothing.

C.S. Lewis, *Mere Christianity,* Book Three, Ch. 12, "Faith (2)"

God, bring to my remembrance this day the Command of Jesus to HAVE FAITH AND TRUST IN GOD. I want to live in moment-by-moment trust in you, in your character, in your goodness, in your care for me and for all the world. Give me both the intellectual vigor and the childlike simplicity of heart to trust you and believe you and have faith in you. Thus, heavenly Father, may I be an instrument in my small corner of the world for the ultimate salvation of mankind. Amen.

62. Do Not Be Called Teacher or Leader

"Do not be called Rabbi; for One is your Teacher...Do not call anyone on earth your father; for One is your Father...Do not be called leaders; for One is your Leader [*Master*—KJV], that is, Christ." (Matthew 23:8-10, NAS)

An entire history of Christendom could be written from the perspective of the slow, steady, continuous *divergence* of Christ's followers from Christ's Commands.

This deviation began early. We tend to idealize the first century church as a paragon of church life. In fact, the church of the first century set this pattern in motion. Paul clearly occupies an exalted position of infallibility for many, yet responsibility surely rests on the heads of those through the years who have taken his words to justify overly doctrinalizing the *work* of Christ such that the *Commands* of Christ have taken a back seat. The inevitable result has been a church more mired in dogma than energized and continually renewed by the daily exampling of Matthew 5-7 and John 13-17. This does not diminish the towering contributions of Paul to Christian thought, especially when he *does* focus on the Commands. But neither can we be naïve. We *must* read all doctrine and teaching—from

Paul to the present—through the lens of the Commands or we will assuredly misunderstand the foundations of the Christian faith.

We are therefore compelled to ask upon what basis the early church set up "leadership labels" within its structure, then to prioritize them into a hierarchy of status. How much more clear could Jesus have been: *Do NOT be called teacher or leader.* Yet we have Paul instructing the churches at length about qualifications, roles, duties, and gifts, defining titles and offices of church leadership. (1 Cor. 12:27-30, Eph. 4:11, 1 Tim. 3, etc.) We have Paul's words to Timothy, "Anyone who aspires to oversight desires a noble work." How does this square with Jesus' words *against* ambition, and that the Christ-life is characterized by servanthood not headship? Jesus specifically rebukes his disciples for desiring to rule. Yet here is Paul saying that such an ambition is worthy and noble. Did Paul's obsession with church titles perhaps stem from his own ambition to be called an "Apostle?" He was not satisfied merely to do the work of an Apostle with the quiet humility of a servant's heart. He insisted on being *recognized* as an Apostle and *calling* himself an Apostle. Something is wrong with this picture.

From this beginning, down through the centuries, the church has been defined by its leadership hierarchy—from Popes and bishops down to local elders and pastors and teachers. Everyone must have a *title.* Teachers want to be *known* as "Teachers." Musicians must be known as "Worship *Leaders.*" Conferences instruct ambitious Christians on the techniques of *leadership.* Schools are founded to teach the inordinately self-presumptuous to step into their role as "Prophets," the highest of all Christian titles behind Apostle.

Has perhaps our confusion stemmed from the words Rabbi and, in some translations, Master? Of course, we flatter ourselves, none of us would allow ourselves to be called *Rabbi* or *Master.* We would never be *that* brazen or audacious.

In the Greek, however, the words Jesus forbids us allowing to be used of ourselves are not so easy to dismiss. (He also excludes use of "Father," PATER, as indicating the source of life, from which *Pope* derives). Jesus says clearly: "...for you have one DIDASKALOS (*teacher*)...Neither be called KATHEGETAI (*master/leader*)..."

Christianity was not intended by its Founder to have defined and identified "leaders" or "teachers" at all, but to be led by the childlike example of obedient *servants.*

Ambition is the desire to be above...and here there is no possibility of comparison with one's neighbour: no one knows what the white stone contains except the man who receives it...Relative worth is not only unknown—to the children of the

kingdom it is unknowable. Each esteems the other better than himself. George MacDonald, *Unspoken Sermons, First Series*, "The New Name"

God, bring to my remembrance this day the Command of Jesus NOT TO BE CALLED TEACHER OR LEADER. May my claim to recognition as your follower be as a servant. Thus, heavenly Father, may I be an instrument in my small corner of the world for the ultimate salvation of mankind. Amen.

63. Do Not be Diverted by Externals, Traditions, and Doctrines, But Look to the Heart

"Well did Isaiah prophesy of you hypocrites…'This people honors me with their lips, but their heart is far from me; in vain do they worship me, teaching as doctrines the precepts of men.' You leave the commandment of God, and hold fast the tradition of men…For from…out of the heart…come evil thoughts…adultery, coveting…deceit… envy…pride, foolishness. All these evil things come from within, and they defile a man." (Mark 7:6-8, 21-25)

The passage from Mark 7 concerning the pharisaic worship of the letter of the law, as manifested by an obsession with clean cups and bowls and hands, gives a singularly important teaching in all the Gospels. Jesus here addresses an inevitable tendency in *all* religions—the susceptibility of truth to degenerate into doctrines and legalisms, defined by what Jesus calls the "traditions of the elders" rather than by constantly renewing reality.

It *happens*. It happens in *all* spiritual movements and churches no matter how vibrant their origins. This tendency infects us *all*. We cannot help it. It is happening around you and me every Sunday as we sit in church. It is happening in the pulpit. It is happening in the lives of those about us. Reality is hardening into the concrete of externals, legalisms, traditions, and doctrines every moment. It is happening inside *our* own hearts.

Many Christians too readily read this passage as a two-thousand-year old exchange between Jesus and his disciples and the Pharisees. But its reality is much closer. Every church in the land possesses its own sacred "traditions of the elders," its doctrinal versions of bowls and pots and cups, its unique rituals and belief systems which must not be tampered with or questioned. If we would read the Gospels with true insight, we must always put ourselves into the story. *We* are the disciples in the boat, terrified at the storm. *We* are they to whom Jesus said, "Do you still not understand?" We are also the Pharisees. This is no mere two-thousand-year old tale. The Gospel is being rewritten anew every day. When he upbraids the Pharisees—*You do your deeds to be seen of men…you love the places of honor…you neglect the weightier matters of the law…you strain at a gnat and swallow a camel*—only the most self-righteous among us would not humbly admit, "Yes, he is speaking to me too. God be merciful to me a sinner!"

If we are to read the Gospels accurately, we are the disciples *and* we are the Pharisees. We love our traditions. We cherish our doctrines. We hold them fast and condemn those who do not adhere to their letter. We love the *externals* of religion more than its deepest truths. God help us! As the Pharisees trivialized, legalized, and ritualized the truths of the Law, so too has the church done with the life-changing truths of the New Covenant.

How then do we avoid the drift of truth into external dogma? By ever renewing our focus on the Commands, and to the inward state of our own hearts. George MacDonald says, "There are 'traditions of men' after Christ as well as before him." These will exercise their allure as surely as the sun will rise tomorrow. We must look to our *hearts*. It is in the *internal* recesses of our being where sin resides, and where Christlikeness is born. Note the startling fact that Jesus places envy, pride, even *foolishness*, alongside evil thoughts, adultery, and murder. Sin in the inward parts is sin. *All* sin must go—foolishness and envy no less than adultery. We are called to internal purity, not to obsess over the external pots and bowls of our doctrines and traditions.

> In Colossians Paul listed some of the outward forms people use to control sin: "touch not, taste not, handle not." He then added that these things "have a show of wisdom in will worship" (Col. 2:20-23, KJV)... "Will worship" may be able to have an outward show of success for a time, but in the cracks and crevices of our lives, our deep inner condition will always be revealed. Jesus described that condition when He spoke of the outward show of righteousness of the Pharisees. "Out of the abundance of the heart the mouth speaks..."
>
> Richard Foster, *Celebration of Discipline,* p. 4-5

God, bring to my remembrance this day the Command of Jesus NOT TO BE DIVERTED BY EXTERNALS, TRADITIONS, AND DOCTRINES, BUT TO LOOK TO THE HEART. Open my eyes to externals and traditions that my own church has put on a pedestal to revere in place of the Commands. Thus, heavenly Father, may I be an instrument in my small corner of the world for the ultimate salvation of mankind. Amen.

64. Don't Fret About Trifles

"Martha, Martha, you are anxious and troubled about many things" (Luke 10:41)

Two individuals in the Gospels occasionally cause the sensitive heart a pang of empathy. In both instances, at first glance we feel that Jesus is a little harsh. Who has not felt that the prodigal's elder brother had a convincing point about his lifelong faithfulness alongside his brother's squandering lifestyle? And who, too, has not felt sympathy for poor Martha? There she was doing all the work involved in welcoming Jesus into their home, preparing a meal, making sure his needs were attended to, while Mary was basically just "sitting around" listening to Jesus. It is the classic dichotomy between the *practical* mind and the *spiritual* mind. Do we not hear the validity of Martha's complaint? Martha was acting the part of a "servant" to the Lord's needs. Jesus' gentle rebuke seems out of place.

To get at the heart of his words, however, and thus lay hold of the Command implied for us by his exhortation, we must go deeper. It is not the spiritual vs. the practical that Jesus was addressing. No doubt he was filled with gratitude for Martha's heart of service. Nor was he telling her that she ought to sit down beside Mary and be more "spiritual."

He was pinpointing Martha's fretful spirit. Martha was *troubled*. That was the source of her inner tension. She had the heart of a servant, but she was not at peace in that servanthood. It is an easily recognizable predicament into which we easily sink—serving out of obligation or duty…but being irritated by being in the position of having to serve. Such annoyance is especially common in family-servanthood—the grumbling service of a sour disposition. Martha was being challenged where servanthood is hardest—in her own family. Out of the tension in Martha's heart, a spirit of resentment grew toward her sister. Therefore Jesus had to redirect her spiritual compass.

It is easy to identify with Martha. Life's trifles, especially in the home, pester and nag like buzzing flies on a hot day. How can we ignore them when they are so ever-present? Interestingly, Jesus *doesn't* tell us to ignore them. He simply tells us, along with Martha, not to *fret* about them—not to be "anxious and troubled" about them. He might as well have said, as he did of the poor, "You will always have nagging trifles with you. Life is full of them. But don't fret about them. They will all be gone one day. They matter eternally no more than a puff of smoke. The only thing that will last is what you are allowing the small things of life to make of you. Therefore, let life's trifles make you a person of peace."

What then are we to do with life's trifles? Attend to them. Deal with them. Cope with them. Be a good steward over them. Handle life's details responsibly and with a cheerful attitude. Just don't *fret* over them. Serve those nearest you without grumbling. Christlikeness is at stake in your attitude. Jesus didn't grumble and complain when he washed his disciples' feet—it was his *privilege* to do so. Jesus calls Martha's worries life's "many things." Perhaps we ought to change our "Things To Do" lists to "Trifles" lists to remind us of this important Command that faces us every day of our lives.

We too dull our understandings with trifles, fill the heavenly spaces with phantoms, waste the heavenly time with hurry. To those who possess their souls in patience come the heavenly visions. When I trouble myself over a trifle...the loss of some little article, say...am I not like the disciples?...God would have me wise, and smile at the trifle...This losing of things is of the mercy of God; it comes to teach us to let them go...I forget that it is live things God cares about—live truths, not things set down in a book, or in a memory, or embalmed in the joy of knowledge, but things lifting up the heart, things active in an active will.

George MacDonald, *Unspoken Sermons, Second Series,* "The Cause of Spiritual Stupidity"

God, bring to my remembrance this day the Command of Jesus to NOT FRET ABOUT TRIFLES. *Help me keep life's details in perspective, relegated where they belong—as but passing ticks on eternity's clock. My response to life's "many things" can either be of peace or of worry. Flood me with the vision of eternity. Instill within me Martha's heart of service and Mary's heart of peace. Thus, heavenly Father, may I be an instrument in my small corner of the world for the ultimate salvation of mankind. Amen.*

65. Do Not Show Goodness and Hospitality Only to Those Who Are Kind to You

"If you love those who love you...And if you do good to those who do good to you, what credit is that to you? For even sinners do the same. And if you lend to those from whom you hope to receive, what credit is that to you? Even sinners lend...to receive as much again. But love your enemies, and do good, and lend, expecting nothing in return; and your reward will be great...When you give a dinner or a banquet, do not invite your friends or your brothers or your kinsmen or rich neighbors, lest they also invite you in return, and you be repaid. But when you give a feast, invite the poor, the maimed, the lame, the blind, and you will be blessed, because they cannot repay you." (Luke 6:32-35; 14:12-14)

So many of Jesus' Commands are interrelated. In these combined passages from Luke, we hear echoes of *Love, Give to the poor, Do more than required, Be a servant, Be kind, Do good, Do not demand back what you have given, Serve the least of humanity as you would Jesus.*

This underscores one of the truly significant points in our study of the Commands. *All* the Commands are interwoven. Jesus is inaugurating (and commanding) an entire lifestyle. His teaching can be neither understood nor lived by emphasizing one or two, or even a dozen of the Commands, or one *type* of Command (the "spiritual" Commands, the "social" Commands, the "belief" Commands, the "blessings" Commands). We all have observed only too well the danger of overemphasis—the pitfall succumbed to by individuals, churches, denominations, groups, and movements who seize upon some one or another of Jesus' teachings to the exclusion of all else. They may truly be said to be *obedient* Christians at the point of their one area of obsession. But rarely do they demonstrate full Christlikeness. Nor have such individuals and movements done much to convince the world that Jesus came from the Father.

The Commands of Jesus come as a package. They are *all* important. This is not to say that none is more important than another. Some *are* more important. But none can be omitted or ignored. They interweave as an all-consuming lifestyle—sixty Command-threads stretching lengthways as the fabric's warp, the other sixty interweaving amongst them as the woof...all together creating a tapestry called the Christlike life.

In this case, little needs be said other than what Jesus himself said. No words of mine can add force to his. The Command stands powerfully and unambiguously on its own. We must simply do what Jesus said.

This is not a complicated Command: Don't be enamored of those who love you in return, those who are rich, popular, "in," and who can repay your kindness. Give to the poor, the downtrodden, the oppressed, those whom everyone else ignores, those whom society looks down on. Do good to and show interest in those on life's fringes, the *un*popular, the *un*lovely, the *un*cool, the awkward, the difficult. When one of life's "beautiful people" walks into the room and all heads pivot to take a second look, turn *your* head instead in the opposite direction, toward the shadows and corners. There you will find Jesus gazing out of the lonely eyes of "the least of these" that everyone else overlooks,

> Self-righteous service requires external rewards. It needs to know that people see and appreciate the effort. It seeks human applause—with proper religious modesty of course. True service rests contented in hiddenness. It does not fear the lights and blare of attention, but it does not seek them either. Since it is living out of a new Center of Reference, the divine nod of approval is completely sufficient.
>
> Self righteous service is highly concerned about results. It eagerly waits to see if the person served will reciprocate in kind...True service is free of the need to calculate results...True service is indiscriminate in its ministry...True service is a life-style. It acts from ingrained patterns of living. It springs spontaneously to meet human need.
>
> Richard Foster, *Celebration of Discipline*, p. 112

God, bring to my remembrance this day the Command of Jesus NOT TO SHOW GOODNESS AND HOSPITALITY ONLY TO THOSE WHO ARE KIND TO ME. Open my eyes with sympathetic compassion to the nearby needy. Give me ways to show goodness and hospitality toward them whether or not they can repay it. Expand the horizons of my compassion. Thus, heavenly Father, may I be an instrument in my small corner of the world for the ultimate salvation of mankind. Amen.

66. Worship the Lord and Serve Him Only

"It is written, 'You shall worship the Lord your God, and him only shall you serve.'"
(Matthew 4:10)

We here encounter a Command made all the more intriguing when we consider to whom Jesus addressed it. He did not speak these words to his disciples or followers or to the crowds. This was his response to *Satan* after the final temptation in the wilderness. Can we then consider it a universal Command which Jesus places upon his followers as well?

It is a question probably more theological than practical. Any practically-minded obedient disciple recognizes instantly in these words echoes from many other of the Lord's Commands, including *You cannot serve God and Mammon,* by which Jesus means *anything* (not money alone) that stands in the way of wholehearted worship of and service to God.

Jesus is not exactly directing a "Command" to Satan. He is meeting the temptation with Scripture, all the more reason for *us* to take his words very personally. When Jesus references the Old Testament, we can be certain that the import upon our lives is highly significant. Jesus is here paraphrasing from Deuteronomy 6:13, a lengthy passage in which Moses warns against the temptations the Israelites will face to worship false gods: "You shall fear the Lord your God; you shall serve him and swear by his name. You shall not go after other gods, of the gods of the peoples who are round about you." (Deuteronomy 6:13-14)

What is it to *worship* God the Father and God the Son? Is *worship* achieved by going to church, by public prayer, by lifting the hands? Is *worship* fulfilled in praise, in song, in jubilation?

If we answer yes, we make a mockery of the forty days of temptation endured by our Lord which this Command triumphantly concluded. The "worship" which, in a sense, Jesus perfected in those forty days, was a worship crowned in suffering, a worship of temptation shunned, that chose the will of God over all the enticements of false gods and lesser objectives, that chose the Best over the good...a worship perfected in obedience.

To worship is to serve. To serve is to obey. To obey is to walk by the Lord's example: *What, Father, would you have me do?*

> We shall now look at the third temptation. The first was to help himself in his need; the second, perhaps, to assert the Father; the third to deliver his brethren.
>
> To deliver them, that is, after the fashion of men...And as in the others, the evil in this last lay in that it was a temptation to save his brethren, instead of doing the Will of his Father.

> Could it be other than a temptation to think that he might, if he would...leap into the chariot of power, and ride forth...? Glad visions arose...of the prisoner breaking jubilant from the cell of injustice; of the widow lifting up the bowed head...of weeping children bursting into shouts at the sound of the wheels of the chariot before which oppression and wrong shrunk and withered...
>
> I will not inquire whether such an enterprise could be accomplished without the worship of Satan...But I will ask whether to know better and do not so well...whether to flatter their pride by making them conquerors of the enemies of their nation instead of their own evil...—in a word, whether, to desert the mission of God, who knew that men could not be set free in that way, and sent him to be a man, a true man, the one man, among them, that his life might become their life...whether, to desert God thus...would not have been to fall down and worship the devil...Nothing but the obedience of the Son, the obedience unto the death, the absolute *doing* of the will of God...could redeem the prisoner, the widow, the orphan...He would not pluck the spreading branches of the tree; he would lay the axe to its root. It would take time; but the tree would be dead at last—dead, and cast into the lake of fire...It would take courage and strength and self-denial and endurance; but his Father could give him all. It would cost pain of body and mind, yea, agony and torture; but those he was ready to take on himself...The great and beautiful and perfect will of God *must* be done.
>
> George MacDonald, *Unspoken Sermons, First Series,* "The Temptation in the Wilderness"

God, bring to my remembrance this day the Command of Jesus to WORSHIP AND SERVE YOU ONLY. Show me the false things I worship. Reveal to me my false worship. Then lead me into the true worship you would have me offer. May I worship you by obeying you. Thus, heavenly Father, may I be an instrument in my small corner of the world for the ultimate salvation of mankind. Amen.

67. Do Not Desire More Than God Gives You

"You cannot serve God and mammon." (Matthew 6:24)
"Do you begrudge my generosity." (Matthew 20:15)
"Take heed, and beware of all coveteousness." (Luke 12:15)

Contrary to what many think, Jesus had nothing against either money or rich people. Many of his closest friends were possessors of means. Who did he and the disciples stay with as they traveled about? Obviously it took large quarters and some degree of prosperity to house and feed such a band. In the early chapters of *Acts*, the meeting place of the fledgling church was the home of wealthy widow Mary, mother of future gospelist John Mark and possibly one of the Gospel "Marys." Knowing how rapidly the movement called "The Way" was growing at that time, it must have been an enormous place—what we might call a "compound." Thinking that Jesus walked about without concern for his earthly needs, expecting everything to be provided as manna from heaven, we easily overlook the fact that he and the disciples actually kept their own little bank account in the form of the money box Judas was in charge of.

The word "mammon" is Aramaic for *riches*. It signifies more than mere money, but the desire to accumulate more and more and more. Money and possessions are not the problem. *Serving* them, *trusting* in them, and *lusting* for more of them, is.

And note, the poor may lust after wealth no less than the rich. There are poor men and women who are as preoccupied with mammon as the rich, who begrudge the rich their wealth. The covetousness in their hearts is no less a sin than the mammon-worship of the greedy miser. Both covetousness and grateful contentment may be cloaked in rags or robes of purple silk. God looks to the heart not to the bank balance, whether it be zero or millions.

Taking all the above passages as one, we see that Jesus is addressing deeper qualities of character than merely one's response to money. Those character qualities are contentment and gratitude. *Covetousness* is the sin, not money or possessions. It is the covetousness of desiring more, of desiring that which another possesses, or as much as someone else has.

We do not usually associate the parable of the workers in the vineyard of Matthew 20 with mammon worship. In fact it may be here that we unlock the high secret of this Command. At first glance, it is a puzzling parable. Comparing wages and work, the payment schedule for the workers is obviously unfair. This is exactly Jesus' point—by human standards it is unfair. This is a parable about gratitude in the midst of life's inequities. Some people are rich, some are poor, and most fall somewhere in the middle…often through no clear difference in their level of diligence. Life's blessings simply fall in many cases according to patterns we cannot understand. God gives more to some, less to others. Will we begrudge him his generosity?

While many of Jesus' words about riches are directed to the wealthy, this is a word addressed to those whose apportioned share in life may be less. *Don't begrudge the rich their wealth,* says Jesus. *For if God chooses to bless them with more, you are still commanded to be grateful, and not to desire more than he gives you. And if you are rich,* he adds, *then do not worship your wealth, use it wisely, give to the poor…and follow me.*

Covetousness is no respecter of persons.

> Nor does the lesson apply to those only who worship Mammon, who give their lives, their best energies to the accumulation of wealth: it applies to those equally who in any way worship the transitory; who seek the praise of men more than the praise of God; who would make a show in the world by wealth, by taste, by intellect, by power, by art, by genius of any kind, and so would gather golden opinions to be treasured in a storehouse of earth.
>
> George MacDonald, *Unspoken Sermons, First Series,* "The Heart with the Treasure"

God, bring to my remembrance this day the Command of Jesus NOT TO DESIRE MORE THAN YOU GIVE ME. *Keep me from the lethal responses of envy and greed. Reveal the hidden corners of coveteousness, whatever else I may call it, that I have allowed to lurk in the shadows. Forgive me even for desiring an easier time of it, for by this, too, I am being less than grateful for the life you have ordained for me. Thus, heavenly Father, may I be an instrument in my small corner of the world for the ultimate salvation of mankind. Amen.*

68. Do Not Pray Ostentatiously and With Empty Phrases

"In praying do not heap up empty phrases." (Matthew 6:7)

This is a *very* interesting and seriously convicting Command. And one mostly ignored by the vast majority of Christendom's churches. For what are most church prayers but memorized dissertations aimed vaguely in God's direction but recited in unison from a prayer book, or composed in advance to sound lofty, pious, and compassionate for each other's benefit. In their publicly-read prayers our pastors and priests make sure that every possible base of prayer-need is covered—seemingly directing their laundry lists more to the congregation than to God.

And which of us have not participated in prayer meetings and uttered the stock words of prayer appropriate in times of sickness, financial need, relational stress, spiritual trial, and decision-making uncertainty. Every group and sect and church in Christendom has its own lexicon of prayer-jargon. And how many millions the world over pray with the rosary, in direct violation of this Command—using memorized phrases and thinking they will be heard for their many words? Where have all these traditions of the prayer book, the pastoral prayer, the rosary, and prayer meeting phraseology originated? Not in the red letters.

I am as guilty of these misdirected so-called prayers as anyone. I am aghast to read Jesus' words and realize how often I have prayed *exactly* as he commands us not to—with empty phrases and many words. I have used the stock phrases and the familiar verbiage on occasions too numerous to count. In a circle of prayer, I grow uncomfortable with the heavenly hush. It is difficult to *listen* in the silence, to attune oneself to the still small Voice that may be trying to speak. It is far easier to begin babbling in what we call prayer, but is more accurately the heaping up of many words that drowns out the Divine whispers that would speak to the heart.

If I was lost on a desert island, alone with no one but God, how different would my prayers be? Would I pray prayer-book prayers? Would I pray memorized prayers? Would I sit down to compose my prayers beforehand, making sure they sounded lofty, illustrious, and holy, and then stand and with pious intonation, increased volume, and appropriate hand gestures, turn my face upward and read my composition?

If my prayers would be different on a desert island than in church or a prayer meeting, then the question is self-evident: Who am I praying for? Or perhaps...Who am I praying *to*?

The word "ostentatious" comes from Luke 18:11-13, where Jesus compares the prayers of two men. *Two men went up into the temple to pray, one a Pharisee and the other a tax collector. The Pharisee stood and prayed thus with himself, "God, I thank thee that I am not like other men, extortioners, unjust, adulterers, or even like this tax collector. I fast twice a week, I give tithes of all that I get." But the tax collector, standing far off, would not even lift his eyes to heaven, but beat his breast, saying, "God, be merciful to me a sinner!"*

Let us not too quickly dismiss the applicability of the lesson. Jesus usually uses extreme examples to drive home his point. Our own pomposity in prayer will not be so absurdly visible as this. Ostentation in religion is as easy to perceive as it is to disguise. But Jesus' final words (Luke 18:14) rip the mask from both those who try to hide what they are but can't, as well as those who successfully veil their self-righteousness: *Every one who exalts himself will be humbled, but he who humbles himself will be exalted.*

> The prayer of faith, presupposes that the prayer of guidance is perpetually ascending to the Father. We must hear, know and obey the will of God... "There is a way of ordering our mental life on more than one level at once. On one level we may be thinking, discussing, seeing, calculating, meeting all the demands of external affairs. But deep within, behind the scenes, at a profounder level, we may also be in prayer...and a gentle receptiveness to divine breathings." (quoted from Thomas Kelly's *A Testament of Devotion*, pp. 125, 35)
>
> Richard Foster, *Celebration of Discipline*, pp. 35, 40

God, bring to my remembrance this day the Command of Jesus NOT TO PRAY WITH EMPTY PHRASES. *May my heart's prayers be always and only directed to <u>you</u>, and you alone. Thus, heavenly Father, may I be an instrument in my small corner of the world for the ultimate salvation of mankind. Amen.*

69. Remain Gratefully Aware of Your Spiritual Need

"Blessed are the poor in spirit, for theirs is the kingdom of heaven." (Matthew 5:3)

There are many "firsts" in the Gospel story—the first disciples called, the first Command, the first sermon, the first *Follow me*, etc. We have noted some of these as we have progressed through the Commands. One of the most instructive such firsts occurs in Matthew 5:3: *Blessed are the poor in spirit, for theirs is the kingdom of heaven.* These are Jesus' first New Testament words of teaching, as he opens what we call the Sermon on the Mount with the Beatitudes. And this is the *first* Beatitude.

Obviously, then, something of major importance is here. Why does Jesus begin his teaching of what comprises a life of righteousness with *Blessed are the poor in spirit?*

What does it mean to be "poor in spirit"? The words are familiar, yet hazily understood. We might assume it to refer to "spiritual poverty"—in other words, an *unspiritual* man or woman. But then why would such a one be called blessed and happy? It is only those who are *rightly* related to God—truly "spiritual" men and women—who know the greatest joy of life.

Being "rightly related" to God begins in understanding who God is, and who I am. He is everything, I am nothing. He is the Creator, I am the created. He is the Potter, I am the clay. My very life depends on him each moment. He holds my every breath in the palm of his hand. My need and dependency upon God is total.

This is the foundation of spirituality—humbly recognizing my need of God. In and of myself, I am utterly impoverished—naked and alone before the universe, powerless even to control the next beat of my heart and surge of my lungs. Yet in that state, God *loves* me and *sustains* me. He not only gives me life, he desires relationship and friendship with me. He lavishes goodness upon me. Thus, in my impoverishment, I am *not* destitute—I am wealthy and blessed beyond comprehension. The very life of God, the kingdom of heaven itself, is mine…if I will take it!

Thus, the great dichotomy of the spiritual life—in ourselves we are spiritually poor, but in God we are spiritually rich. Keeping this essential equation of life constantly before us is indeed the key to happiness. "Blessed" are we indeed because we are "poor in spirit" And it is those who recognize this relational equation between Creator and created who are most blessed of all. Not only are they blessed, Jesus concludes the beatitudes by saying, *Rejoice and be glad.*

In other words: Blessed are those who are humble, who know who they are before God and who recognize their spiritual need. Be thankful if you are such a one. Be grateful that you are spiritually poor, because in God you are so spiritually rich that the kingdom of heaven is yours.

*The presence of God…*in my opinion, contains the whole spiritual life…

There is not in the world a kind of life more sweet and delightful than that of a continual conversation with God: those only can comprehend it who practise and experience it: yet I do not advise you to do it from that motive; it is not pleasure which we ought to seek in this exercise; but let us do it from a principle of love, and because God would have us.

Were I a preacher, I should above all other things preach the practice of the presence of God; and, were I a director, I should advise all the world to it: so necessary do I think it, and so easy too.

Ah! Knew we but the want we have of the grace and assistance of God, we should never lose sight of Him, no not for a moment.

"Brother Lawrence," Nicholas Herman, from *The Practice of the Presence of God,* XV,1685

God, bring to my remembrance this day the Command of Jesus to REMAIN GRATEFULLY AWARE OF MY SPIRITUAL NEED. *Remind me of my spiritual need...a recognition of my need of you. Poorness of spirit, and the humble self-awareness before you that accompanies it, is the very doorway into the kingdom of heaven. May I walk through that door anew every day, knowing who I am, because I am yours. I am grateful for my need, because in that need is my childship born. Thus, heavenly Father, may I be an instrument in my small corner of the world for the ultimate salvation of mankind. Amen.*

70. Take Up Your Cross

"If any man would come after me, let him deny himself and take up his cross daily and follow me."
(Luke 9:23)

The cross has become the essential symbol of Christianity. It was not so, however, when Jesus spoke these words. People throughout the Roman Empire knew well enough that the cross signified the ultimate penalty of Roman justice. But when the disciples heard Jesus say that a man must *take up his cross,* it is doubtful that the words carried much meaning. Their first thought must have been, "What is he talking about!" No one *willingly* takes up a cross. The cross was imposed *against* one's will. Even in the Lord's case, his *Not my will* prayer tells us clearly that it was *not* his will to suffer crucifixion. And how can a cross be taken up *daily*? You can't die more than once. What could Jesus possibly mean?

We find ourselves facing an enormous question. Did Jesus know that death on a cross was his predetermined fate? He surely knew that his confrontation with the Jewish leaders would end in martyrdom. It seems, however, that stoning, not crucifixion, would have been the more likely outcome. Indeed, it had already been tried twice. His quarrel from the beginning was with the spiritual corruption of Judaism. Jesus had little argument with Rome. His mission was a spiritual not a political one. Having perhaps prepared himself for the fate which later befell Stephen, one wonders if Jesus was as taken by surprise as were the disciples at the turn events took at the end of his life—finding his ultimate destiny in Pilate's hands rather than the High Priest's. Could the gradual realization that crucifixion awaited him, rather than the execution prescribed by

Mosaic Law, have been the cause of his anguished prayer in Gethsemane?

To what, then, was he referring with the words that a man must *take up his cross?* Though the figurative cross of this passage indeed became the literal cross of his crucifixion, it seems likely that his primary intent here was *not* to foretell his death. Jesus was using the familiar image to give his disciples a picture of what he had brought to the world. The cross was an image of the life he was exampling before their very eyes. He was describing life with God. He was not speaking of the *future*, he was giving them a vivid illustration of the *now*.

Thus he uses the phrase that we must take up our *own* cross. His use of "daily" reveals the Lord's high meaning. It is an *ongoing* cross. Had his reference been to his crucifixion, he would have said that we must *submit* to or *endure* the cross. But no—we must *take up* our cross. We *choose* the cross. We must crucify *ourselves*. Of this process, George MacDonald writes in his sermon *Justice*: "The only vengeance worth having on sin is to make the sinner himself its executioner." It is on the self-chosen cross of moment-by-moment self-denial that we kill our own sin, deathing our wills into God's will. This we do over and over...*daily*.

The eternal power of the crucifixion was accomplished in Gethsemane. It was in the Garden that the Son of God perfected in the heavenlies that which he lived out on earth the next afternoon on the hill of Golgotha. It is in Gethsemane that the true sacrifice took place—the final relinquishment of his will into the Father's. It is there that Jesus culminated and perfected the same life he had been living all along: *Not my will, but yours be done.* Every day of his life he chose to *take up* his cross before the will of the Father. The cross is the visible symbol of self-relinquishment, symbolizing the lifting of empty hands of faith and nailing them to the cross ourselves—dying to all but the will of the Father.

> Jesus rose at once to the height of his being, set himself down on the throne of his nature, in the act of subjecting himself to the will of the Father...When he died on the cross...he completed and held fast the eternal circle of his existence in saying, "Thy will, not mine, be done!"
>
> George MacDonald, *Unspoken Sermons, Third Series*, "The Creation in Christ"

God, bring to my remembrance this day the Command of Jesus to TAKE UP MY CROSS. *May I grow in daily, moment-by-moment relinquishment of my will into yours. Give me the will and the courage to death my own sin on the cross of self-chosen sacrifice, and with Jesus say continually, "Thy will, not mine, be done." Thus, heavenly Father, may I be an instrument in my small corner of the world for the ultimate salvation of mankind. Amen.*

SERIES EIGHT

"THE JAMES SON OF ALPHAEUS COMMANDS"

The Golden Rule

LIFE'S MOMENT-BY-MOMENT GUIDE TO CONDUCT

James, son of Alphaeus, also referred to as James the Younger, or James the Less, is another disciple about whom nothing is known for certain. Yet his name itself is significant. For Matthew is also called the *son of Alphaeus* (Mark 2:14). This identification can hardly be coincidental. It seems all but certain that Matthew and the unknown James were brothers.

Great human drama always exists between the lines of the Gospel. Capernaum, was a Jewish village on the Sea of Galilee large enough to have a synagogue, but small enough that "everybody knew everybody." Not only do we know the name of Alphaeus' two sons, we also know his wife as one of the several New Testament "Marys." Whether or not significance can be attached to Matthew being given the name *Levi,* we cannot know. But is it possible his father had priestly aspirations for his eldest son?

However, Levi must have been an ambitious young man. Being a tax collector was not the sort of job one acquired by accident. He had to seek the position. What kind of young Jew would want such a job? Throwing in with Herod and the Romans, then squeezing his own people for personal gain, required a level of betrayal beyond the mere desire for gain. It is hard to imagine anyone *wanting* such a job. But this was Matthew's chosen career.

What did his family think? How close were he and his brother when *James'* taxes came due? As Matthew was no doubt the black sheep of the family, the whole household was probably stained in the public eye. As is common in our time, a family black sheep often results in gossip about what the parents must have done wrong for the prodigal to have gone astray. One can imagine the scribes and Pharisees shunning Alphaeus and Mary as well.

Then Jesus came. When Mark so powerfully says, "Jesus came into Galilee, preaching the Gospel of God," he came to *people.* Among those people was the household of Alphaeus. The only details we know are that two young men called James and Levi (or Matthew) were soon among Jesus' closest friends, became his disciples, and were both appointed among the Twelve.

Reconciliation and healing came to the whole family. Obviously Matthew and James must have been wonderfully reunited as brothers. But the life-changing power of the Gospel was not limited to the two brothers. In one of the tiny details of the Gospel account we encounter a wonderful fact.

Fast forward three years. In Mark 15, Mark says that "some women" were watching the crucifixion "from a distance." Among the group were Mary Magdalene, Salome (wife of Zebedee and mother of James and John,) and *Mary the mother of James the younger.* If the above family associations are accurate, we now see that not only the sons, but also the mother had become one of Jesus' close followers. She was with the other women and mothers at the end, even after the disciples themselves, possibly two of her own sons, had fled.

χρηστός : CHRĒSTOS—*Kind* (CHRĒSTOTĒS—*Kindness*)

An investigation into the origins of the Greek words translated "kind" and "kindness" reveals several fascinating truths. The primary word used by Jesus to describe God in Luke 6:35 ("for he is kind") is χρηστός—CHRĒSTOS. However, two additional words take scriptural kindness to a higher level. AGATHOS (literally "good") is also translated "kind." And PHILANTHRŌPIA (literally "loving man") also denotes "kindness." Intriguingly, CHRĒSTOS only differs by one letter from CHRISTOS, or "Christ." And AGATHOS stems from the same root as AGAPĒ. The connections between love, goodness, philanthropy, Christlikeness and *kindness* are clear. No wonder Jesus used CHRĒSTOS to describe God. As God is AGAPĒ, God is also χρηστός—*kind.* If we would be like God, simple human kindness is where it begins.

Series Eight

Life's Moment-by-Moment Guide to Conduct

71. Do and think toward others as you would have them behave toward you.

72. Don't judge.

73. Deal with your own faults before thinking of the faults of others.

74. Ask, seek, knock.

75. Enter through the narrow gate.

76. Come to me with your burdens and find rest.

77. Take my yoke upon you.

78. Don't swear.

79. Judge rightly not by appearances.

80. Give the world its due and give God the things that are his.

71. Do and Think Toward Others As You Would Have Them Behave Toward You

"So whatever you wish that men would do to you, do so to them; for this is the law and the prophets." (Matthew 7:12)

Throughout the Commands, we have repeatedly emphasized that this or that word from Jesus is THE essential, THE first, THE foundational Command. "Wait a minute," some may object. "If *this* is the most important Command…how can *that* be the most important?"

In a sense, this dichotomy uncovers a great truth—*all* the Commands are foundational. How can we rank the relative importance of *Love God, Love man, Follow me, Deny yourself, Believe, Abide in me, Obey my Commands*? These and many others are *all* the most important.

There is only one Command, however, which Jesus says sums up all the Law and the Prophets. That obviously places it very high on any ranking of significance. Yet amazingly, it is also probably the *most* practical and the *least* "spiritual" of the Commands. It is nothing but the familiar "Golden Rule"—*Do unto others as you would have them do unto you.*

Imagine it. Jesus says that all spirituality is summed up in being nice to others. It is a matter of consistency. Treat others as you want to be treated. Think about others as you want to be thought about. Speak to others as you want to be spoken to. It is simple character consistency going both directions—what we want to come *in* toward ourselves, we send *out* to others.

Do you want to be given the benefit of the doubt? Then give others the benefit of the doubt. Do you want to be criticized? Of course not. Then don't criticize others. Do you want people to smile at you? Then smile at them. Do you want people to think good thoughts of you? Then think good thoughts of them. Do you want to be forgiven when you blunder? Then forgive others their blunders. Do you want people to be patient with you? Then be patient with them.

Jesus is saying that life is a gigantic mirror that reflects actions, thoughts, attitudes, and responses. What we project *into* the mirror will be reflected back to us. Anger will be met by anger. Blessing will be met by blessing. Selfishness will be met by selfishness. Generosity will be met by generosity. Criticism will be met by criticism. Kindness will be met by kindness. Smiles will be met by smiles.

It is truly an incredible thing to consider the astonishing magnitude of what it would be to think and behave toward others *as we want them to think and behave toward us.*

Stop and ponder it! The very idea is beyond comprehension!

Yet the high and magnificent thing is so close. It is in my grasp in the next five minutes if I but *do* what Jesus said. I therefore resolve to treat the next person who crosses my path as I would like to be treated myself.

> This is very probably the most universally famous thing that Jesus ever said. With this commandment the Sermon on the Mount reaches its summit and its peak. This saying of Jesus has been called "the capstone of the whole discourse." This saying is the topmost peak of social ethics, and the Everest of all ethical teaching.
>
> It is possible to quote rabbinic parallels for almost everything that Jesus said in the Sermon on the Mount; but there is no real parallel to this saying. This is something which had never been said before. It is new teaching, and a new view of life and life's obligations...
>
> In its negative form this rule is in fact the basis of all ethical teaching, but no one but Jesus ever put it in its positive form. Many voices had said, "Do not do to others what you would not have them do to you," but no voice had ever said, "Do to others what you would have them do to you."
>
> William Barclay, *The Gospel of Matthew, Vol. 2*, pp. 276-77, 279

God, bring to my remembrance this day the Command of Jesus to DO AND THINK TOWARD OTHERS AS I WOULD HAVE THEM BEHAVE TOWARD ME. Explode into my consciousness the absolutely shocking, revolutionary, incredible yet unbelievably simple and moment-by-moment power of doing as I would be done by. Jolt my senses awake in the midst of every interaction with another of my kind—that I can truly treat others as I want to be treated. Thus, heavenly Father, by doing as I would be done by, may I be an instrument in my small corner of the world for the ultimate salvation of mankind. Amen.

72. Don't Judge

"Judge not, and you will not be judged." (Luke 6:37)

Many of the Commands are implied, but this is a direct, clear, forceful, and unyielding Command—*Judge not.* The Lord's words in Luke 6:37 are absolutely total and consuming—*Don't judge, don't condemn. Instead forgive.* Matthew adds the pithy image of trying to take a speck out of someone else's eye when there are blind spots in our own life the size of logs.

But it is so *easy*, so natural, enjoyable, and satisfying to the flesh to notice those blind spots in everyone else. They are so glaring. They jump out for all the world to see—those annoying mannerisms, those obvious examples of self-centeredness, those immaturities, that propensity always to talk about oneself, the hogging of the limelight, that critical spirit, that habit of interrupting, of having to be right, of always getting the last word, of never having anything good to say, of talking incessantly and never letting another person get a word in edgeways.

All these traits are so *obvious*. How can they not see them?

Imagine the eye-opening shock if we truly saw ourselves as others see us. All these little specks we see in others…they detect the same things in us—and more besides!

They are saying about you and me, and about *our* faults and inconsistencies and immaturities, "They are so obvious. How can they not see them?" You and I are blind too!

When Jesus says that we will be judged and forgiven by the same measure with which we judge and forgive others, he is not saying that God will *refuse* to forgive us if we judge others harshly. He is merely stating a fact of life—everyone by nature judges others more harshly than they do themselves. Turn that principle around, he says. Look to your *own* sins and weaknesses and selfishnesses first. Show leniency and understanding and forgiveness to others, and lo and behold…you will find that same spirit of generosity and kindness coming back to you.

In truth, however, this principle represents a basic tenet of first-grade spirituality. When we move into graduate level Christlikeness, the weakness of others ceases to move the compass needle of our thoughts a hair's breadth. We choose to see those whose paths cross ours as God sees them—by looking *into* them. We choose to behold not what they may be now, but what God is making of them. We do not focus on the outer shell of weak humanity, but rather upon the radiant seed of eternal God-ness struggling to come to life within them. We rejoice in those aspects of their being that reflect God's image. For such purpose they were created.

As for ourselves, we turn the searchlight of our prayers inward, toward no one but ourselves. We ask for the illumination of the Holy Spirit to give us sight to see our *own* blind spots, that we may walk humbly before God, and before our brothers and sisters, fully aware what small and fragile and weak and self-centered creatures we are. With David, the prayers of the 19th and 51st Psalms breathe silently from our lips: *Cleanse me from my hidden faults…Wash me thoroughly from my iniquity, and cleanse me from my sin…purge me…Create in me a clean heart, O God, and renew a right spirit within me.*

There were some movements which…disagreed with each other as well…They agreed in discarding anything that was not expressly authorized by Scripture, but disagreed on what was authorized. They wished to return to…primitive Christianity…but disagreed on what that was. They liked simple forms of worship…but did not always like each other's. They believed that…The 'world'…one day would have to hear in answer to their 'Lord, we didn't know' the judgment reply, 'Well, you know now,' while the small company of elect would be tucked up cosily in their undercrowded heaven... They have been with society ever since in a thousand shapes.

David Christie-Murray, *A History of Heresy*, pp. 160-61

God, bring to my remembrance this day the Command of Jesus NOT TO JUDGE. *Judgment is so slippery. Subtle judgments against others sneak in easily, unseen, and seem so reasonable, so full of truth, even so helpful, that I do not recognize them as the evil they are. Truly I need your help, desperately, continuously! Open my eyes to my judging heart! Thus, heavenly Father, by my stout refusal to judge others, may I be an instrument in my small corner of the world for the ultimate salvation of mankind. Amen.*

73. Deal with Your Own Faults Before Thinking of the Faults of Others

"Why do you see the speck that is in your brother's eye, but do not notice the log that is in your own eye? Or how can you say to your brother, 'Let me take the speck out of your eye,' when there is the log in your own eye? You hypocrite, first take the log out of your own eye, and then you will see clearly to take the speck out of your brother's eye." (Matthew 7:3-5)

No pithier visual imagery exists in Jesus' teaching than his clever use of the speck and log in the matter of fault-finding. He presents a picture so ludicrously absurd it's hard not to laugh when calling it to mind.

But Jesus was in deadly earnest. When we encounter these words, we sense no humor in his tone. Indeed, I sense an earnestness that borders on righteous anger toward the all-too-common cancer within humankind to notice the faults of others before heeding our own. We feel no tenderness in his voice when, *You hypocrite!* slams into our ears. He means his listeners to take fault-finding very, very seriously. He wants us to recognize it for the sin it is—a sin that produces spiritual blindness.

Jesus' command here pinpoints a tendency that is so close to the surface in most of us as to be frightening. Truly heeding our own "logs" of spiritual blindness, indeed we might exclaim, "Now *that's* scary!" It ought to frighten us more than a little when a thought of criticism toward somebody else comes to mind, and with it the further idea that perhaps we should *help* him or her by pointing out the fault we have noticed. It's the decent thing to do, after all. They obviously don't see it. They *need* to see it. Surely they will *thank* us for caring enough to call it to their attention.

Such justifications indeed ought to scare us! For that is the very moment when Jesus turns, not to the one about whom we feign such concern, but to you and me, and says with a tone of considerable warmth and feeling, *You hypocrite, you should know better!*

Let us say it again: *Fault-finding is a sin.* Fault-finding is a sin that produces spiritual blindness.

Notice an interesting detail. Jesus does not imply that your brother (or sister) has no faults. Perhaps there *is* a speck in his or her eye. He simply says, "You are not the one to address it. It's none of your business. You've got faults of your own. Deal with them."

Imagine if everyone in the world heeded this simple prescription. There would be no need for criticism at all. Every individual would be scrupulously and diligently focused on his or her own individual weaknessness, shortcomings, faults, and blunders. No one would worry about the faults of others because, all taken together, everything was covered. We would all be "taking heed to ourselves." All sin would be attended to.

That's the incredibly practical corollary to Jesus' Command—our fault-finding does no good anyway. Nobody else can get rid of my faults. Only I can do that. And I am powerless to get rid of anyone else's.

> To persuade the heart, the will, the action, is alone worth the full energy of a man. His strength is first for his own, then for his neighbour's manhood. He must first pluck out the beam out of his own eye, then the mote out of his brother's—if indeed the mote in his brother's be more than the projection of the beam in his own. To make a man happy as a lark, *might be* to do him grievous wrong: to make a man wake, rise, look up, turn, is worth the life and death of the Son of the Eternal.
>
> George MacDonald, *Unspoken Sermons, Second Series*, "The Hardness of the Way"

God, bring to my remembrance this day the Command of Jesus to DEAL WITH MY OWN FAULTS BEFORE THINKING OF THE FAULTS OF OTHERS. *When criticism or fault-finding rises in my brain, sting me with a reminder of the sobering rebuke of Jesus toward speck hunters—You hypocrite! When I am being a hypocrite, painful though it is, I want to know it. Open my eyes to the beams in my eyes. Thus, heavenly Father, may I be an instrument in my small corner of the world for the ultimate salvation of mankind. Amen.*

74. Ask, Seek, Knock

"Ask, and it will be given you; seek, and you will find; knock, and it will be opened to you. For every one who asks receives, and he who seeks finds, and to him who knocks it will be opened." (Matthew 7:7-8)

The familiar passage from Matthew 7 is usually associated with prayer, and the promise of answered prayer: *Ask, and it will be given you; seek, and you will find; knock, and the door will be opened to you.*

Jesus may indeed have had prayer in mind. However, all his teachings and Commands are multi-dimensional. That is why we may study the Gospels all our lives, and continue to find ever deepening, ever more practical, ever more expansive meaning from their pages. The Commands are inexhaustible in their practicality, in their wisdom, and in their revelation of Father and Son.

It may be, then, that there is more to *Ask, Seek, Knock* than meets the eye. Jesus may also be speaking about, not merely one's approach to prayer, but about one's approach to all of life. To use several familiar idioms, Jesus may be urging his followers to take life by the horns, to go for it, to approach what we do with gusto.

We discover here another of those many dichotomies where the Commands seem to point in multiple directions, emphasizing again that they cannot be taken or left as if they are presented us as a spiritual smorgasbord. The Commands come to us as a totality. They outline a practical yet complex unity of conduct, attitude, and character. So whereas we are commanded to trust, and to relax in the face of life's anxieties, to approach life as the birds of the air and lilies of the field, to seek God's kingdom and not worry about the things of earth...we are also commanded to bring energy, determination, vision, and forcefulness into our walks with God. *Pluck* is perhaps the operative word. Jesus wants followers who do not give up, who knock on closed doors, who ask the impossible, who seek what others only dream of, who are not easily dissuaded, who, when they are knocked out of the saddle, get up again and continue on. Followers with *pluck* and *energy* and *vigor*.

The great Old Testament spy Caleb was such a one. He and Joshua were the only two of the twelve spies with faith to believe that they could take the land. Thus they were the only two who remained alive to enter Canaan years later. When that time came, as an old man, Caleb's determination and vision were no less valiant than when he was a youthful spy. He boldly said to Joshua in Joshua 15, "I was forty years old when Moses the servant of the Lord sent me...to spy out the land...And now, behold, the Lord has kept me alive, as he said, these forty-five years since...I am this day eighty-five years old. I am still as strong to this day as I was in the day that Moses sent me; my strength now is as my strength was then, for war, and for going and coming. So now give me this hill country...and I shall drive them out as the Lord said...So Hebron became the inheritance of Caleb, the son of Jephunneh." (Numbers 14:7-14)

At eighty-five, Caleb's vision and strength were undimmed. He was ready for war! *Give me that mountain, and I will drive them out!*

Caleb asked, Caleb sought...and Caleb got his mountain.

In Greek there are two kinds of imperative; there is the *aorist* imperative which

issues one definite command. "Shut the door behind you," would be an aorist imperative. There is the *present* imperative which issues a command that a man should always do something or should go on doing something. "Always shut the doors behind you," would be a present imperative. The imperatives here are *present* imperatives; therefore Jesus is saying, "Go on asking; go on seeking, go on knocking."
William Barclay, *The Gospel of Matthew, Vol.* 1, p. 276

God, bring to my remembrance this day the Command of Jesus to ASK, SEEK, AND KNOCK. Help me discern the balance between trusting you, resting in you, and walking in submission to your will, and at the same time being an energetic disciple with pluck and vision. Give me faith to seek you for big things, humility to be content in small things, and the wisdom to know the time for each. Thus, heavenly Father, may I be an instrument in my small corner of the world for the ultimate salvation of mankind. Amen.

75. Enter Through the Narrow Gate

"Enter by the narrow gate; for the gate is wide and the way is easy, that leads to destruction, and those who enter by it are many. For the gate is narrow and the way is hard, that leads to life, and those who find it are few."
(Matthew 7:13-14)

Most commentators, theologians, pastors, and teachers, through the years have interpreted this passage through a salvationary lens. The contrast they see as between the saved and the unsaved, believers and unbelievers, his disciples and the Pharisees, and ultimately heaven and hell. This view is bolstered by Jesus' word that the wide, easy gate leads to *destruction*, which they read as an obvious reference to hell. Paraphrased, according to this prevailing perspective, they hear Jesus saying, "Get yourself saved." It may be, however, that a more subtle reading strikes closer to home, and perhaps probes more meaningfully to the heart of Jesus' intent.

The final fifteen verses of the Sermon on the Mount, begun by this passage, are clearly a unity. Jesus is offering a stark differentiation between "religion" as commonly understood ("You have heard that it was said...") and the life of righteousness he has been proposing ("But I say to you...") As the great "sermon" moves to a climax, he concludes with a triumphant progression of contrasts:

The narrow gate vs. the wide and easy gate. Grapes and figs vs. thorns and thistles. The sound tree vs. the bad tree. He is not contrasting belief and unbelief. The entire context takes place *within* belief. Jesus is speaking of *false* religion and *true* religion. His warning in verse 15 is not against atheism but against false *spirituality*: "Beware of false prophets."

Jesus is talking about the Commands. He is contrasting those who obey the Commands and those who don't. His point could not be more clear: "Not every one who says to me, 'Lord, Lord,' shall enter the kingdom of heaven, but he who does the will of my Father." The rest of the passage is blunt, ending with the chilling words, "And then will I declare to them, 'I never knew you; depart from me you evildoers.'"

Jesus is not here addressing the unbelieving world with a Command to get saved. He is speaking about believers, men and women of all brands and stripes who pretend to be spiritual but don't do what he says. The wide and easy gate is not atheism, but *religion without obedience.* This passage has nothing to do with salvation. It has everything to do with obedience. The narrow gate is nothing more nor less than The Commands.

Jesus' final contrast, climaxing this brief series of contrasts, and indeed summarizing the entire Sermon on the Mount, is between a wise man and a foolish man. What is the difference between the two? Some people do his words…others don't.

"Every one then who hears these words of mine *and does them* will be like a wise man."

We may thus paraphrase Jesus: *Enter through the narrow gate, which is obedience to my words. For the gate is wide and the way is easy that makes an outward show of religion but pays little heed to The Commands. But spirituality of the wide gate will only lead to destruction in the end. For every one who hears these words of mine and does not do them will be like a foolish man who built his house upon the sand; and the rain fell, and the floods came, and the winds blew and beat against that house, and it fell; and great was the fall of it. Therefore, enter through the narrow gate. Obey the Commands.*

> To every man there openeth a way and ways and a way;
> And the high soul treads the high way, and the low soul gropes the low;
> And in between on the misty flats the rest drift to and fro;
> But to every man there openeth a high way and a low;
> And every man decideth the way his soul shall go.
> John Oxenham, from William Barclay's *The Gospel of Matthew, Vol. 1,* p. 282

God, bring to my remembrance this day the Command of Jesus to ENTER THROUGH THE NARROW GATE. *Keep me from the wide gate complacent satisfaction of business-as-usual Christianity. Help me be a narrow gate obedient believer who hears your words and does them—a 24/7 not a 1-in-7 Christian. Thus, heavenly Father, may I be an instrument in my small corner of the world for the ultimate salvation of mankind. Amen.*

76. Come to Me with Your Burdens and Find Rest

"Come to me, all who labor and are heavy laden, and I will give you rest." (Matthew 11:28)

There are two ways to read Jesus' invitation, *Come to me, all who labor and are heavy laden, and I will give you rest.* We can't forget that the Jews to whom he was primarily speaking in the first century were laboring under a morass of legalistic ritual and regulation. The more faithful the man or woman, the more impossible was the pharisaic law to keep. Religion was indeed a heavy burden. In one sense, then, Jesus is simply saying, "I came to deliver you from the heavy burdens of legalism. In the living water that I bring, you will find sustenance, and rest for your souls."

In another sense that comes close to us all, he is saying nothing more than, "I know that life is hard, life is unfair, life is burdensome…it is hard work, it is disappointing, discouraging, painful. Therefore, bring me your burdens. Let them go. Release them. Hand them over to me. Let me carry the heartaches that are weighing you down. I will take them for you. Rest, just *rest*…in me."

Is it easier said than done?

Of course.

Yet is it *possible*…anytime…anywhere…at any moment? Again, of course! It is perhaps the most possible thing in the world, simply to center down into that inner place of silent intimate prayer, close the eyes, relax, exhale the stress, and say, "I'm sorry, I forgot. I picked up my burdens again. I hadn't even realized I was carrying them myself. Here, Jesus—take them. I will let you carry them for me now."

> "Of all words that ever were spoken, were ever words gentler, tenderer, humbler, lovelier…than these…'Come unto me, all ye that labour and are heavy-laden, and I will give you rest. Take my yoke upon you, and learn of me; for I am meek and lowly in heart: and ye shall find rest unto your souls. For my yoke is easy, and my burden is light.'?
>
> "Surely these words, could they but be heartily believed, are such as every human heart might gladly hear! What man is there who has not had, has not now, or will not have to class himself amongst the weary and heavy-laden?…
>
> "Come then, sore heart, and see whether his heart cannot heal thine. He knows what sighs and tears are, and if he knew no sin in himself, the more pitiful must it have been to him to behold the sighs and tears that guilt wrung from the tortured hearts of his brethren and sisters. Brothers, sisters, we *must* get rid of this misery of ours. It is slaying us. It is turning the fair earth into a hell, and our hearts into its fuel. There stands the man, who says he knows: take him at his word. Go to him who says in the might of his eternal tenderness and his human pity—Come unto me, all ye that labour and are heavy-laden, and I will give you rest. Take my yoke upon you, and learn of me; for I am meek and lowly in heart: and ye shall find rest unto your souls. For my yoke is easy and my burden is light."
>
> George MacDonald, *Thomas Wingfold, Curate*, Chapter 46

God, bring to my remembrance this day the Command to COME TO JESUS WITH MY BURDENS AND FIND REST. I forget so easily that you are with me and beside me every moment, Jesus, willing and eager to share my load and carry my burdens for me. Remind me of your presence. Remind me continually. Take the burdens and anxieties of my life that weigh me down. I give them to you. I know they are light for you. It is your joy to carry them for me. May I likewise know joy in giving them to you. Thus, heavenly Father, may I be an instrument in my small corner of the world for the ultimate salvation of mankind. Amen.

77. Take My Yoke Upon You

"Take my yoke upon you, and learn from me; for I am gentle and lowly in heart, and you will find rest for your souls. For my yoke is easy and my burden is light." (Matthew 11:29-30)

The unfortunate image conjured up by this passage in the minds of many is of a poor suffering beast of burden, a hundred-pound slab of oak laced to his neck, a plow tied behind, laboring in the hot sun from sunup to sundown. Not a very appealing life!

What a dramatically different image Jesus intended to convey! What he is actually saying is this: "Because I am lowly in heart, my only desire is to submit myself to my Father's will as the one good, and my one joy in life. I do not live for myself—I live for him. This is the yoke I bear—a *chosen* yoke, an *easy* yoke, a *joyous* yoke. I would do no other than live for him! It is a burden altogether light to bear. It is no burden at all! Therefore, learn from me. Take this same yoke for your own. In obedience to the Father you will find rest for your souls."

There is little further that needs be said, except to add the following beautiful exposition of this passage by William Barclay:

"The Jews used the phrase *the yoke* for *entering into submission to.* They spoke of the yoke of the Law, the yoke of the commandments, the yoke of the Kingdom, the yoke of God. But it may well be that Jesus took the words of His invitation from something much nearer home than that. He says, 'My yoke is *easy.*' The word *easy* is in Greek CHRĒSTOS, which can mean *well-fitting*. In Palestine ox-yokes were made of wood; the ox was brought, and the measurements were taken. The yoke was then roughed out, and the ox was brought back to have the yoke tried on. The yoke was tailor-made to fit the ox. Now there is a legend that Jesus made the best ox-yokes in all Galilee, and that from all over the country men came to Him to the carpenter's shop to buy the best yokes that skill could make. In those days, as now, shops had their signs above the door; and it has been suggested that the sign above the door of the carpenter's shop in Nazareth may well have been: 'My yokes fit well.' It may well be that Jesus is here using a picture from the carpenter's shop in Nazareth where He had worked throughout the silent years." (*The Gospel of Matthew,* Vol. 2, p. 19)

"He wants them to have peace—*his* peace—peace from the same source whence he has it. For what does he mean by *Take my yoke upon you, and learn of me?* He does not mean *Wear the yoke I lay upon you, and obey my words.* I do not say he might not have said so, or that he does not say what comes to the same thing at other times, but that is not what he says here—that is not the truth he would convey in these words. He means *Take upon you the yoke I wear; learn to do as I do, who submit everything and refer everything to the will of my Father, yea have my will only in the carrying out of his: Be meek and lowly in heart, and ye shall find rest unto your souls.* With all the grief of humanity in his heart, in the face of the death that awaited him, he yet says, *For my yoke, the yoke I wear, is easy, the burden I bear is light.* What made that yoke easy,—that burden light? That it was the will of the Father."...

Whoever, in the commonest duties that fall to him, does as the Father would have him do, bears His yoke along with Jesus; and the Father takes his help for the redemption of the world—for the deliverance of men from the slavery of their own rubbish-laden waggons, into the liberty of God's husbandmen. Bearing the same yoke with Jesus, the man learns to walk step for step with him, drawing, drawing the cart laden with the will of the father of both, and rejoicing with the joy of Jesus.

George MacDonald, *Thomas Wingfold, Curate,* Chapter 46; *The Hope of the Gospel,* "The Yoke of Jesus"

God, bring to my remembrance this day the Command to TAKE UPON MYSELF JESUS' YOKE. *With Jesus I choose to wear the yoke of obedience and submission to your will. As it was Jesus' joy to be fit with the yoke of obedience, I choose to share in the same life that he lived, and thus enter into his joy as well. Thus, heavenly Father, by my willing, chosen, and joyous submission to your will, may I be an instrument in my small corner of the world for the ultimate salvation of mankind. Amen.*

78. Don't Swear

"You have heard that it was said to the men of old, 'You shall not swear falsely...' But I say to you, 'Do not swear at all.'" (Matthew 5:33-34)

Literalists eager to discover loopholes in the Commands will easily be able to dismiss a blanket injunction against obscenity. They will correctly note that the "swearing" condemned by Jesus in Matthew 5 and later in Matthew 23 was not profanity, but the sealing of a word or agreement by an oath. When he speaks of *swearing* by heaven, Jerusalem, the temple, the altar, or even by one's head, he was condemning the use of holy things to enforce a binding pledge. It is the same sense used in court when one places a hand on a Bible, raises the other, and says, "I swear that the testimony I am about to give is the truth..." Or, in less august settings, we have all heard statements like, "I swear on a stack of Bibles that..." or, "I swear by all that's holy that..." or, "I swear on my grandmother's grave that..."

What does all this have to do with profanity—with what we commonly call "swearing?" As we have stressed many times, we have to seek the heart of Jesus' intent. Here we can see that he was laying down no legalistic code about oaths. He was speaking rather about the entire nature of how we express ourselves—in particular about employing holy things to punctuate and enforce our speech. What is such loose talk but "swearing"—adding force and emphasis by the use of holy or profane terms.

All loose, crude, unthinking, irreverent talk, all oaths and exclamations whether holy or vulgar, used to add "color" to speech, or shouted in outbursts of anger, are an abomination to God's ears. How much worse are those vulgar "curses" which are spoken against others, variations of the *You fool!* which Jesus says makes one liable for hell. Our minds have been polluted by such expletives from constant exposure. In the world we are barraged from morning to night with filthy, degrading, coarse, lewd, and suggestive expressions. But God *hates* such talk. May we never cease to be shocked and appalled by it.

Worst of all, however, must be the ease with which the world has accustomed itself to using God's name in vain. The use of the holy name *God* to punctuate careless speech has become an epidemic in our time. How shocked would be the unthinking young person to count the number of times *God* is sprinkled through speech as if it is no more important a word than *the* or *and*. Yet Jesus says that we will be held accountable for *every* careless word. How much more will we be held accountable for the careless use of his name. Sadly, Christians have adopted this dreadful habit as well. What will they think when ten thousand such violations of the third commandment are held up to the mirror of their conscience, and God says, "How could you speak of me so irreverently?"

Indeed, as James says, the tongue is a fire. Loose speech may seem like one of the most insignificant of sins. But in truth, the tongue is an open window into the soul. The words it speaks are one of the most accurate measures of what lies deep inside. Careless talk reveals careless habit patterns.

> Let the words of my mouth and the meditation of my heart be acceptable in thy sight, O Lord, my rock and my redeemer. (Psalm 49:14)
>
> All the words of my mouth are righteous; there is nothing twisted or crooked in them. (Proverbs 8:8)
>
> The words of a man's mouth are deep waters...a fool's lips bring strife...a fool's mouth is his ruin. (Proverbs 18:4, 6, 7)
>
> The tongue of the wise brings healing. (Proverbs 12:18)

God, bring to my remembrance this day the Command of Jesus NOT TO SWEAR. *Whenever my tongue would speak loosely and thoughtlessly and light unintentional fires, I ask you to step in and silence my tongue before any damage is done. May the words of my mouth be an expression of my heart, and may both reflect my reverence for you, for your name, for your character and goodness, as well as my respect for my brothers and sisters and all humanity. Thus, heavenly Father, by the simple example of my gracious speech, may I be an instrument in my small corner of the world for the ultimate salvation of mankind. Amen.*

79. Judge Rightly Not by Appearances

"Do not judge by appearances, but judge with right judgment." (John 7:24)

Most Christians are well familiar with Jesus' injunction against condemnation: *Judge not.* We are less acquainted with the form of judgment he *does* tell us to make.

It is impossible to go through life without making judgments. We constantly weigh various factors and draw conclusions. We make decisions based on our evaluation of the evidence before us. In all these ways, Jesus says that we are to judge with what he calls *right judgment.*

This is easier said than done. The natural tendency is to judge too quickly, and to judge by appearances. We are especially guilty with people. We are drawn to attractive, outgoing, fun, and interesting people. We rarely approach relationships by asking about character, integrity, selflessness, and humility. If it's a pretty face, we are drawn toward it. If not, we shy away. Unbelievably, many are captivated by the loudest and most self-centered person in a group. Humility is the last character trait many find appealing. What is it that makes heads turn when someone walks into a room? Not righteousness or meekness, but *looks.* We are notoriously obsessed with appearances. How many ill-advised marriages fail precisely because neither husband nor wife judged with "right judgment." There are many ways of judging wrongly. But Jesus singles out just this one—don't judge by *appearances.*

It is not merely in dealings with our fellow man that appearances are deceiving. Right judgment is also required to discern *truth.* In the incident described in John 7, which prompted Jesus to command judging with right judgment, he was responding to the wrong judgment being directed against him and his teaching. Nowhere is right judgment so imperative as in matters of belief. Yet here too, Christians judge by appearances. Doctrines and theologies, fads and teachings, pastors and churches, are all evaluated superficially. The preposterous prosperity teaching that continues to exercise such a hold within certain elements of Christendom represent an idea whose "appearance" is appealing but which cannot withstand the scrutiny of "right judgment." Many such teachings exist which the unsuspecting and unthinking swallow hook, line, and sinker.

When taught from the pulpit, from a charismatic pastor or teacher who conveys confidence and authority, they *appear* to make sense. But do we bring diligent thought and prayerful "right judgment" to our aid in evaluating them? Are we asking enough questions? Are we relying too heavily on what is being served from the pulpit though it may be a spiritual diet suitable only for infants? Perhaps right judgment occasionally requires delving deeper into the heart of the Gospel than using its proof texts to fill in the sermon notes in the bulletin.

The wise discernment of right judgment asks not merely what would Jesus *do*, but also what would Jesus *think*. How would Jesus weigh truth and falsehood, wisdom and immaturity, in this individual, this church, this decision, this teaching, this doctrine? We are reminded again that the Book of Proverbs is one of the most important and practical aids used constantly by the wise, right judging man or woman in carrying out this Command in the daily affairs of life. Proverbs is the Bible's *Manual of Right Judgment*. It clarifies how right judgment is to be made in business, in love, in friendship, in finances, in families, and in spiritual matters. We need right judgment most of all when looking in the mirror.

> My son, if you accept my words and store up my commands within you, turning your ear to wisdom and applying your heart to understanding, and if you look for it as for silver and search for it as for hidden treasure, then you will understand the fear of the Lord and find the knowledge of God. For the Lord gives wisdom, and from his mouth come knowledge and understanding...Then you will understand what is right and just and fair—every good path. For wisdom will enter your heart, and knowledge will be pleasant to your soul. Discretion will protect you and understanding will guard you.
>
> Proverbs 2:1-6, 9-11, NIV

God, bring to my remembrance this day the Command of Jesus to JUDGE RIGHTLY AND NOT BY APPEARANCES. I make Solomon's words the prayer of my heart. I call out for your insight, I cry for understanding. I ask you to fill me with the right judgment of your wisdom. Thus, heavenly Father, may I be an instrument in my small corner of the world for the ultimate salvation of mankind. Amen.

80. Give the World Its Due and Give God the Things That Are His

"Render to Caesar the things that are Caesar's, and to God the things that are God's."
(Mark 12:17)

Many of the Commands of Jesus emerged out of free-flowing conversations with those around him. It can therefore be difficult to perceive his higher intent in the midst of a specific exchange. A good example exists in the matter of rendering to Caesar what is his, and to God what is his. The query posed to Jesus was very specific: *Is it lawful to pay taxes? Should we pay them?* The nature of the question, bolstered by the incident of the coin in the fish's mouth which Jesus instructed Peter to use to pay their taxes, leads to the interpretation of "render to Caesar" as: *Pay your taxes. Be a dutiful, law-abiding citizen.*

Yet is that all there is to it? If so, the parallel between Caesar's things and God's things breaks down immediately. God levies no taxes at all. Therefore, something greater than mere payment of taxes, and even greater than obeying the laws of the land, must be here. What higher truth was Jesus thinking of?

Jesus' teachings give no ground to formula. They underline eternal truths of character, conduct, and attitude. We must ruthlessly guard against turning them into clichés. All the Commands emphasize high principles. They cannot be obeyed one-dimensionally. Even a seemingly specific Command such as, *Give the world its due and give God the things that are his*, is not so simple as it looks. It is about far more than dutifully paying taxes. Jesus is speaking of an entire worldview, of the nature of our citizenship in God's kingdom, of what it means to be in the world but not of the world, about the focus of one's heart and life's priorities.

Jesus turns these two questions about taxes into a high teaching about one's entire life-focus and perspective of allegiance. Where is my heart—on the things of earth and its passing priorities and systems, or on the things of eternity? The question at its most fundamental is: Where lies my citizenship?

Many Christians feel duty bound to engage in the political process, and seek to influence the laws and programs of nations. Three questions must be asked. Is this how *Jesus* changed the world? Is he, or is he not, our example? If so, then why are so many of his followers trying to change the world by methods *contrary* to his example? It is fearfully easy for allegiances to blur, for temporal concerns to dilute eternal perspective. Does eternal citizenship require something other than political activism? What, in fact, *are* the "things of God" that Jesus says we must give to him? One cannot help wonder if much of the political fervor felt by Christians stems from rendering a little too much of the passionate allegiance we owe to God…to Caesar.

The Gospel of Jesus Christ cannot be forced upon an unwilling world by political coercion. The truths of God are birthed in the heart. It is there, not in Washington D.C., London, or elsewhere, that our citizenship has its foundations. Jesus' followers can only hope to change the world by keeping their eyes on the prize, not on the distractions of Caesar's passing world.

Pilate asks Jesus if he is a king. The question is called forth by what the Lord had just said concerning his kingdom, closing with the statement that it was not of this world...The rank and rule of this world are uninteresting to him...He might from Jerusalem have ruled the world, not merely dispensing what men call justice, but compelling atonement. He did not care for government. No such kingdom would serve the ends of his father in heaven...What was perfect empire to the Son of God, while he might teach one human being to love his neighbour, and be good like his father! To be love-helper to one heart, for its joy, and the glory of his father, was the beginning of true kingship! The Lord would rather wash the feet of his weary brothers, than be the one only perfect monarch that ever ruled in the world. It was empire he rejected when he ordered Satan behind him.

George MacDonald, *Unspoken Sermons, Third Series,* "Kingship"

God, bring to my remembrance this day the Command of Jesus to GIVE THE WORLD ITS DUE AND GIVE GOD THE THINGS THAT ARE HIS. Keep my eyes on the prize. Never let me forget that all this will pass away, and that your kingdom cannot be legislated. Thus, heavenly Father, may I be an instrument in my small corner of the world for the ultimate salvation of mankind. Amen.

SERIES NINE

"THE THOMAS COMMANDS"

Truthfulness

SPEAKING AND BEHAVING WITH HONEST CONSISTENCY

Thomas has been dealt a cruel blow by posterity. The whole world knows the phrase "a doubting Thomas." Judas may deserve his reputation, but Thomas probably doesn't deserve his. Indeed, we owe Thomas a greater debt of gratitude than many realize.

We primarily know Thomas, also called Didymus (twin), for supposedly doubting the resurrection. His response to the reports, paraphrasing John 20:25, was, *I'll believe it when I see it.* However, we can interpret Thomas' statement differently. What if it wasn't doubt that prompted his statement, but a desire to be absolutely sure of the *truth*? Perhaps his nickname, instead of doubter, should be "Thomas the lover of truth." The moment he saw Jesus in the flesh, he instantly embraced the truth of the resurrection with the triumphant declaration that resounds through all time, "My Lord and my God!"

Thomas was also courageous. His first onstage appearance in the Gospels comes in John 11 when Jesus announced his plan to go to Bethany because his friend Lazarus was sick. Knowing the danger of possible stoning that awaited them in Jerusalem, the other disciples hesitated and urged him not to go. But Thomas spoke up. "Thomas, called the Twin, said to his fellow disciples, 'Let us also go, that we may die with him.'"

It is not for either of these two statements that we owe Thomas the greatest debt, but for a question he posed in the upper room. Again, the nature of his question highlights Thomas' hunger for truth. Jesus had just made his wonderful promise of going to prepare a place for the disciples. Thomas speaks up, voicing the question that must have been on all their minds: "Lord, we do not know where you are going; how can we know the way?" Jesus replies with one of the most powerful and well-known statements in Scripture; "I am the way, and the truth, and the life; no one comes to the Father, but by me." How thankful we are for Thomas' question! It prompted one of the foundational creeds of Christianity.

Thomas was a man who was not afraid to speak up, and who said what he thought. His *yes* was yes and his *no* was no. No hidden agendas. If he did not understand something, he *wanted* to understand. He was not afraid to voice his questions and doubts in *trying* to understand. He was what we would call a bold thinking disciple.

ἀλήθεια: ALĒTHEIA —*Truth*

When Jesus said "truth (ALĒTHEIA) will make you free," he was speaking not merely of himself as the Truth, but of *truth* as defining the entire personal character of one committed to living by God's principles. The Greek ALĒTHEIA literally means "nonconcealment." What a powerful concept! How much about life and the world is veiled from our understanding. God is the greatest mystery of all. And in the world of relationships, what stupendous energy is devoted to *hiding* our true selves.

From such etymological origins, ALĒTHEIA obviously stands in direct contrast to what is "concealed." What is a lie but an attempt to conceal and hide? To *tell the truth* is to reveal everything and conceal nothing. When Jesus says, "I tell you the truth," he is about to solemnly introduce a teaching in which things hidden and obscure before are about to be revealed.

ALĒTHEIA points not only toward *telling* the truth, but being a man or woman *of* truth. It speaks against all that is hidden, to what IS—without falsehood, dishonesty, or duplicity. *Nonconcealment* is light, revelation, understanding, wisdom. In *truth,* we are given an image of the essence of character, of real, authentic, honest, genuine personhood.

Series Nine

Speaking and Behaving With Honest Consistency

81. Love truth, speak truth, do truth.

82. Do not speak carelessly.

83. Acknowledge your discipleship.

84. Let your yes be yes and your no be no.

85. Do not doubt.

86. Speak graciously with words of peace.

87. Let people injure you without retaliating.

88. Show mercy.

89. Proclaim the kingdom of God.

90. Don’t insult or call anyone a fool.

81. Love Truth, Speak Truth, Do Truth

"He who does what is true comes to the light." (John 3:19)

One of Jesus' most familiar "I am" declarations in John's gospel is, *I am the truth.* To love Jesus, therefore, one must love truth. Nowhere are we commanded, as many would seem to think, to love doctrine, to love church, to love theology, to love spiritual jargon. We are to love Jesus by loving *truth.*

For many Christians, loving truth means learning the ideas and doctrines they have been taught *about* Christianity. That is a far different thing than loving truth. Indeed, in some cases the most dreadful falsehoods about God and his work have been foisted on gullible congregations in the name of truth. And not merely in times long past. Many are the subtle persuasions being taught and perpetuated to this day by smoothly articulate teachers and pastors and priests which do not represent God's truth at all. The first necessity in loving truth is to beware of falsehood. Jesus called those who taught falsely about his Father wolves in sheep's clothing. They may be closer than you think. They may be in your own pulpit. They may be the author of a book you are reading. They may be your favorite Christian television personality.

We are not commanded to love what we are taught...but to love *truth.* There may be a difference. Loving truth implies hungering for truth, seeking to know what is true. A lover of truth is a *thinker,* not one who merely parrots back learned phrases of orthodoxy—whether political, spiritual, or other kind of orthodoxy. He digs to discover truth for himself.

Out of love for truth proceeds *speaking* truth.

Speaking truth does not mean speaking *up* for truth—arguing and debating and defending Christianity in the face of challenge. Perhaps in some instances that is called for. But that is not what Jesus is speaking of when he says *Do not bear false witness.* He is pointing rather to character—being a man or woman of truth, one whose word is their bond, whose every word is utterly reliable, who would never lie, who would never even stretch the truth. Bearing false witness is simply speaking untruly. Even a little white lie, a fib, an exaggeration, in its own way, is to bear false witness. A lover of truth does not countenance even minor violations. Truth, to the obedient disciple of Jesus, is holy. It is *never* to be toyed with.

Finally, Jesus says that in *doing* truth we will live in his light. What does it mean to do truth? The phrase itself may be unfamiliar. It means nothing more than being an individual of character who walks in truth. Loving truth and speaking truth culminate in the man or woman of integrity and virtue living in all ways by the truth, and thus *doing* truth. What greater aspiration could one strive for and pray for, what greater approbation could one hope for, than for it to be said at the end of one's life, "There walks a man, there walks a woman, of truth."

> A fact which in itself is of no value, becomes at once a matter of life and death...when a man has...the imperative choice of being true or false concerning it. When the truth, the heart, the summit, the crown of a thing, is perceived by a man, he approaches the fountain of truth whence the thing came, and perceiving God by understanding what is, becomes more of a man, more of the being he was meant to be...But far higher will the doing of the least, the most insignificant duty raise him. He begins thereby to be a true man. A man may delight in the vision and glory of a truth, and not himself be true. The man whose vision is weak, but who, as far as he sees, and desirous to see farther, does the thing he sees, is a true man...Man is man only in the doing of the truth, perfect man only in the doing of the highest truth, which is the fulfilling of his relations to his origin...The very nature of a man depends upon...these relations. They are truths, and the man is a true man as he fulfils them. Fulfilling them perfectly, he is himself a truth, a living truth.
>
> George MacDonald, *Unspoken Sermons, Third Series*, "The Truth"

God, bring to my remembrance this day the Command of Jesus to LOVE, SPEAK, AND DO TRUTH. Through my obedience, make me into a man of truth, which is the idea of me that is in your divine mind for me to become. Bring to blossom the truth of my being, which is Jesus perfected in me. Increase my love of truth. May I show my love of truth by speaking truth and doing truth. Thus, heavenly Father, may I be an instrument in my small corner of the world for the ultimate salvation of mankind. Amen.

82. Do Not Speak Carelessly

"I tell you, on the day of judgment men will render account for every careless word they utter; for by your words you will be justified, and by your words you will be condemned."
(Matthew 12:36-37)

It continues to be astonishing, once we see it, how much of Jesus' teaching concerned the simple things of life—such "unspiritual" things. Where is all the theology and doctrine? Of course we can turn to *Romans* or *Ephesians* if we want that sort of thing. But where is it in the Gospel*s*? It's not there.

What a superb example of the Lord's practicality. I cannot but wonder if in the distant background we hear faint echoes of Mary's or Joseph's teaching in the home and carpenter's shop many years before in Nazareth: *Speak nicely to your brothers and sisters. Let your words be kind and gracious. Don't criticize or gossip. Never speak a rude word.*

It cannot be accidental that the most practical books of the New Testament concern the teaching of the two brothers who grew up side by side in that home—Jesus and James. Most of the New Testament is heavily doctrinal. But the Gospels and Letter of James are utterly down to earth. And both Jesus and James strongly emphasized the power of speech.

James' memorable words shock our complacency awake with a hot blast of searing insight: *If any man thinks he is religious, and does not bridle his tongue but deceives his heart, this man's religion is vain...The tongue is a fire. The tongue is an unrighteous world among our members, staining the whole body...and set on fire by hell...No human being can tame the tongue—a restless evil, full of deadly poison.* (James 1:26; 3:6, 8)

Wow! Strong words. Did James get his dire view of the power of speech from his brother's words, "Men will render account for every careless word they utter?" Or did both, perhaps, glean the same perspective from the gracious speech and teaching of their mother and father?

It is obvious, if we are paying heed to both the sons of Mary, that words *matter.* How we speak during the small moments throughout every day, adds up. How many thoughtless words do we utter in the course of a day? How many *flippant* words, how many words about others that border on gossip, how many words about things that are none of our business, how many subtle rumors passed on to tickle another's ears, how many joking words that are not in the best of taste, how many coarse words, how many chatty words, how many unnecessary words, how many critical words, how many unkind words, how many trivial words, how many opinionated words, how many heated words?

James' image of the tongue as a *restless evil* is pregnant with insight. Give us a secret, a juicy bit of gossip, and the tongue fairly itches with restlessness until it can pass it on. It doesn't matter if it's true! We are compelled to tell what we heard, true or not! How many fires do our words set ablaze and we never know it? Truly can maturity be judged on the basis of this great principle: The mature man *can* tame his tongue. The tongue of a mature woman is *not* a restless evil full of deadly poison. The tongue of a wise man is harnessed and in control for the spreading of light, love, compassion, sympathy, understanding, wisdom, kindness, and blessing.

"I tell you, on the day of judgment men will render account for every careless word they utter." Therefore...*Do not speak carelessly.*

> But flippancy is the best of all. In the first place it is very economical....Among flippant people...every serious subject is discussed in a manner which implies that they have already found a ridiculous side to it. If prolonged, the habit of Flippancy builds up around a man the finest armour-plating against the Enemy that I know...It is a thousand miles away from joy: it deadens, instead of sharpening, the intellect.
> C.S. Lewis, The Screwtape Letters, "XI"

God, bring to my remembrance this day the Command of Jesus NOT TO SPEAK CARELESSLY. *Keep my speech free from reckless frivolity and petty trivialities. Harness my tongue from being a setter of fires. The moment a hint of gossip begins to rear its head, may I take refuge in silence. Thus, heavenly Father, by my gracious, careful, and respectful speech, may I be an instrument in my small corner of the world for the ultimate salvation of mankind. Amen.*

83. Acknowledge Your Discipleship

"Every one who acknowledges me before men, I will also acknowledge before my Father." (Matthew 10:32)

It is easy to hear words such as, "He who is ashamed of me and my words…of him will the Son of Man be ashamed" (Mark 8:38, Luke 9:26), and read ourselves right out of the text. Of course I would not do *that*, we say. I would never be *ashamed* of Jesus.

It is not enough to read the negative Commands of what we are *not* to do. We have to invert them, turn them around, and translate them into *positive* qualities of character and behavior. Vigorous, dynamic, character-transforming, world-changing Christianity is a lifestyle of active positive faith lived by men and women asking what they are to DO as the Lord's followers. *Not* doing is a mere beginning. Disciples march forth into the world every day *doing* as Jesus did.

Thus, we translate "Do not exalt yourself" into *Treat others with honor.*

"Don't judge" becomes *Think the best of others.*

"Don't swear" becomes *Speak with integrity, gentleness, and grace.*

"Guard against hypocrisy" becomes *Be a man or woman of transparent consistency.*

"Don't call anyone a fool" becomes *Speak respectfully of everyone.*

We must carry out this "translation" of the negative into positive attributes of character every time we read the Commands. In the same way, we are always looking to discern the larger and more encompassing perspective. While *obeying* the specificity, we are also looking *beyond* specificity to the high eternal truths toward which Jesus would point us. Thus, as we have seen, *Give God the things that are his* speaks not just about paying taxes but about one's entire outlook and citizenship while we yet dwell in a temporal world.

In the case of this Command, we find that Matthew in his parallel text has translated it into its positive form already. It is not sufficient *not to be ashamed* of Jesus, we are called to *acknowledge* our discipleship before men. Suddenly we are in the realm of vigorous *do.*

Does this mean we pass out tracts and turn every conversation onto spiritual themes? Of course not. We acknowledge our beliefs by who we are. At the same time people have to know *why* we are who we are. We are not merely trying to be "nice people"—as intrinsic as *niceness* is to Christlikeness. But there are loftier truths in play. We have dedicated our lives to the high attempt to model ourselves after Jesus. We are not mere "believers." We are *disciples*. There is a world of difference. His Spirit dwells within us. Eternally supernatural forces are at work. We are in the process of being transformed. We are in training as God's sons and daughters.

Therefore, to each will come moments in life when we are called to stand and be counted, when we are required to say, "Here I stand...this I believe...I am a citizen of God's kingdom...the Lord Jesus Christ is my master." While few are called to be street preachers, and it may be a legitimate question whether some street preachers actually further or hinder the kingdom of God, nor does it accomplish much to bring the Four Laws into every discussion, we yet cannot lightly dismiss the Command upon us to acknowledge our discipleship when those moments come that our beliefs are on the line.

Notice that Jesus does not add persuasion to the Command. We don't have to convince anybody of anything. No debate births truth. That is the Holy Spirit's job, not ours. He only says, *Acknowledge me before men.* The quiet, unassuming, spoken *and* unspoken witness, "Here I stand, this is why," is the most powerful acknowledgment that can be made.

> I will not then tell you what I think, but I will tell any man who cares to hear it what I believe...
>
> I believe in Jesus Christ, the eternal Son of God, my elder brother, my lord and master; I believe that he has a right to my absolute obedience...I believe that he died that I might die like him—die to any ruling power in me but the will of God.
>
> George MacDonald, *Unspoken Sermons, Third Series,* "Justice"

God, bring to my remembrance this day the Command of Jesus TO ACKNOWLEDGE MY DISCIPLESHIP. *When opportunities come, give me quiet, humble boldness to speak. Thus, heavenly Father, may I be an instrument in my small corner of the world for the ultimate salvation of mankind. Amen.*

84. Let Your Yes Be Yes and Your No Be No

"Let what you say be simply 'Yes' or 'No'; anything more than this comes from evil." (Matthew 5:37)

Again we encounter Jesus making a point with overstatement. No one seriously expects us to go through life saying nothing but *yes* and *no*. Jesus himself did not do so either. Once more we gain further insight into his words from the Lord's brother James, who gave this Command in its more familiar form: *Let your yes be yes, and your no be no.* (James 5:12) The two brothers continue to be remarkably in sync. It may be, too, that James was attempting to formulate, in the form of a brief address to the churches, an intensely practical restatement of the essence of his brother's teaching. If so, it is no surprise that he would amplify Jesus' own words.

In this case, James is making a simple but profound point: *Say what you mean.* He is building upon the earlier Command. Not only do not speak *carelessly*, speak *accurately*.

The implications are enormous in a time when people use language so casually. Nor is it merely a question of speaking carefully and truthfully. It is larger than that. James is speaking of dependability, commitment, follow-through, predictability, accountability. Not just *say* what you mean, *do* what you mean: *Do what you say you will do.*

If you say you will be somewhere...*be* there. If you promise to do something...*do* it.

The Lord's people are meant to be men and women you can trust implicitly. Their words can be depended on. Their promises can be depended on. Their entire character can be depended on. All this, and more besides, is drawn up into the magnificent challenge that touches every aspect of life—*Let your yes be yes, and your no be no.*

Sadly, there are Christians so mesmerized by spiritual concerns that they don't stop to consider what flighty, inconsistent, unreliable, erratic unpredictability says to a watching world. Their yes means if they get around to it. Their no means maybe. They are perennially late, enamored of every new fad and teaching, full of plans, dreams, schemes, but little comes of them. They move from church to church, the last people you would depend on in a pinch. Staying power, constancy, steadfastness, a long obedience in the same direction—these do not enter into the calculus of their spiritual focus. But they are not worried—grace covers all.

Being an individual whose yes means yes and whose no means no contains important implications about how one conducts himself or herself in conversation. Ideas, opinions, and plans are measured out judiciously. Another of James' injunctions—being slow to speak—is always on the mind of one whose yes means yes and whose no means no, lest, speaking too hastily and without forethought, a word might later have to be withdrawn and it will turn out that yes wasn't *exactly* yes, and no wasn't *quite* no. Of course circumstances arise and there are times we must change our minds. But life will be full of less awkwardness the fewer times commitments must be broken. Better to keep one's own counsel and remain silent until certain that the *yes* or *no* can be spoken with confidence, and with the staying power to back it up.

Fewer more accurate windows into character exist than the reliability of one's words. In all likelihood, one whose yes means yes and whose no means no will be an individual of maturity in other areas of life as well.

Vigorous writing is concise. A sentence should contain no unnecessary words, a paragraph no unnecessary sentences...This requires not that the writer make all his sentences short, or that he avoid all detail and treat his subjects only in outline, but

that every word tell.—William Strunk, Jr., *The Elements of Style.*
Say what you mean.—Rudolf Flesch, *Say What You Mean*

God, bring to my remembrance this day the Command of Jesus to LET MY YES BE YES AND MY NO BE NO. *Keep me from frivolous chatter and unwise commitments I have not thought through. Check the scattered ideas that come and go in my brain at the door of my mouth. Make me known as a person who says what he means, who does what he says he will do, and whose word is his bond. Thus, heavenly Father, may I be an instrument in my small corner of the world for the ultimate salvation of mankind. Amen.*

85. Do Not Doubt

"If you have faith and never doubt…if you say to this mountain, 'Be taken up and cast into the sea,' it will be done." (Matthew 21:21)

We have spoken several times about Jesus' use of hyperbole, exaggeration, and metaphor. We do not actually "eat his flesh" when participating in a communion or Eucharist service. He does not *really* want his followers to "cut off" their hands or "pluck out" their eyes to rid their lives of sin. These are symbols and images which Jesus used skillfully to get his points across.

But the Command toward faith and against doubt is more difficult. Jesus is using a vivid picture. He obviously is not speaking literally. We *aren't* going to pray and see mountains cast into the sea. He did no such thing himself. Nor does he expect his followers to do so.

He did, however, still the winds on Galilee. And it was a withered fig tree that prompted the discussion that led to this statement in Matthew 21:21. Therefore, many through the years have taken these words as a basis to pray for huge things, even outlandish things. They have used this seeming promise as scriptural justification to pray against the natural order of God's creation (mountains and wind and fig trees)—against storms, sickness, even death itself. How many urgent prayers have begun with some version of, "Lord, you promised if we believed that the very mountains would be cast into the sea, therefore, in faith we pray…"

Yet many such prayers are met with disappointment. So what kind of faith was Jesus urging upon us? Are the "mountains" to be taken as seemingly impossible circumstances blocking our way, filling us with discouragement, which, if we pray faithfully against them, will disappear and our way be made straight? Perhaps. Such mountains of circumstances are certainly worthy objects of prayer. Yet this remains a very interpretive passage for which there are no one-dimensional readings universally applicable in every situation.

Equally perplexing are Jesus' words about doubt. *Never* doubt? This is a difficult word. Even Jesus *himself* doubted. His prayer in Gethsemane is riddled with uncertainty. His anguished prayer-cries on the cross betray the doubt of having been forsaken by his Father. We read his discussions with the Jewish teachers in the Temple at twelve as indicating the honest doubts of the young Son of God questioning the old teaching he would replace and fulfill with his new wine eighteen years later. It was *necessary* to question the old orthodoxy before he could fully recognize the truth of the new covenant he had come to bring.

If doubt *itself* is no sin, why did Jesus say to *never* doubt? The question is particularly probing in that we see from his own example that doubt is sometimes actually required. If orthodoxies are untrue, though believed by the majority and taught by the spiritual leadership, they *must* be questioned, as Jesus questioned the teachers in the Temple.

Yet such honest doubt must not give way to unbelief. Perhaps Jesus is not so much speaking against doubt, but against unbelief. When he says, *Do not doubt*, he may have been saying, "Believe…keep believing…never disbelieve." Doubt itself—*good* doubt, *honest* doubt, *believing* doubt, *faithful* doubt, *trusting* doubt—is not the opposite of faith. Unbelief is faith's opposite. Therefore Jesus exhorts us, "Do not lapse into unbelief. *Always believe*." Such were Jesus' doubts in Gethsemane and on Calvary—the faithful, honest, *believing doubt* that trusted his Father even in the face of death looming before him.

> A man may be haunted with doubts, and only grow thereby in faith. Doubts are the messengers of the Living One to rouse the honest. They are the first knock at our door of things that are not yet, but have to be, understood; and theirs in general is the inhospitable reception of angels that do not come in their own likeness. Doubt must precede every deeper assurance; for uncertainties are what we first see when we look into a region hitherto unknown, unexplored, unannexed.
>
> George MacDonald, *Unspoken Sermons, Second Series,* "The Voice of Job"

God, bring to my remembrance this day the Command of Jesus NOT TO DOUBT. Use my doubts to deepen my knowledge of you, my understanding of your ways, and my faith in your promises. Thus, heavenly Father, may I be an instrument in my small corner of the world for the ultimate salvation of mankind. Amen.

86. Speak Graciously with Words of Peace

"Blessed are the peacemakers." (Matthew 5:9)

"As you enter the house, give it your greeting…your blessing of peace." (Matthew 10:12-13, NAS)

"Have salt in yourselves, and be at peace with one another." (Mark 9:50)

Curiously, Jesus did not address the mode and manner of how we are to conduct ourselves in the normal flow of daily conversation. His comments about speech are very specific (*Let your yes be yes and your no be no...When you pray, do not heap up empty phrases...Do not swear...Use no careless words.)* Therefore, this is another case where we must probe between the lines to discover what Jesus *meant*, and what he wants from us.

Jesus speaks of being an individual of peace, of bringing peace, of making peace, of entering homes and giving greetings and blessings of peace. How else is this to be done but by the way we communicate—in speech and word and manner? If thankfulness, gratitude, and rejoicing are to characterize our responses to life's circumstances, surely these will be reflected in our patterns of speech as well. They combine to convey a spirit of grace.

In seeking to understand and obey the Commands, however, we must look at the whole picture, not merely focus on those we find convenient or that confirm our own predilections. The Commands of Jesus come to us as a whole, not as a pick-and-choose assortment of optional suggestions.

Honesty, therefore, compels us to note—with some perplexity perhaps—the second half of the passage in Matthew 10. After telling his disciples to give their greeting and blessing of peace to households they find worthy, he also tells them to *withhold* their blessing from those who do not listen to them, and to shake the dust from their feet as they leave. What do we make of this, that in some cases Jesus instructs us to *rebuke* rather than speak with words of grace and peace? Is "withhold your blessing" a universal Command or one intended only for the twelve in the immediate aftermath of being sent out? Is Jesus perhaps instructing mere silence in such circumstances, not verbal rebuke? These are difficult questions. Some Christians feel that the strong word, even the rebuke, should indeed be regularly included in a Christian's conversational lexicon. They also point to the rebuke Jesus instructs against a sinning brother in Luke 17:3.

Similarly, the salt passages in the Gospels (Matthew 5:13, Mark 9:49-50) give commentators a wide berth for enormous interpretation. But it might not be so complicated at all. It may be that Jesus uses the image of salt to describe the seasoned and gentle speech that brings a soothing "peace additive" into the stresses and tensions of the world. Do we gain further insight into this image from Paul? Surely he is thinking of Jesus' words when he writes to the Colossians, "Let your speech always be gracious, seasoned with salt." (Col. 4:6)

Ever the practicalist, as we have recently seen, James' warnings are not ambiguous in the least: "The tongue is a fire." (James 3:6)

When Jesus says, "Have salt in yourselves, and be at peace with one another," is he saying no more nor less than: *Speak graciously. Season your words with gentleness, kindness, and peace?* If so, in those few words he has given us a practical conversational guide every time we open our mouths.

> The tongue is an unrighteous world among our members, staining the whole body…no human being can tame the tongue—a restless evil full of deadly poison…From the same mouth come blessing and cursing. My brethren, this ought not to be." (James 3:6, 8-10)

God, bring to my remembrance this day the Command of Jesus to SPEAK GRACIOUSLY WITH WORDS OF PEACE. Remind me every time I open my mouth what James says about the tongue. Sting my conscience the very moment criticism, harshness, rebuke, unkindness, gossip, complaint, faithlessness, or preoccupation with myself begins to pour forth from me. Teach me the glorious lesson of being able to listen. Season my speech with blessing, peace, kindness, goodwill, cheerfulness, and graciousness. Thus, heavenly Father, may I be an instrument in my small corner of the world for the ultimate salvation of mankind. Amen.

87. Let People Injure You Without Retaliating

"If any one strikes you on the right cheek, turn to him the other also." (Matthew 5:39)

This is surely one of the Bible's most well-known verses. Its succinct proverb is a part of everyday conversational idiom everywhere. The Command might therefore have been rendered in its more familiar form as simply: *Turn the other cheek.*

But do these four words capture the full essence of what Jesus is commanding? It may be that we have to look deeper, and broaden our inquiry to include far more than a literal slap across the face.

How many of us have actually been struck on the cheek? It's not what we would call an everyday occurrence. Maybe two or three times, maybe for some people a half dozen times, in a lifetime. But Jesus doesn't usually give Commands that are to be obeyed so rarely. Most of the Commands can be obeyed every day—even *many* times a day.

So we have to look at the "slap on the cheek" as an analogy for *any* form of personal injury, rebuke, insult, criticism, rebuff, snub, condemnation, or rejection. Suddenly the Command hits much closer to home. We are now in a world of *daily* application. Even an unkind look or abrupt word from a clerk in a store may qualify as a tiny metaphorical slap on the cheek of our sensibilities.

What is the normal first response to an unkind rebuke, insult, or unkind act we feel directed toward us? Retaliation…defense…a stinging word or a scowl of disapproval shot back. How it especially grates to be criticized or judged *unfairly*. Of course we have to respond! We have to set the record straight! We have to be strong for truth. We mustn't let injustice stand! We live in an era when personal rights reign supreme.

It is exactly at this point where Jesus steps in. Let people criticize you, he commands. Let people judge you, rebuke you, speak falsely about you, let all manner of injustice be hurled against you…*without* retaliating. If you are my disciple, he says, your only *right* is the right of love. The rights of self are to be nothing to you.

His own followers, anyone who chooses to go by the sacred name *Christian*, he goes on, are much further to be distinguished from the world than by mere silence. He commands us to turn the *other* cheek—to allow yet *more* grievances, wrongs, affronts, and slanders to come…and *still* do nothing to respond in kind. Turn it graciously. Turn it with a smile. Turn it without condescension. Especially turn it without pride.

Christians live in the world of the second cheek.

> Lord, make me an instrument of thy peace;
> where there is hatred, let me sow love;
> where there is injury, pardon;
> where there is doubt, faith;
> where there is despair, hope;
> where there is darkness, light;
> where there is sadness, joy.
> O, Divine Master, grant that I may not so much seek to be consoled, as to console;
> to be understood, as to understand,
> to be loved, as to love;
> for it is in giving that we receive,
> it is in pardoning that we are pardoned,
> and it is in dying that we are born to eternal life.
> St. Francis of Assisi, "Prayer of St. Francis"

God, bring to my remembrance this day the Command of Jesus to LET PEOPLE INJURE ME WITHOUT RETALIATING. *The words, glances, and silent criticisms can hurt most of all. When they come, bring a smile of response quickly to my lips—the smile of the second cheek, the smile of forgiveness, of good cheer, of graciousness. Make me worthy to be called the brother or sister of that dear saint of Assisi. Like him, may the prayer constantly rise from my heart, "Lord, make me an instrument of thy peace." Thus, heavenly Father, may I be an instrument in my small corner of the world for the ultimate salvation of mankind. Amen.*

88. Show Mercy

"Be merciful, even as your Father is merciful." (Luke 6:36)

How far into eternity will God's mercy extend? It is one of the great historic theological conundrums. We are told only a handful of characteristics that actually *define* God's character. The Bible clearly states: God IS love, God IS kind, God IS merciful. It is curious that most afterlife theologies view justice as more eternal even than these three. In the final analysis, they imply that God's *justice* toward the unrepentant will prevail, while love, kindness, and mercy will at some point reach their limit and, in a sense, give up. Justice, which does NOT define God's character, they say, will trump love, mercy, and kindness which DO define his character. So, at least, implies the common theology of the afterlife. One can only conjecture with amazement how such a doctrine came into being in ancient Christendom when it would seem to violate the character of God. (The Second Council of Constantinople set this late-developing doctrine in stone in 553, declaring, "Whosoever says or thinks that the punishment of demons and of the wicked will not be eternal, that it will have an end…let him be anathema.")

Curiously, the passage from the pen of the beloved disciple that defines God's essential character as love (1 John 4:8) comes from the same letter stating that God is also *just.* According to John, however, his justice points in a very specific direction. He says that God is faithful and just *to forgive.* How sadly intriguing that justice is most often cited as the supreme justifying principle to bolster the view that God will NOT forgive in eternity. John gives no time limit to his resounding declaration. "If we confess our sins, he is faithful and just, and will forgive us our sins and cleanse us from all unrighteousness." (1 John 1:9)

This brief excursion into the theology of the Justice vs. Mercy controversy is far from intellectual. Upon one's perspective hangs an entire view of the divine nature. Are God's qualities infinite or not? Is his *mercy* infinite, or will there come a point in eternity where it will be withdrawn? Without a clear answer before us, our daily obedience to the Command, *Be merciful* suddenly becomes muddled. If there are those to whom God will ultimately NOT show mercy, we can easily justify withholding mercy in certain instances ourselves. This is indeed a most practical bit of theology. It affects our outlook on everything.

The Bible is clear: God IS merciful. He is eternally and everlastingly merciful. Mercy belongs to the divine nature. Jesus commands us to reflect that nature by also being merciful. There is no *if* to the Command. We are to be merciful without conditions. Whether John's "*If* we confess our sins…" limits God's forgiveness will no doubt continue to be hotly debated among Christians until we all reach the other side. But here and now we are simply commanded, "Be merciful," without qualification. While making no excuses for ourselves, we are to make *every* excuse possible for others—not overlooking sin, but showing infinite, even undeserved mercy, sympathy, grace, compassion, and kindness toward every individual we meet.

> We are enjoined to forgive, to be merciful, to be as our father in heaven...We are required to forgive, with the argument that our father forgives...Every attribute of God must be infinite as himself. He cannot be sometimes merciful, and not always merciful. He cannot be just, and not always just. Mercy belongs to him, and needs no contrivance of theologic chicanery to justify it...
>
> Justice and mercy are simply one and the same thing; without justice to the full there can be no mercy, and without mercy to the full there can be no justice; that such is the mercy of God that he will hold his children in the consuming fire of his distance until they pay the uttermost farthing, until they drop the purse of selfishness with all the dross that is in it, and rush home to the Father and the Son, and the many brethren—rush inside the centre of the life-giving fire whose outer circles burn. I believe that no hell will be lacking which would help the just mercy of God to redeem his children.
>
> George MacDonald, *Unspoken Sermons, Third Series*, "Justice"

God, bring to my remembrance this day the Command of Jesus to SHOW MERCY. Again I pray with St. Francis, Lord, make me an instrument of thy peace...for it is in pardoning that we are pardoned. May love of mercy outshine my desire for justice. Thus, heavenly Father, as I grow into a tiny reflection of your mercy, may I be an instrument in my small corner of the world for the ultimate salvation of mankind. Amen.

89. Proclaim the Kingdom of God

"Preach as you go, saying, 'The kingdom of heaven is at hand.'" (Matthew 10:7)
"As for you, go and proclaim the kingdom of God." (Luke 9:60)

Most of the Commands Jesus gives to his disciples when he sent them out two by two must be viewed as being too specific to be considered universally incumbent upon all his followers throughout all time. *Don't go to Gentiles...take no money...don't take two tunics...shake the dust off your feet*—while such Commands may be used by God's Spirit to speak occasional words of guidance, conviction, or insight into individual lives, it is doubtful that we can universalize them as applying to all Christians in all circumstances.

A few of them, however, must certainly be regarded as applying to you and me and all Christians today. *Proclaim the Kingdom of God*, is one such Command. It is clearly universal, as evidenced by the variety of ways Jesus commanded many of those individuals we encounter in the Gospels to speak up for God's truth: *Shout it from the housetops...Go home to your friends and tell them how much the Lord has done for you...As for you, go and proclaim the kingdom of God.*

With it comes an important question. Is the Command to *Preach* universal? Are we to "preach" the kingdom of God? Does "proclaim" mean *preach*? Is every witness to be a *verbal* declaration? Many, indeed, believe that Christ's Great Commission in Matthew says exactly that. But this is a misunderstanding. The Great Commission does not command us to preach the Gospel at all. We are told to "make disciples" of all nations *by teaching them to obey the Commands.* Therefore, the Lord's Command to his disciples when he sent them out must be individualized. Not all are called to "preach." Yet we all are commanded to share concerning the Kingdom, to illuminate its principles to a watching world, and thus bear witness to the kingdom of God, each in our own way.

The most effective means, of course, by which such proclamation is made is by our own character, by our visible discipleship as followers of Jesus Christ. It is entirely possible for a mute to proclaim the kingdom loud and clear. Indeed, the street preacher might gain valuable insight by reflecting on the fact that *words* are not the most valuable commodity for communicating the principles of the kingdom. Actually, they are far down the list. As you and I intermix with people in the world every day, we are proclaiming *something* simply by the people we are. What are our lives proclaiming—the kingdom of God or the kingdom of man?

To *proclaim the kingdom of God* occasionally requires *acknowledging your discipleship* openly and visibly for those around you to see and hear. Only you and I can make the determination when such a moment has come. No proclamation of the Kingdom can be made or will be effective if we are trying to conform to anyone else's standard. God will lead us each to proclaim his truths in our own individual and unique way. But he will not let any of us go through life silent.

Where do we stand? Who knows it?

> "Hear the words of this covenant, and speak to the men of Judah and the inhabitants of Jerusalem. You shall say to them, Thus says the LORD, the God of Israel: Cursed be the man who does not heed the words of this covenant which I commanded your fathers when I brought them out of the land of Egypt...saying, Listen to my voice, and do all that I command you. So shall you be my people, and I will be your God..."
>
> The LORD said..."Proclaim all these words in the cities of Judah, and in the streets of Jerusalem: Hear the words of this covenant and do them. For I solemnly warned your fathers when I brought them up out of the land of Egypt, warning them persistently, even to this day, saying, Obey my voice."
>
> Jeremiah 11:1-4, 6-8

God, bring to my remembrance this day the Command of Jesus to PROCLAIM THE KINGDOM OF GOD. *Reveal to me how you want <u>me</u> to proclaim your truth, your kingdom, and obedience to your Commands. Give me courage to speak when you want me to speak. Give me patience when you want me to proclaim your kingdom by silence. May my character speak loudest of all. Thus, heavenly Father, may I be an* *instrument in my small corner of the world for the ultimate salvation of mankind. Amen.*

90. Don't Insult or Call Anyone A Fool

"Whoever insults his brother shall be liable to the council, and whoever says, 'You fool!' shall be liable to the hell of fire." (Matthew 5:22)

In how many ways we each break this Command—often, even daily! When it comes to the "Commands of personal conviction," this must certainly rank up near the top of the list.

I do not think I have ever actually *said* the words, "You fool!" to anyone in my life. Am I therefore excused from all the times (probably thousands) when I have *thought* another foolish, when an insult or inward scolding has risen in my mind but remained unspoken? Am I excused by the letter of the Command even though I have violated its spirit?

If we are looking for excuses to absolve us from dwelling in the strict region of obedience, they are not hard to find. Excuses are easy enough to fabricate. But I am not interested in excuses. The prayer of my heart is to be pure, to be Christlike, to think and speak toward others as Jesus would.

Therefore, I read this Command and I am deeply convicted of my failure to give others the same benefit of the doubt I want them to give me. I can only say, "Be merciful to me, Lord, a sinner." Then I must rise from my knees, remembering also the Command to *Show mercy*, and feast my eyes, freshly aglow with the compassion of Jesus, upon the low, mean, sometimes foolish, slow of heart, selfish brothers and sisters of my fellow humanity, and *love* them as they are. For they are just like me! I too am low, sometimes mean and foolish, slow of heart, and selfish. Jesus loves me amid my fallen, struggling humanity. How can I not love them likewise?

A great theological conundrum is raised by this passage not unrelated to the question of God's mercy. Does calling another "Fool" *really* make one liable to the fires of hell, or was Jesus speaking hyperbolically? It seems like an extreme judgment against what might be considered a trivial sin. We are accustomed to thinking of the entrance requirements for hell being unbelief and greater wickedness than merely thinking poorly about others. Yet here is Jesus speaking of a relatively minor offence making one liable for hell.

This single verse raises a complex question: What is the nature and purpose of hell? If it is to *punish* unbelief, what is Jesus talking about here? Is it possible that there exists a more far-reaching and eternal purpose, a "deeper magic from before the dawn of time"? Do we get a hint of it in 1 John 1:9, considered earlier in connection with God's justice and forgiveness—that God's *ultimate* purpose is perhaps not to *punish* sin, but to drive sin out of the universe, and, in us his children, "to cleanse us from all unrighteousness"? If hell's purpose is cleansing, healing, restoring, and purifying, suddenly Jesus' statement makes all the sense in the world.

I know not how others may respond to this query. It may cut cross-grain to all you have been taught about the afterlife. At this point, I speak only for myself and the deeply probing words of Jesus' Commands. And I say that if it takes the loving fire of God's consuming Presence and his purifying furnace to cleanse me from *all* unrighteousness, including my critical attitude toward the foolishness of others…I eagerly welcome it.

> On a huge hearth a great fire was burning, and the fire was a huge heap of roses, and yet it was fire…and the heat of the flames of them glowed upon his face…
>
> "Curdie," she said… "you have stood more than one trial already…now I am going to put you to a harder…It needs only trust and obedience…It will hurt you terribly, Curdie, but…no real hurt but much good will come to you from it…Go and thrust both your hands into that fire."…
>
> Curdie dared not stop to think. It was much too terrible to think about. He rushed to the fire, and thrust both of his hands right into the middle of the heap of flaming roses.
>
> George MacDonald, *The Princess and Curdie,* Chapter 8

God, bring to my remembrance this day the Command of Jesus NOT TO INSULT OR CALL ANYONE A FOOL. *Oh, how quickly the silent, acceptably-phrased, "You fool!" leaps into my mind when I see or hear foolishness and selfishness around me. People may be foolish, but forgive me my judging spirit. If it takes the fire to purge it from me, Lord, then do what you must to make me pure. Thus, heavenly Father, may I be an instrument in my small corner of the world for the ultimate salvation of mankind. Amen.*

Series Ten

"The Thaddaeus Commands"

Obedience

The Mark of a Disciple

Though Thaddaeus, also called Judas son of James, has two names in the Gospels, he is the one of the Twelve about whom nothing whatever is known. Matthew and Mark list him among the apostles as Thaddaeus, Luke calls him Judas son of James.

William McBirnie, in his *The Search For the Twelve Apostles,* suggests that Thaddaeus was probably the youngest of the disciples, and was in fact the son of James, brother of John, and thus the grandson of Zebedee. This would also make him cousin to Jesus. William Barclay, in his *The Master's Men,* suggests further that Thaddaeus, along with Simon the Zealot, Judas Iscariot, and James the son of Alphaeus, were all Jewish nationalists. Barclay sees his question during the last supper as tinged with nationalistic uncertainty. Both are mere conjectures with some support in legend and tradition, but with no actual facts upon which to base them.

Thaddaeus' only "on stage" appearance comes in John's gospel, where he is also referred to as Judas. Like Philip and Thomas, he was paying keen attention during that final evening in the upper room. When he posed the question for which he would forever be remembered, his question elicited from Jesus the towering declaration that he and the Father manifest themselves in no other way than by obedience (keeping his word), and that without obedience there is no love.

"Judas (not Iscariot) said to him, 'Lord, how is it that you will manifest yourself to us, and not to the world?' Jesus answered him, 'If a man loves me, he will keep my word, and my Father will love him, and we will come to him and make our home with him. He who does not love me does not keep my words; and the word which you hear is not mine but the Father's who sent me.'" (John 14:22-24) ὑπακοή: HUPAKOĒ—*Obedience*

The Trinity is founded in rule, obedience, and revelation. But whereas Fatherness is its originating foundation, the Son's *obedience* gives the Godhead its vital life-energy. In his sermon "The Creation in Christ," from *Unspoken Sermons, Third Series,* George MacDonald posits that a misplaced period in John 1:3-4 has given an erroneous impression of what actually was the "creative" work of God's Word, his λογος. The familiar text reads: "All things were made through him, and without him was not anything made that was made. In him was life, and the life was the light of men." MacDonald says that the period between *made* and *In* should perhaps come three words earlier, yielding a much more sensible and powerful reading: *All things were made through him, and without him was not anything made. That which was made in him was life, and the life was the light of men.* This *life,* MacDonald goes on, made through him, was the life of obedience, "created in Christ" toward the Father. It is this obedience that gives the Godhead its pulsating life, outflowing and correspondent, between Father and Son.

The Greek HUPAKOĒ is comprised of two roots—HUPO (under) and AKOUŌ (to hear). The verb form, HUPAKOUŌ is thus defined as to *listen and attend,* then to place oneself *beneath—to submit to what has been heard.*

In brief, then, obedience can be succinctly defined as: *To hear it and do it.*

Jesus, therefore, perfected his obedience by *listening* to the Father (John 14:31—*I do as the Father has commanded me*), and then placing himself *under* the authority of what the Father has told him (John 8:28—*I do nothing on my own authority, but speak thus as the Father taught me*).

Series Ten

The Mark of the Disciple

91. Rule your life by the will of God.
92. Settle disputes promptly and privately.
93. Ask the Lord of the harvest to send workers.
94. Partake of the symbols of my body and blood.
95. Do for the least of humanity as you would for me.
96. Do not give way to anger.
97. Do not close your eyes to the Holy Spirit's work.
98. Give generously, and not merely from your abundance.
99. Don't heed false prophets.
100. Obey the commandments.

91. Rule Your Life by the Will of God

"Whoever does the will of God is my brother, and sister, and mother." (Mark 3:35)

A few of the Commands are so all-encompassing that, if they were followed perfectly, none of the other Commands would be necessary. They draw all the Commands into them.

This is certainly one such Command: *Rule Your Life by the Will of God.* It is what Jesus was doing all the time. In one sense, it is the only thing he did. He said it in a variety of ways: *I seek not my own will but the will of him who sent me.* (John 5:30) *I have come down from heaven not to do my own will, but the will of him who sent me.* (John 6:38) Obviously, then, to follow Jesus is to follow that same life pattern.

What is "the will of God?" Simply what God wants. To live by the will of God is to live according to the principles, truths, priorities, and objectives that God has made clear he wants us to live by. That's why God the Father sent his Son to live on the earth among men—to make those principles, truths, priorities, and objectives crystal clear. This Jesus did by telling us what they were, and by living them himself. He illuminated God's will in two ways—by *teaching* and by *example*. We live God's will by *following his example* and *obeying his teaching*.

God has revealed his will on three levels: His *eternal* will for the universe, his *general* will for mankind, and the specific *personal* application of that will in your life and mine.

1) At the highest level, God's eternal will for the universe is revealed by his character and his created universe. Unity, for example, is a principle that defines God's character ("The Lord our God is one") and which also defines his eternal purpose in the universe, that all creation will be brought to oneness and unity and wholeness.

2) Out of God's eternal will for the universe, given definition by his character and creation, proceeds God's general will for mankind. Love, kindness, purity, humility, accountability, patience, gentleness, diligence, and forgiveness are qualities of character that God wills for *all* men and women to make ruling principles in their lives. These are general principles of his will that apply to everyone, without exception. They represent the manifestations in human life and character of high and eternal truths embodied within the nature and character of God himself. When we are kind, we are living out an eternal truth of God's nature where it intersects with daily life. In showing kindness, therefore, we can be said to be living according to God's will.

3) As we live by these general principles, *specific* application emerges for decisions and life directions unique to each individual. As we make the

daily choices that define our progress through life, God reveals specific aspects of his "will," built upon a foundation of obedience to the general principles of his will, that vary from person to person. His specific will for me in the situations I face will be distinct from his specific will for you in the situations *you* face. These different directions he may reveal to us by the voice of conscience, through Scripture, through circumstances, from wise counselors and mentors in our lives, as well as by other means.

All three levels of God's will are revealed and given clarity through the Commands. Jesus gave the Commands precisely so that we would know *how* to live as he lived—ruling our lives by the will of God.

> There is only one who...said he knew God's Will for all humankind—a man who lived in it, and taught his followers to do likewise...Jesus is the door into the discovery of God's practical, daily, live-able Will. Without Jesus one may be able to discern a great deal about God...However, when it comes to translating high truth...into our daily workplaces, choices, decisions, and attitudes—what we are supposed to *do* and *not do,* Jesus is...our guide into the practical realities of what comprise God's Will.
>
> Michael Phillips, *Leben 5.*

God, bring to my remembrance this day the Command of Jesus to RULE MY LIFE BY THE WILL OF GOD. Thank you for the example and teaching of Jesus that illuminates what your will is. Thank you for his Commands that bring all aspects of your will into practical reality in my life. Thus, heavenly Father, as I learn to discern your will and live in your will, may I be an instrument in my small corner of the world for the ultimate salvation of mankind. Amen.

92. Settle Disputes Promptly and Privately

"Make friends quickly with your accuser..." (Matthew 5:25)

"If your brother sins against you, go and tell him...between you and him alone." (Matthew 18:15)

The examples Jesus uses to address the settling of disputes are, in a sense, unfortunately narrow of focus. In both Matthew 5 and Luke 12, his words seem less concerned with reconciliation than keeping us out of jail. In Matthew 18 and Luke 17, his emphasis appears more pointed toward rebuking a brother for his sin than forgiving him. It is fearfully easy to overlook the beam in our own eye. To get to the true essence of Jesus' heart in the matter of disputes, we can never forget that all reconciliation is a two-way street.

Though Jesus says that it *may* occasionally be necessary to point out another's sin, there are strict rules governing the process. Those rules are spelled out in the rest of the Commands: Love, don't judge, show mercy, take the beam out of your own eye, etc. The Commands must be obeyed as a unity. So as Jesus speaks about the necessity of rebuking a brother for his sin, he says *at the same time*—Be kind, show mercy, don't judge, and so on.

This highlights the constant imperative to seek the heart of Jesus' intent. What did he *mean*? Usually his meaning is directed toward our *own* attitudes. It is impossible to settle disputes correctly or to show a brother his sin...if we are not looking first to ourselves. The foundation of settling disputes, and working toward reconciliation in the midst of conflict, is not built on *another's* wrong but on my *own* accountability. That's why this Command cannot be read apart from the Command: Deal with your own faults before thinking of the faults of others.

This double-sided coin of dispute settling is beautifully articulated in Luke 17:3-4. But the scope of the Command is easy to miss if one is intent to seize upon a justification to look at another's sin. Note the opening foundation. Our *own* attitude of mercy, non-judgment, and forgiveness must lead the way: "*Take heed to yourselves;* if your brother sins, rebuke him, and if he repents, forgive him; and if he sins against you seven times in the day, and turns to you seven times, and says, 'I repent,' you must forgive him."

Staying out of jail and rebuking others are not the primary focus. Heeding ourselves, forgiveness, and reconciliation provide a threeway foundation that gets to the heart of Jesus' intent. For the disciple of Jesus, reconciliation and oneness are always the objectives.

Those...who are growing pure in heart through hunger and thirst after righteousness, are indeed the children of God; but specially...those...who, on their way home, are peace-makers in the travelling company...The true idea of the universe is the whole family in heaven and earth...[T]he life-germ at the root of the world...is its relation to God the father of men. For the development of this germ in the consciousness of the children, the church...is one of the passing means. For the same purpose, the whole divine family is made up of numberless human families, that in these, men may learn and begin to love one another...Now the primary necessity to the very existence of a family is peace...Wherever peace is growing, there of course is the live peace, counteracting disruption and disintegration...The peace-makers quiet the winds of the world ever ready to be up and blowing; they tend and cherish the interlacing roots of the ministering grass; they spin and twist many uniting cords, and they weave many supporting bands; they are the servants...of the great universal family....They are the true children of that family, the allies and ministers of every clasping and consolidating force in it; fellow-workers they are with God in the creation of the family; they help him to get it to his mind, to perfect his father-idea...for like him they would be one with his creatures...

The main practical difficulty, with some at least of the peace-makers, is, how to carry themselves toward the undoers of peace, the disuniters of souls. Perhaps the most potent of these are...those powers of the church visible who care for canon and dogma more than for truth, and for the church more than for Christ...for the disintegration of the body of Christ...the party-liars of politics...[and mostly] the babbling liars of the social circle, and the faithless brothers and unloving sisters of disunited human families.

George MacDonald, *The Hope of the Gospel*, "God's Family"

God, bring to my remembrance this day the Command of Jesus to SETTLE DISPUTES PROMPTLY AND PRIVATELY. *In all I do, may I be a peacemaker, working for the unity of the human family. Give me your wisdom in applying the mechanics of unity into all the relationships of which I am part. Thus, heavenly Father, may I be an instrument in my small corner of the world for the ultimate salvation of mankind. Amen.*

93. Ask the Lord of the Harvest to Send Workers

"The harvest is plentiful, but the laborers are few; pray therefore the Lord of the harvest to send out laborers unto his harvest." (Luke 10:2)

Here we encounter another highly specific Command. While said by Jesus only once, it is yet difficult to include in any other grouping or summary of Commands. Like other such specific Commands, its meaning is not instantly apparent. Jesus was a master of metaphor—Take up your *cross*...let your *light* shine...enter through the *narrow gate*...bear *fruit*...take my *yoke*...be shrewd as *snakes* and innocent as *doves*. Metaphor is especially apparent in the most specific of the Commands. What is *salt?* What are *pearls* that we oughtn't to cast before swine?

In this case, what is the *harvest*, who are the *laborers?* Read in conjunction with the parable of the tares and wheat and other "harvest" teachings of the Gospels, along with "judgment" and "hell" mentioned several verses later, it is easy to imbue Jesus' words with an evangelistic, sheep and goats, get-people-saved meaning. Reading with this interpretation, there is no metaphor at all. It's straightforward. The laborers are Christians sent out to witness in the world and get as many into the fold before the harvest of death and the final judgment come.

But is this the full essence of what Jesus has in mind? Might the "harvest" not be one whose yield is measured in *souls* (the saved and the unsaved), but rather a harvest of *fruit* in the lives of God's people? When Jesus speaks of fruitfulness in John 15, it is not with the black-and-white perspective of you're either in or you're out. He speaks of fruitfulness as an ongoing quality of the abiding life. His faithful disciples are pruned that they might bear *more* fruit. Those branches that do not bear fruit are burned. The judgment of fire in this case is between fruitful disciples and non-fruitful disciples.

The harvest, then, is the season when the fruit of growth is gathered in. Though certainly all the Commands carry multiple layers of meaning, Jesus may not primarily be comparing the saved and the unsaved. I believe he is speaking of the harvest of fruitfulness that life with him is supposed to produce. I believe he is speaking about you and me, and the harvest our *own* lives are yielding. Are we producing the fruit of Christlikeness that results from abiding in him? Paul calls this harvest the "fruit of the Spirit."

When Jesus says that the laborers are few, therefore, he is lamenting the fact that so few of those who claim to be his followers are in fact growing the fruit of the Spirit that is the intended crop of the discipleship-harvest. Read with such deeper meaning in mind, this Command cannot be understood apart from John 15:5-6. The fruit Jesus expects to see growing may not be a harvest of souls from witnessing, but fruit within *us*—the fruit of the Spirit.

In obedience to this Command, I believe Jesus is telling us to pray that God will send out more Christians who will be serious about living by his Commands, and thus bear the good fruit of thirty, sixty, and hundredfold Christlikeness that the harvest is intended to produce. Only that fruit will change the world by the power of its example, and produce a yet greater harvest within the souls of mankind in the end.

> The Lord not only promises the greatest possible reward; he tells his disciples the worst they have to expect. He not only shows them the fair countries to which they are bound; he tells them the truth of the rough weather and the hardships of the way. He will not have them choose in ignorance. At the same time he strengthens them to meet coming difficulty…All this is part of his preparation of them for his work, for taking his yoke upon them, and becoming fellow-labourers with him in his father's vineyard. They must not imagine, because they are the servants of his father, that therefore they shall find their work easy; they shall only find the reward great.
>
> George MacDonald, *The Hope of the Gospel,* "The Reward of Obedience"

God, bring to my remembrance this day the Command of Jesus to ASK THE LORD OF THE HARVEST TO SEND WORKERS. *Grow fruit within my character worthy of a bountiful harvest. May I be a diligent laborer for truth in the vineyard of the*

Commands, where the fruits of the Spirit grow. Thus, heavenly Father, may I be an instrument in my small corner of the world for the ultimate salvation of mankind. Amen.

94. Partake of the Symbols of My Body and Blood

"He who eats my flesh and drinks my blood abides in me, and I in him." (John 6:56)

Probably few other Commands of Jesus have been interpreted with such wide latitude as the Command to "eat the bread" and "drink the cup" in remembrance of the last supper on the night before his crucifixion. Whether one calls it "communion" or the "Eucharist," no other ritual is so central in Christendom. Yet practice varies to an almost unbelievable extent—open or closed…bread or wafer…wine or grape juice…celebrated daily, weekly, monthly, or even yearly…administered by priest or passed among congregation…symbol or transubstantiation?

A careful reading of the last supper passages of the Gospels reveals the perhaps startling, and surely controversial, fact that in none of the gospel accounts is Jesus recorded as commanding a perpetual repetition of the events of the last supper upon his followers. When he passed the loaf around the table and said to his disciples, "Take of this and eat," he added nothing about turning that gesture into a ritual they were to repeat on a regular basis. It was Paul who added to the Lord's statement the words that are now repeated during many communion services: "This is my body which is broken for you. Do this in remembrance of me…This cup is the new covenant in my blood. Do this as often as you drink it, in remembrance of me." (1 Corinthians 11:24-25)

This ambiguity inherent in the communion Command highlights the deeply personal nature of "remembrance" that is called for. Though partaking of the symbols of the Lord's body and blood is usually carried out publicly, in mass or a worship service, it is one of the most personal, private, and prayerful exchanges of the Christian life.

One thing the remembrance of the last supper must *not* be is a ritual. Whether Catholic or charismatic, whether Lutheran or Mennonite, partaking of the bread and wine, perhaps more than at any other moment in Christian experience, drives us inwardly to our knees, humbly reflective of the life-ruling reality that the Lord has called us not merely to *remember*, but to follow his example. It is an example of self-denial, self-abandonment, and relinquishment of self-will on the Gethsemane altar of *Not my will but yours be done.*

The symbol of his body and blood drive us into the depths of the garden where the Father of Jesus Christ awaits us.

To learn of Me seek the olive tree,
though near its trunk, blood stains the ground.
The disciple's path leads through Gethsemane,
and the thorns I wore gave me my crown.

The way is steep up that lonely hill.
It is hard to yield what you want to do.
But if you would find My Father's will,
ask what He would have of you.
(Michael Phillips, *Kings Crossroads*, Chapter 3)

It is with the holiest fear that we should approach the terrible fact of the sufferings of our Lord. Let no one think that those were less because he was more. The more delicate the nature, the more alive to all that is lovely and true, lawful and right, the more does it feel the antagonism of pain, the inroad of death upon life; the more dreadful is that breach of the harmony of things whose sound is torture. He felt more than man could feel, because he had a larger feeling...These sufferings were awful indeed when they began to invade the region about the will; when the struggle to keep consciously trusting in God began to sink in darkness; when the Will of The Man put forth its last determined effort in that cry after the vanishing vision of the Father...Yet never was God nearer him than now. For never was Jesus more divine...

Thus the Will of Jesus, in the very moment when his faith seems about to yield, is finally triumphant.

George MacDonald, *Unspoken Sermons, First Series,* "The Eloi"

God, bring to my remembrance this day the Command of Jesus to PARTAKE OF THE SYMBOLS OF HIS BODY AND BLOOD. Whenever I partake in a service to commemorate the last supper, still my heart to hear what you would speak to me. Lord Jesus, enter with me into the inner sanctum of my own heart where you and I can probe the depths of Gethsemane together. May I enter into the agonizing reality of the prayer you prayed that fateful night as if I had been there with you. May I then appropriate that reality on this day of remembrance, and every day. Thus, heavenly Father, may I be an instrument in my small corner of the world for the ultimate salvation of mankind. Amen.

95. Do for the Least of Humanity As You Would For Me

"'For I was hungry and you gave me food, I was thirsty and you gave me drink, I was a stranger and you welcomed me, I was naked and you clothed me, I was sick and you visited me, I was in prison and you came to me...Truly, I say to you, as you did it to one of the least of these my brethren, you did it to me.' (Matthew 25:35-36, 40)

This is the second time we have used this passage from Matthew 25 to highlight one of the Commands. And for good reason. This must surely be one of the most powerful passages in all the Bible. It is so powerful that it is regularly trotted out by liberal politicians who have not the slightest interest in obeying the full scope of the Commands of Jesus. Yet they find in this Command support for various social policies and programs.

But Jesus is not here talking to the world. He is speaking to his disciples. He is speaking to those who call him *Lord.* He is speaking to Christians not politicians. He is saying, "*I* am that sick, hungry, thirsty, naked, lonely, imprisoned man or woman. Would you minister kindness if you knew it was me? Well it *is* me."

This is not a passage merely about ministry to the poor, hungry, and downtrodden, as important as that is. It speaks too of the afterlife, of the judgment, of the division between sheep and goats. But this division is not between saved and unsaved. Read it carefully—this is NOT a saved vs. unsaved judgment. *All* those described consider themselves believers. *Both* sheep and goats call Jesus "Lord." There are no atheists here. There are no God-mockers. Jesus is drawing a line between *obedient believers* and *disobedient believers*. The fires of hell awaiting the goats are the purifying fires necessary to purge self-righteousness from the disobedient among those who call Jesus *Lord*. This furnace of purification is described in Malachi 3 and is for the purpose of healing the hearts of the Levites, not the heathen. Whatever other purposes hell may serve, the judgment of Matthew 25 speaks no word about the eternal fate of unbelievers. It describes the chastening, refining, fiery purification of self-righteous believers that will be required in the next life.

Little can be added to what Jesus said. The words themselves are powerful and convicting. Let us each read them with hearts of prayer.

When the Son of Man comes in his glory, and all the angels with Him, then He will sit upon His glorious throne; and all the nations will be gathered into His presence. And He will separate them one from another, just as a shepherd separates the sheep from the goats; and will make the sheep stand at His right hand, and the goats at His left. Then the King will say to those at His right , "Come, my Father's blessed ones, receive your inheritance of the Kingdom which has been divinely intended for you since the creation of the world. For when I was hungry, you gave me food; when I was thirsty, you gave me drink; when I was homeless, you gave me a welcome; when I was ill-clad, you clothed me; when I was sick, you visited me; when I was in prison, you came to see me." "When, Lord," the righteous will reply, did we see Thee hungry, and feed Thee; or thirsty, and give Thee drink? When did we see Thee homeless and give Thee a welcome" or ill-clad, and clothe Thee? When did we see Thee sick or in prison, and come to see Thee?" But the King will answer them, "In solemn truth I tell you that in so far as you rendered such services to one of the humblest of these my brethren, you rendered them to me." Then He will say to those at His left , "Begone from me, with the curse resting upon you, into the Fire of the Ages, which has been prepared for the devil and his angels; for when I was hungry, you gave me nothing to eat; when I was thirsty, you gave me nothing to drink; when homeless, you gave me no welcome; ill-clad, you clothed me not; sick or in prison, you visited me not." Then they will also answer, "Lord, when did we see Thee hungry or thirsty or homeless or ill-clad or sick or in prison, and not come to serve Thee?" But he will reply, "In solemn truth I tell you that in so far as you withheld such services from one of the humblest of these, you withheld them from me." And these shall go away into the Punishment of the Ages, but the righteous into the Life of the Ages.

Jesus to his disciples, Matthew 25:31-46 (*Weymouth New Testament,* 1903 edition)

God, bring to my remembrance this day the Command of Jesus to DO FOR THE LEAST OF HUMANITY AS WE WOULD FOR HIM. Lord, what would you have me do today...to whom would you send me today...how can I minister today...in obedience to your Command? Thus, heavenly Father, by my selfless compassion for those less fortunate than myself, may I be an instrument in my small corner of the world for the ultimate salvation of mankind. Amen.

96. Do Not Give Way to Anger

"I say to you that every one who is angry with his brother shall be liable to judgment." (Matthew 5:22)

Paul's famous statement in Ephesians (4:26), "Be angry but do not sin; do not let the sun go down on your anger," is often used to excuse anger, so long as we don't let it go on *too* long. Nothing to worry about if we eventually get over it. Anger is normal, a natural human response. How stringent are we going to be—we can't condemn ourselves just for getting angry, as long as we don't let it fester into bitterness. Surely it's no *sin* to get angry.

Isn't this what Paul says—that anger *itself* is no sin? This is the justification used by those whose outbursts make them feel better. "I needed to get it off my chest," they say. "Now I can forget it and move on. I just had to say what I felt and get my anger out."

This dichotomy between the Lord's words and Paul's illustrates why the Commands of Jesus must be the last word for the focus of our obedience. What can we conclude but that Paul may have misspoken? Jesus says that it *is* a sin to get angry with a brother, that anger is liable to judgment. Anger that results in insult and rebuke, Jesus continues, is liable to the fires of hell. His words are plain—anger is not to be taken lightly. Those who justify an outburst of temper as merely "getting something off their chest" need to think again. Temper is a *sin.*

But this is the wonderful genius of Paul—though he sometimes blunders, his wisdom in interpreting the Gospel into daily life has few equals. So even though he perhaps goes a bit too far in excusing anger in the first half of this passage, the second half contributes a beautiful practicality that shows us *how* to deal with anger. We need to read it as, "If you have sinned and become angry, do not let the sun go down on your anger." Rather than justifying our anger, we bring another of the

Commands to our aid: *Repent.* The way to "move on" and to conquer "bitterness" and to "be reconciled with your brother" is not with an outburst of temper that is excused as "normal," but through repentance.

What role, then, in the life of the Christian is occupied by what we call "righteous indignation"—that form of truly justifiable anger that Jesus displayed toward the hypocrisy of the Pharisees? Is there an anger which we too occasionally *ought* to feel on behalf of God, on behalf of Jesus, on behalf of an individual who has been wronged, on behalf of truth? The answer, of course, is *yes.* The more deeply we share the heart-pulse of God's own heart the more will the injustices and wrongs of the world fill us with indignation at their causes, and toward the selfishnesses and hypocrisies that perpetuate them.

Feeling these things, however, we can never forget the Lord's repeated words, *Take heed to yourselves.* The mirror is always our guide. We may indeed *feel* God's anger. But rare will be the occasions when we are called to act upon it. While we are yet in the flesh, we are not capable of completely extinguishing the stirrings of self. "Righteous indignation," therefore, is mostly a prayerfully painful *felt* response of the God-infused heart, not a *vocal* response from a Christian hothead.

> There is a wrath of God, and there is a wrath of man that worketh not the righteousness of God. Anger may be as varied as the colour of the rainbow. God's anger can be nothing but Godlike...at one with his love, helpful, healing, restoring...There is the degraded human anger, and the grand, noble, eternal anger. Our anger is in general degrading, because it is in general impure.
>
> It is to me an especially glad thought that the Lord came so near us as to be angry with us. The more we think of Jesus being angry with us, the more we feel that we must get nearer and nearer to him—get within the circle of his wrath, out of the sin that makes him angry, and near to him where sin cannot come...O Christ...let not our faults pass as if they were of no weight. Be angry with us, holy brother, wherein we are to blame; where we do not understand, have patience with us, and open our eyes, and give us strength to obey, until at length we are the children of the Father...Make us able to be angry and not sin; to be angry nor seek revenge the smallest; to be angry and full of forgiveness. We will not be content till our very anger is love.
>
> George MacDonald, *Unspoken Sermons, Third Series, "The Displeasure of Jesus"*

God, bring to my remembrance this day the Command of Jesus NOT TO BE ANGRY. *Forgive me not only for the sin of my anger, but for justifying my anger by calling it anything less than sin. Thus, heavenly Father, may I be an instrument in my small corner of the world for the ultimate salvation of mankind. Amen.*

97. Do Not Close Your Eyes to the Holy Spirit's Work

"Whoever speaks against the Holy Spirit will not be forgiven." (Matthew 12:32)

Probably the most feared sin in the world, "the Great Sin," is what we commonly refer to as blasphemy against the Holy Spirit. Its most hideous portrayal is given in the grossly inaccurate translation of the King James Version in Mark 3:29: "But whoever blasphemes against the Holy Spirit never has forgiveness but is in danger of eternal damnation." The NIV's horrendous mistranslation "will never be forgiven" adds a yet greater burden to an already difficult text.

The apparent irrevocable judgment of this passage has weighed heavily on the hearts of multitudes through the years, producing a totally erroneous view of God, and probably keeping many out of his kingdom. It has surely caused as much fear and confusion as any verse in the Bible. It is no exaggeration to say that for some this passage is the single great stumbling-block preventing a life of intimacy with God. Guilt may be at root. But a deeper problem exists than that—the corrosive effect it has on our portrayal of God's nature.

All this misunderstanding is based on an *incomplete* and *inaccurate* translation not found in the Greek original. What we read in our Bibles are not only *translations* of the Greek, but also *interpretations* bolstered by tradition and passed down from one version of the Bible to the next, continuing to support the orthodoxy of the translators. Thousands, if not millions have been misled as a result to wrong perspectives about God.

To dig between the lines of this verse, and get to the true meaning of this Command, most of us will have to forget what we have been taught about the extent of God's forgiveness. There is no such thing as an "unforgivable sin." God wants to forgive *all* sin. But he is only *able* to forgive when the door to forgiveness is open. The verse speaks not about God's *willingness* to forgive, but about the *conditions* in which forgiveness can operate. If those conditions are wrong, there is simply no way for forgiveness to get in. MacDonald writes: "This is the condemnation…" (ie—not the sins that men have committed, but the condition of mind in which they choose to remain.) "In this sin against the Holy Ghost, I see no single act alone…but a wilful condition of mind." (*Unspoken Sermons, First Series*, "It Shall Not Be Forgiven")

What Jesus is speaking of here is no blasphemous outburst, but an overall perspective toward God's work among men. The "blasphemy" is no sudden curse, but an outlook. The Pharisees were attributing the miracles of Jesus to the devil. They did not recognize the source of those miracles. They were closing the door, blocking truth from their hearts. As long as they refused to acknowledge truth's Source, the Holy Spirit of God, there could be no forgiveness. They had closed the door against it. The Spirit had no means of entry.

What Jesus is commanding here, then, when he says, *Do not speak against God's work,* is simply this: "To fall in with God's truth, you must recognize that his Spirit is the source of forgiveness, then embrace and welcome it. As long as you willfully refuse to recognize the truth, God's forgiveness has no door into your life. *You* have closed the door by refusing to recognize the Spirit's work. Therefore, embrace the Spirit's work and let in God's forgiveness. Forgiveness is *always* waiting to rush in like a flood. Open the door. Recognize God's work."

> Let us now turn back to the beginning of the verse to ask what it means to "blaspheme" against the Holy Spirit. Is it an *act,* or a *condition* of mind and heart?...It is the non-recognition of the Holy Spirit's work...It is thus a *condition of heart,* not a single act, spoken word...As long as such an attitude persists, forgiveness cannot find a home. Not recognizing the work of the Spirit closes the only door through which forgiveness can enter...Forgiveness cannot be manifested until its Source is recognized.
>
> Michael Phillips, *Leben 7,* "The Great Sin"

God, bring to my remembrance this day the Command of Jesus NOT TO CLOSE MY EYES TO THE HOLY SPIRIT'S WORK. Reveal the ways I overlook, disregard, or diminish what the Holy Spirit may be doing in my life or around me. Give me eyes to see the Source of all you do. Keep the doors of my brain and heart open. Thus, heavenly Father, may I be an instrument in my small corner of the world for the ultimate salvation of mankind. Amen.

98. Give Generously, and Not Merely from Your Abundance

"This poor widow has put in more than all of them; for they all contributed out of their abundance, but she out of her poverty put in all the living that she had." (Luke 21:3-4)

Giving, for many Christians, is founded on legalistic obligation based on the Old Testament tithe. It is doubtful, however, that a strong case can be made in the New Testament for the perpetuation of the tithe as commonly taught. Yet it is hardly a surprise that the tithe continues to be urged upon Christians by churches and pastors and ministries dependent upon it. The entire edifice of their work depends upon people feeling duty-bound to give 10% of their income to the church or the ministry of their choice. How else could they support themselves? So the tithe-obligation is pressed upon Christians week after week, sometimes subtly, and in the cases of certain television evangelists not so subtly, prior to the passing of the box or plate or bag or end-of-telecast pitch.

But is giving to the "church" really what Jesus had in mind? It is debatable that a *paid* church staff, with lavish church buildings to house their enterprises resembling a corporate headquarters or a country club, exists anywhere in the New Testament, except in the second or third chapter of *Revelation*. The first century movement called "The Way" was mostly a *volunteer* enterprise. The bloated bureaucracy that came to be known as "the church" centuries later, which pressed upon its ignorant listeners excessive financial requirements to sustain itself, was not an institution whose roots can be found in the Gospels. It is true that Jesus did not condemn the priesthood, the Temple, or the giving that supported them. He usually spoke respectfully toward them. Yet we are still left with the inescapable reality that a "professional" Christianity is nowhere to be found in the pages of the New Testament.

If we would understand the giving that Jesus commands, therefore, we must look beyond the collection plate. If one wants to give to keep pastors, priests, church staffs, or televangelists supplied with their monthly paychecks, that is fine. There is nothing wrong with giving to help a church meet its budget. Obviously missions organizations do their work because of the generous giving of Christians the world over. Indeed, the widow of the above passage gave to the Temple treasury, and Jesus lauded her giving even knowing that her two copper coins were going to feed a corrupt Temple system. In so doing, however, we need to recognize that Jesus was addressing another kind of giving altogether. He did not point to the woman because of the two coins, but because of the eternal example of generosity and sacrifice that lay in her heart.

Therefore, we have to appropriate this Command on a higher plane. Jesus would urge upon us not a mere dutiful giving rule governed by mathematical percentage, but rather a generosity of lifestyle toward *people*, toward the needs one meets the other six days of the week in the market-place and work-place. Church giving may be optional. *People-giving* is required. It was this compassion toward the needs of the *brethren*, not to a church building and professional full-time staff, that prompted Paul on several occasions to urge generous giving between the fellowships of believers throughout the Mediterranean. They were not bound by the tithe, but by need. The money was collected not for a huge mortgage payment, but for food.

If one feels obligated to tithe to a church, it cannot be assumed that such giving satisfies the requirement of this Command. Giving to a church mostly supports that *church*. We are called upon to use our resources to meet the needs of *people*. The generosity of this Command of Jesus takes up where church-giving leaves off.

Do not withhold good from those who deserve it, when it is in your power to act. Do not say to your neighbor, "Come back later; I'll give it tomorrow"—when you have it with you now. (Proverbs 3:27-28, NIV)

God, bring to my remembrance this day the Command of Jesus to GIVE GENEROUSLY AND NOT MERELY FROM MY ABUNDANCE. *Give me opportunities to give and not delay, to minister kindness and not delay, to give more than is comfortable and not delay. Free me from obligatory giving. Thus, heavenly Father, may I be an instrument in my small corner of the world for the ultimate salvation of mankind. Amen.*

99. Don't Heed False Prophets

"Beware of false prophets." (Matthew 7:15)

Jesus often couched his teachings in the form of metaphors and parables for the curious purpose, if we are to take him at his word, of *preventing* those who are not in earnest about obeying him from understanding him. The truths of the kingdom, he says, are *mysteries*. They reveal themselves only to the obedient. To "those on the outside" (by which he means those who have *not* made obedience their life's priority) those truths remain hidden. George MacDonald's wonderful insight bears repeating, "Obedience is the opener of eyes."

This winnowing process whereby obedience leads to *greater* understanding, while excuse, delay, and disobedience lead to the *loss* of even what understanding one may possess, is not a principle merely dividing the spiritual from the unspiritual mind. It is also operative within Christendom. It is at work at this very moment. There will be those whom every Command drives to their knees, for whom the mirror of prayerful self-reflection is always speaking. There will be others who excuse the imperative of obedience by discussion, intellectualization, rationalization, and by thinking of all the people they know *who really need to hear this*.

Three lethal responses to the Commands will constantly exert their allure upon us. We have had occasion to remind ourselves of them repeatedly already.

Pitfall 1—Reading the Commands through the lens of *another's* need for obedience rather than our own. *Pitfall 2*—Reading the Commands and immediately seizing upon loopholes that excuse us from looking into the mirror of self-examination. *Pitfall 3*—Reading the *Don't* Commands and automatically thinking, "Oh, but I would never do *that*."

It will be the easiest thing in the world to assume, "I would *never* pay attention to a false prophet." Don't be too sure. All around us are pastors, teachers, authors whose every word is taken as gospel by gullible

Christians. Yet some of these are teaching subtle falsehoods about God. There are famous, respected, and best-selling authors and ministers and Christian teachers, many of whose names you would recognize, who will be revealed by the light of eternity to be nothing less than false teachers. Some are among the most well-known names in Christendom. Jesus says that false prophets come dressed in sheep's clothing. Their teachings snare us precisely because we *don't* recognize them. They *sound* pleasing. They tickle the love of intellectual, experiential, emotional, relational, and doctrinal religiosity. But they do not point toward the imperative of obedience. Nor do they proclaim the true nature and character of God.

Twenty years ago I met a man who, to all appearances, was a godly man. His words sounded right, his prayers earnest, his knowledge of Scripture vast. It took time and the stress of conflict to reveal the cancer at the core of his faith. He was a wolf in sheep's clothing. But I was taken in by his winning manner and the engaging appeal of his personality and friendship. My carelessness in heeding this all-important Command caused our family to be ripped apart by a false man and a false teaching. We still have not entirely recovered. I must bear the responsibility myself. I was not paying close enough attention.

Those who teach subtle and disguised falsehoods about God may be nearer than you think.

> How have we learned Christ? It ought to be a startling thought, that we may have learned him wrong. That must be far worse than not to have learned him at all: his place is occupied by a false Christ, hard to exorcise! The point is, whether we have learned Christ as he taught himself, or as men have taught him who thought they understood, but did not understand him.
>
> George MacDonald, *Unspoken Sermons, Second Series*, "The Truth in Jesus"

God, bring to my remembrance this day the Command of Jesus NOT TO HEED FALSE PROPHETS. *Keep my mind and senses fully awake to deceptions, however subtle. Without judgment, enliven my perceptions to the validating stamp of character over ideas in determining whether a teaching and its teacher are of the truth. Make me of the truth, by obedience, so that I will recognize truth as well as falsehood. Thus, heavenly Father, may I be an instrument in my small corner of the world for the ultimate salvation of mankind. Amen.*

100. Obey the Commandments

"You know the commandments: 'Do not kill, Do not commit adultery, Do not steal, Do not bear false witness, Do not defraud, Honor your father and mother.'" (Mark 10:19)

This may appear on the surface to be identical with the first Command: *Obey my Commands*. From Jesus' conversation with the man we call the "rich young ruler," however, the inference can be made that Jesus is specifically speaking of the Ten Commandments of Exodus 20. His response makes it clear that Jesus considers it obvious, implicit, a *given*, that the Ten Commandments are to serve as the undergirding law of life. We have already noted the intriguing addition Jesus makes in Mark's version of the account, including *Do not defraud* along with other of the more familiar of the commandments.

In our day, "the Ten Commandments" are often referred to *en masse* as a blanket summary of Old Testament moral law—more as a historical fact than a model for life. Most people do not often stop to ponder them individually and prayerfully as universally applicable practical guides to daily behavior, attitude, conduct, and character. In Jesus' time, however, "the Commands" which regulated all aspects of life were none other than these magnificent and formative ten. His Commands which we are reflecting on in this book are but amplifications and extensions of the original ten given by God to Moses on Sinai, and by Moses to the people.

Foundational to the Commands of Jesus, therefore, are certainly these ten "commandments." If they ruled Jesus' life as "the Commands" to which he had pledged *his* obedience, they are obviously Commands which are absolute and inviolate in our daily lives as well. How disheartening that at least three are regularly and flagrantly disregarded in nearly every Christian church in the land, with one or two others on the endangered species list. No wonder the world is paying so little attention to our witness, when we are paying so little attention to the Life-Commandments commanded by Jesus himself.

It is good to remind ourselves of these ten as imperatively among the most foundational of the Commands of Jesus. Let us read and prayerfully ponder each one as among the "Top Ten" of the Commands. They come directly from God himself.

1. You shall have no other gods before me.
2. You shall not make for yourself or serve or bow to any idol or likeness.
3. You shall not use the name of the Lord your God in vain.
4. Remember the Sabbath day to keep it holy. Six days you shall work, and on the seventh rest.
5. Honor your father and mother.
6. You shall not kill.
7. You shall not commit adultery.
8. You shall not steal.
9. You shall not bear false witness.
10. You shall not covet.

> Then the road to eternal life is the keeping of the commandments! Had the Lord *not* said so, what man of common moral sense would ever dare say otherwise? What

else can be the way into life but the doing of what the Lord of life tells the creatures he has made, and whom he would have live for ever, that they must do? It is the beginning of the way. If a man had kept all those commandments, yet would he not therefore have in him the life eternal; nevertheless, without keeping of the commandments there is no entering into life; the keeping of them is the path to the gate of life; it is not life, but it is the way—so much of the way to it. Nay, the keeping of the commandments, consciously or unconsciously, has closest and essential relation to eternal life.

George MacDonald, *Unspoken Sermons, Second Series,* "The Way"

God, bring to my remembrance this day the Command of Jesus to OBEY THE COMMANDMENTS. *Remind me daily, not merely of the Commands but also of the Commandments. Bring Psalm 119 alive in my heart—deepen my love for your laws, your statutes, your principles, your commandments. Thus, heavenly Father, may I be an instrument in my small corner of the world for the ultimate salvation of mankind. Amen.*

Series Eleven

"The Simon the Zealot Commands"

Gladness

The Quiet Joy of Following Christ

The second Simon among the twelve Apostles is twice called Simon the Cananaean and twice called Simon the Zealot. The "Canaanite" of the King James is an incorrect rendition of the Greek. *Cananaean* (Hebrew) and *Zealot* (Greek) are actually the same word and mean one who is jealous for God. Though nothing is known about this Simon personally, we can deduce something about his beliefs and background before becoming Jesus' disciple.

Since the onset of the Roman occupation of Palestine, Jewish nationalist groups dedicated themselves to throwing off the yoke of Roman oppression. Herod the Great managed to keep a lid on the simmering hostility by working with the Romans to gain privileges for his country and keep it at peace. After Herod's death in 4 B.C., his diplomatic skills were not shared by his sons. Violence and insurrections broke out, notably in Galilee. During this time the party of the "Zealots" arose. For the next two generations they were the most fanatical of the Jewish nationalists. Whatever spiritual notions they had originally adopted to preserve the purity of the Jewish faith, the Zealots soon became mere terrorists. They were called the *sicarii,* from the *sica,* a small curved dagger or sword that could easily be hidden in a robe. Their enemies were not only Romans, but also Jews they considered traitors. They were committed to murder and guerrilla warfare against whole towns and villages if it suited their purposes.

Imagine, then, a group of men that included Simon the Zealot and Matthew the tax collector. We can only conjecture how Simon first came to lay down his *sica* and dedicate himself to changing the world a different way. As that change in his heart gradually took place, we can also imagine the fanaticism that once burned within him being transformed to quiet joy

χαρά: CHARA—*Gladness*

In the Lord's towering prayer of John 17 on the eve of an excruciating death, when he would feel abandoned by the Father himself, he speaks of his *joy*. We cannot imagine that Jesus was feeling the exhilarating emotions we associate with joy. Yet he not only spoke of his joy, he prayed that his joy would be fulfilled in us:

"I am not praying for the world but for those whom thou hast given me...that they may have my joy fulfilled in themselves." (John 17:9, 13)

The word Jesus used is a form of the Greek χαρά—CHARA, often translated gladness. It is distinct from the word he uses in Luke 6:23 when he says, "Leap for joy." On the night before his crucifixion, Jesus was not praying for his disciples to have "leap for joy" happiness, but to have the quiet gladness of χαρά fulfilled in us.

It is a *quiet gladness* that expresses a continuous state of gratitude for one's life in God. It cannot be defined by up-and-down fluctuations and momentary feelings. "Leap for joy" happiness comes and goes. Quiet gladness remains.

That's what it means to live "in the state" of being glad. It is our home. I *am* glad to be alive. Feelings of joy, and the specific things that make me *feel* gladness throughout the day, are changeable. But I live in quiet gladness.

There are times when life is hard, when the sun is not shining, when discouragement seems overwhelming, and we cannot see God's presence through the fog. But I am still glad to be alive, glad to be God's child, glad that my life has meaning in the midst of its emotional valleys.

Thus, gladness as a component of joy is both emotional and intellectual. I *feel* joy (emotion), and I *am* glad (intellectual). Gladness can be our home, whether the sun is shining or not. Such is the quiet contentment Jesus prayed would be fulfilled in us.

Series Eleven

The Quiet Joy of Following Christ

101. Be glad in all circumstances.

102. Give up everything.

103. Don't resist evil men.

104. Do not lead others into sin.

105. Teach the nations to obey what I have commanded.

106. Do not follow the example of those who preach but do not practice.

107. Don't cast your pearls before swine.

108. Do not test the Lord.

109. Wash one another's feet.

110. Be wise as snakes and innocent as doves.

101. Be Glad in All Circumstances

"Blessed are you when men revile you and persecute you and utter all kinds of evil against you falsely on my account. Rejoice and be glad, for your reward is great in heaven." (Matthew 5:11-12)

As we have noted before, many of Jesus' specific words must be broadened to incorporate the fullness of what he intended as Commands of obedience upon his followers. In this case, he specifically told his listeners to rejoice under the following conditions:

—*When you are reviled.*

—*When you are persecuted.*

—*When all kinds of evil is spoken against you falsely.*

From the parallel passage in Luke's gospel (6:22-23), we can add:

—*When you are hated.*

—*When you are excluded.*

Drawing upon additional interpretations given to the above (from the *Revised Standard Version*) from other Bible translations, we might add:

—*When you are insulted. (NIV)*

—*When you suffer every kind of calumny* [false accusation; abusive attack on character] *for Jesus' sake. (NEB)*

—*When men denounce you and excommunicate you. (Moffatt)*

—*When you are blamed and ill-treated. (Phillips)*

—*When cruel things are said about you. (Weymouth)*

Can any honest thinking Christian doubt that Jesus meant for his followers to rejoice, not only in the face of cruelty, attacks, hatred, and persecution, but in *all* things and *all* circumstances? Surely Paul was speaking on behalf of the Lord when he said, "Rejoice always...give thanks in *all* circumstances." (1 Thess. 4:16, 18)

Here, then, we encounter another of those remarkable Commands that flagrantly oppose the world's perspective. If it were truly obeyed by Christ's followers, this alone would make the world stand up and say, "Wow, who *are* these unusual people!" In the same way that sexual morality, if the world observed a dramatic distinction of purity within Christendom, would set Christians noticeably apart, so too would obedience to this rejoice-Command. Can you imagine the response if Christians everywhere actually returned cruelty, persecution, hatred, and insults with quiet gladness and smiles and graciousness and kind words? The world's way is to give full vent to complaint, to express dissatisfaction by looks, gestures, and words whenever our wishes and rights and conveniences are infringed upon. How different would it be if Christians everywhere did *not* express dissatisfaction, if complaint was *never* heard from their lips?

But who are "Christians everywhere?" There really is no such thing as "universal" Christendom. There is only *individual* discipleship. Christians everywhere is *you* and *me*. The *everywhere* is where you and I live today. We are not called to change the whole world, we are called to obey the Commands where we live, to influence our little corner of the world now, today, in the next five minutes, by *being glad in all circumstances.*

> Rejoice in the Lord always; again I will say, Rejoice...And the peace of God...will keep your hearts and your minds in Christ Jesus...Whatever is true, whatever is honorable, whatever is just, whatever is pure, whatever is lovely, whatever is gracious, if there is any excellence, if there is anything worthy of praise, think about these things...I have learned, in whatever state I am, to be content. (Philippians 4:4, 8, 10, 11)

God, bring to my remembrance this day the Command of Jesus to REJOICE WHATEVER MY CIRCUMSTANCES. Are there those who dislike me, who have spoken against me, then give me the fortitude to rejoice. Perhaps I am not happy from the effects of it, help me to rejoice anyway. I may not feel like turning cartwheels or shouting for joy. I may be hurting from the ill-treatment I have received. Help me to rejoice anyway. Help me to rejoice in faith, inwardly, quietly, obediently—in spite of my feelings. Keep me from the natural responses of complaint and annoyance. Remind me to keep my dissatisfactions to myself. Remind me, and help me, to REJOICE WHATEVER MY CIRCUMSTANCES. Thus, heavenly Father, may I be an instrument in my small corner of the world for the ultimate salvation of mankind. Amen.

102. Give Up Everything

"Whoever of you does not renounce all that he has cannot be my disciple." (Luke 14:33)

All the Commands are subject to misunderstanding, overemphasis, and underemphasis. The Commands of Jesus can be taken so out of context and misapplied, that they can even become false gods and idols that blind vision from the true nature of the Commands.

A dear friend of many years prided himself that he was truly *living* this Command. He literally gave up everything. He left wife and family, lived in his car picking up what odd jobs he could, ministering as he viewed it to street people, all the while condemning Christians who remained in the "world." He and I were close, but that divide always separated us. I knew he considered me a lukewarm Christian, one who had not given up everything to be the Lord's disciple. My friend died a few years ago early one morning, falling to the street at a bus stop...alone. The sad state of his dysfunctional life breaks my heart to this day. Yet I honor his memory with deep affection. As out of balance as it perhaps was, he made the attempt so few make to give up everything. I never want to forget that Jesus commands me to renounce everything too. Therefore, when Jesus makes this demand none of us can take the probing question lightly.

In Mark 10, Peter says, "We have left everything and followed you." But did they all really leave *everything*? Peter still had his house, possibly with a mother-in-law unit besides. And in Mark 3:19, we read four positively fascinating words that refer to Jesus: "Then he went home."

Home! Jesus had a home? Whose was it? Who *owned* it? The fact is, *someone* owned a house that Jesus called "home." This house served as the General Headquarters for Jesus and his followers in Capernaum. When we fast forward to the book of *Acts* and the burgeoning movement called The Way, another fact becomes clear. It wasn't just a movement of street people. There were men and women of means. All of them *hadn't* given up everything. Many of the Lord's first century followers kept their possessions, their homes and wealth and put them to use for the cause. The home of Mark's mother Mary, the wealthy widow of Jerusalem, likely site of the upper room, became the headquarters for the movement in the first years after the crucifixion, just as the home of unknown ownership had been in Capernaum earlier.

Yet neither can we blithely dismiss this Command as merely symbolic, and thereby excuse never really giving up anything. The example of my friend's life remains. There *is* a renouncement that is required. It is a real *giving up,* not an imaginary one. It *may* involve money and houses and jobs and lands. The imperative upon you and me is to discover what that relinquishment means to *us*. The most healthy mindset, therefore, is the realization that "everything is on the table." Nothing is permanent. It all belongs to God. We are merely using what he gives us. A question always to keep in the forefront is a simple but probing one: What could I not walk away from? It may be time to loosen some strings.

And whereas the "everything" may involve possessions, what we must renounce most of all is self-motive, the desire to have my own way. In learning to pray, *Not my will,* everything else falls into line, including houses and lands. Everything must be put on the altar. What God chooses for us to keep and use afterwards, that is up to him.

> Give up your self, and you will find your real self. Lose your life and you will save it. Submit to death, death of your ambitions and favourite wishes every day…submit with every fibre of your being, and you will find eternal life. Keep back nothing. Nothing that you have not given away will ever be really yours. Nothing in you that has not died will ever be raised from the dead. Look for yourself, and you will find in the long run only hatred, loneliness, despair, rage, ruin, and decay. But

look for Christ and you will find Him, and with Him everything else thrown in.
C.S. Lewis, *Mere Christianity,* "The New Men"

God, bring to my remembrance this day the Command of Jesus to GIVE UP EVERYTHING. *Deepen into every corner of my being the truth that only in letting go, in relinquishment, in submission, do I possess life's most eternal treasures. Only what I have put on the altar will ever be truly mine. Thus, heavenly Father, may I be an instrument in my small corner of the world for the ultimate salvation of mankind. Amen.*

103. Don't Resist Evil Men

"Do not resist one who is evil." (Matthew 5:39)

The Command to "turn the other cheek," which we considered earlier as *Let people injure you without retaliating*, is actually a two-part Command. The passage in its entirety reads, "You have heard that it was said, 'An eye for an eye and a tooth for a tooth.' But I say to you, Do not resist one who is evil. But if any one strikes you on the right cheek, turn to him the other also." (Matthew 5:38-39)

Turn the other cheek, in context, thus carries much larger implications than merely not responding to injury. The reference to "evil men" is full of interest. What does Jesus actually mean here by telling us not to *resist* them?

Two observations may bring helpful insight. One, the imaginary cheek-striker was an *evil* man. The strike on the cheek to which Jesus tells us not to retaliate was malicious. It was *evil.* One would be within his or her rights to retaliate. Striking back would be entirely justified. In common legalese, it would be "self-defense." Jesus says, *Don't retaliate anyway.*

Secondly, looking at the incident from a larger perspective to draw a general conclusion, we might paraphrase Jesus' words to reflect another well-known truth from his lips: *You will always have evil with you; don't try to resist it.* In the same way that we will never rid the world of poverty, we will never rid the world of evil. This does not mean that we do not combat poverty and evil. But we have to combat them according to Jesus' methods, not the world's. We must recognize that the world is the world. These conditions will continue within a fallen humanity. Jesus' methods come at both scourges of the Fall, not head-on, but from the side.

Jesus makes his Commands *personal*...powerfully, pointedly personal. *You will never rid the world of poverty,* he says. *So don't imagine that a political program will accomplish it. Don't turn my words about God's Fatherhood into a political gospel. <u>But as for you—give to the poor.</u> You will never rid the world of evil. Don't imagine that you can devise a social* *program that will rid people of their sin. Don't try to conquer evil with an anti-sin campaign. But as for you—turn the other cheek.* Jesus is instructing us in the true nature of the war he came to wage against poverty and evil. It is a personal war. You and I are its foot-soldiers.

Don't resist evil men...resist evil itself. Resist evil by conquering it within yourself, says Jesus. *The urge to retaliate is itself evil. The urge to retaliate is no less evil than the evil which struck you on the cheek. Therefore, conquer evil. Lay down your arms. Trust my Father to be your advocate. Thus will sin be eradicated by degrees from the world—bringing poverty and the evil that lies within men's hearts in its vanishing train to be burned in the purifying fires of Malachi's furnace—as men observe your obedience. Show them by your example how to turn to me and allow me to take men's poverty and evil to the cross and put their power to death.*

There is a war to be waged, he concludes. *Fight it my way. Resist the evil that would rise within you, and thus prove to the world that you are my disciples.*

> How can we love a man or a woman who is cruel and unjust...who is mean, unlovely...self-righteous, self-seeking, and self-admiring?...These things cannot be loved...
>
> That person, with the evil thing cast out of him, will be yet more the *person,* for he will be his real self. The thing that now makes you dislike him is separable from him...it is working death in him...When he is clothed and in his right mind, he will be a person indeed...Begin to love him now, and help him into the loveliness which is his.
>
> George MacDonald, *Unspoken Sermons, First Series,* "Love Thine Enemy"

God, bring to my remembrance this day the Command of Jesus NOT TO RESIST EVIL MEN. Selfish, proud, arrogant, greedy, mean-spirited, power-hungry, backbiting people are about me on every side. The world seems more worldly than ever as our society becomes increasingly a post-Christian one. Keep me humbly detached from the spirit of this world, knowing that slaps on my cheek are as inevitable as that I need air to breathe. May I not resist by playing the world's games, but return selfishness with kindness. Thus, heavenly Father, may I be an instrument in my small corner of the world for the ultimate salvation of mankind. Amen.

104. Do Not Lead Others into Sin

"Whoever causes one of these little ones who believe in me to sin, it would be better for him if a great millstone were hung around his neck and he were thrown into the sea." (Mark 9:42)
"Temptations to sin are sure to come; but woe to him by whom they come!" (Luke 17:1)

It is a sobering truth to realize that in God's eyes causing *another* to sin may be more serious than sinning ourselves. It is not merely causing another to sin...merely *tempting* someone in the direction of sin is eternally serious. Jesus does not say "Woe to..." unless the most dire consequences are at stake. Nor is he merely speaking about what we may carelessly bring upon children. The warning against tempting others is not age-specific.

This Command, like all the Commands, is closer to home than we might think. Skimming over the words superficially, we tend to assume when Jesus spoke of *causing* or *leading* another "into sin" that he was talking about huge macro-sins—coercing an unsuspecting protégé to accompany you to the bank when your intent is to pull off a heist.

Again, it's easy to overlook the subtleties. Jesus isn't talking about robbing banks. He isn't just talking about dope dealers. He is talking about the unspoken and easily overlooked influence of our lives. We don't usually lead people into sin by dragging them into crime. But we *may* lead others into sin in ways we never suspect by the laxity of our own obedience.

A child grows up observing the speedometer always inching five or ten miles above the limit and listening to his father mumbling about watching out for cops...thirty years later a fatal traffic accident can be traced directly back to that careless parental example.

A boy observes his father being more friendly than he should to every pretty woman who crosses his path, sending the boy a wink and a grin as he does. Thirty years later two broken marriages and a string of affairs can be laid like the great millstone at the father's doorstep.

A daughter watches her mother always careful with make-up and perfume, dressing with skirts just a tad high and blouses just a tad low, swimming in the summer in a suit obviously designed to draw eyes. When that same daughter, at eighteen finds herself sinning against the Command toward sexual purity, who else but the indiscreet mother can be blamed for tempting her in the directions that led to such sin?

How do the careless words and loose language that fall from our lips invisibly influence those around us? If it is a sin to take God's name in vain by punctuating our speech with, *Oh God* every five minutes, and if those who are watching adopt the same habit, what other conclusion can be drawn but that we have "led them into sin?" What do our business practices, our use of money, our tendency toward gossip, the animosity we let slip with barbed remarks, what does the full example of my life say to a watching world? It should be very sobering that another may be led into sin from something I say or do. Yet I may never know it.

Christians are a *watched* people? What is being observed by the eyes noticing *me*?

> A man may loathe a thing in the abstract for years, and find at last that all the time he has been, in his own person, guilty of it...Of all who will one day stand in dismay and sickness of heart, with the consciousness that their very existence is a sham, those will fare the worst who have been consciously false to their fellows...Except I love my neighbour as myself, I may one day betray him! Let us therefore be compassionate and humble, and hope for every man.

A man may sink by such slow degrees that, long after he is a devil, he may go on being a good churchman...and thinking himself a good Christian. Continuously repeated sin against the poorest consciousness of evil must have a dread rousing. There are men who never wake to know how wicked they are, till, lo, the gaze of the multitude is upon them!

George MacDonald, Unspoken Sermons, Third Series, "The Final Unmasking"

God, bring to my remembrance this day the Command of Jesus NOT TO LEAD OTHERS INTO SIN. Remind me often that my example is influencing others. What habits, what attitudes, what responses are they picking up from me? I pray that because of me, others may be motivated to Christlikeness. If I have inadvertently led any man, woman, or child into sin, reveal it to me, that I may repent and make it right. Thus, heavenly Father, may I be an instrument in my small corner of the world for the ultimate salvation of mankind. Amen.

105. Teach the Nations to Obey What I Have Commanded

"Go therefore and make disciples of all nations...teaching them to observe all that I have commanded you." (Matthew 28:19-20)

The Great Commission of Jesus in Matthew 28 is surely one of the most well-known, important, and yet *misunderstood* and *misapplied* passages in the Bible. Much of this confusion stems from the parallel passage in Mark 16:15-18.

But *are* these four verses actually Mark's version of the Great Commission? Biblical scholars say no. Based on almost irrefutable evidence, liberal scholars, conservative scholars, and everyone in between, recognize that the final twelve verses (9-20) of *Mark* from the King James and earlier editions of the Bible, were not written by Mark at all, but were added later. None of the most ancient Greek manuscripts include these verses. Most contemporary editions of the Bible, therefore, now include them in a footnote rather than in the text of Mark's gospel for the simple reason that they were *not* part of Mark's gospel.

It doesn't take a Greek scholar to see the tonal difference of these verses. Here is Jesus speaking about people being "damned" (KJV) if they don't believe, about signs and wonders, about picking up snakes and speaking in tongues and drinking poison—all things Jesus never emphasized. The later addition of editorialized spiritualizations (something *Mark* never did) is also obvious in verses 14 and 19. The entire passage simply does not ring true.

The greatest damage this counterfeit commission has done through the years comes from verses 15 and 16. We have Jesus' Command reduced to, "Go into all the world and preach the Gospel to every creature." The dreadful implication is that people can be brought to Christ by *preaching*.

This is followed by the equally dreadful implication that what is often a superficial observance (baptism) results in people being "saved" and that unbelievers are "damned." The whole thing has led to a terrible miscarriage of Jesus' actual final instructions to his followers. As a result, *preaching* has been viewed as the primary means by which the Gospel is communicated. "Belief" has been hijacked to convey an intellectual agreement to a set of ideas conveyed by preaching. Mass baptisms of entire races and nations have been conducted to get people "saved," all on the erroneous implications of these two verses. Preaching and conversion have thus been almost the sole focus of Christian evangelism.

But it is all wrong. Preaching and conversion are *not* the focus Jesus intended to convey. How different is his true commission! He did not command his disciples to preach or make converts at all. *He commanded them to teach obedience.* Nothing more. Nothing less. He urged the making of *disciples,* not "converts." His words are as plain as can be: "Make disciples…teaching them to observe all that I have commanded you."

The evangelism of the Great Commission is the Commands. These Commands. We are to take the Commands into all the world, and teach people to become disciples by doing them. Nowhere are we commanded to make converts. Nowhere are we commanded to take people to church. Nowhere are we commanded to persuade people to accept the ideas of Christianity. We are to *do* the Commands, and to teach others to do them by our own example, and thus to become disciples of Jesus. No evangelism will succeed in making disciples other than the example of our own courageous, sacrificial, humble, steady, cheerful, enduring obedience.

> He instructs his messengers to go [to] all nations, "teaching them to observe all things whatsoever I have commanded you." Tell me it is faith he requires…and is not faith the highest act of…the human mind…But faith in what? Faith in what he is, in what he says—a faith which can have no existence except in obedience—a faith which is obedience. To do what he wishes is to put forth faith in him.
>
> George MacDonald, *Unspoken Sermons, Second Series,* "The Truth in Jesus"

God, bring to my remembrance this day the Command of Jesus to TEACH THE NATIONS TO OBEY WHAT HE HAS COMMANDED. *Make of me a true evangelist—one who teaches, encourages, and examples life lived according to the Commands of Jesus. Thus, heavenly Father, by my obedience to the Great Commission, may I be an instrument in my small corner of the world for the ultimate salvation of mankind. Amen.*

106. Do Not Follow the Example of Those Who Preach but Do Not Practice

"The scribes and the Pharisees sit on Moses' seat, so practice and observe whatever they tell you, but not what they do; for they preach, but do not practice." (Matthew 23:2-3)

The proverb "practice what you preach" is so common in everyday parlance that most probably do not realize that it was Jesus who coined the phrase. The context of the Command is intriguing. For Jesus actually told his listeners to obey what the Pharisees instructed them to do, but not to follow their example. In other words, to obey their *teachings* but not their *deeds*.

How far we are obligated to adhere to the first half of the Command, therefore, is open to question. Are we really expected to obey the teachings of hypocritical religious leaders? It seems doubtful. Jesus was clearly talking about Moses' Law, which even the hypocrisy of the Pharisees could not entirely pollute. The Law remained sacred, even though the example of the Pharisees was an abomination. The parallel in our own time might be a spiritual leader whose teaching is sound—who emphasizes obedience to the Commands, for example—but whose own example is of a life lived contrary to the Commands. In such a case, we might easily imagine Jesus saying something similar.

All this, however, is really not to the point. Jesus is not merely counseling wisdom in how we determine the spiritual leaders and teachers after whom we model our lives—as important as that is. More significant may be the reminder that it is our *own* example that other people will be watching more than our words. We are not immune from the pharisaism about which Jesus spoke either. This is a two-sided Command, especially for those in leadership and any to whom people are listening. The Command might just as well be inverted to read, "If you occupy Moses' seat as a teacher of spiritual truth, be very careful what you urge people to do. They will observe your practice more than your teaching."

We can therefore turn this Command into its most familiar form: "Practice what *you* preach."

I have no desire to change the opinion of man or woman. Let everyone for me hold what he pleases. But I would do my utmost to disable such as think correct opinion essential to salvation from laying any other burden on the shoulders of true men and women than the yoke of their Master; and such burden, if already oppressing any, I would gladly lift. Let the Lord himself teach them, I say. A man who has not the mind of Christ—and no man has the mind of Christ except him who makes it his business to obey him—cannot have correct opinions concerning him; neither, if he could, would they be of any value to him: he would be nothing the better, he would be the worse for having them. Our business is not to think correctly, but to live truly; then first will there be a possibility of our thinking correctly. One chief cause of the amount of unbelief in the world is, that those who have seen something of the glory of Christ, set themselves to theorize concerning him rather than to obey him. In teaching men, they have not taught them Christ, but taught them about Christ. More eager after credible theory than after doing the truth, they have speculated in a condition of heart in which it was impossible they should understand; they have presumed to explain a Christ whom years and years of obedience could alone have made them able to comprehend. Their teaching of him, therefore, has been repugnant to the common sense of many who had not half their privileges, but in whom, as in Nathanael, there was no guile. Such, naturally, press their theories, in general derived from them of old time, upon others, insisting on their thinking about Christ as they think, instead of urging them to go to Christ to be taught by him whatever he chooses to teach them. They do their unintentional worst to stop all growth, all life. From such and their false teaching I would gladly help to deliver the true-hearted. Let the dead bury their dead, but I would do what I may to keep them from burying the living.

George MacDonald, *Unspoken Sermons, Third Series*, "Justice"

God, bring to my remembrance this day the Command of Jesus NOT TO FOLLOW THE EXAMPLE OF THOSE WHO PREACH BUT DO NOT PRACTICE. Without judging, and with a pure heart and motives, give me discernment to see with your wisdom into the hearts and motives of those I listen to and associate with. Give me love for all, but give me wisdom to know when to be skeptical. Above all, keep me from the spiritually lethal snare of preaching and teaching what I do not practice. Thus, heavenly Father, may I be an instrument in my small corner of the world for the ultimate salvation of mankind. Amen.

107. Don't Cast Your Pearls Before Swine

"Do not give dogs what is holy; and do not throw your pearls before swine." (Matthew 7:6)

We have already spoken of those few Commands too specific and unclear of meaning to be grouped with others. Near the top of the list are surely, *Have salt in yourselves* and, *Don't cast your pearls before swine.* In neither case is the context illuminating. In the matter of the pearls and the swine, the verse is sandwiched between two passages whose unity are plain. The first five verses of Matthew 7 concern judging. Verses 7-11 concern asking, giving, and receiving. Stuck between the two, disconnected from either theme, is the curious verse quoted above.

Scholars uniformly recognize that many of the Lord's sayings in the first three "synoptic" gospels were organized by the three gospelists from what was originally a compilation of random "sayings" of Jesus. One of these conjectured documents is known simply as Q. It is recognized as the foundational source, especially for Matthew's and Luke's gospels. However, to incorporate the Lord's sayings into their sequential narratives, all three writers occasionally had to find places for certain statements that did not flow naturally out of what had come before. Such is probably the case here.

The term "dog" was a common Old Testament reference to Gentiles. When the Syrophenician woman of Mark 7 (a Gentile) sought Jesus to cast a demon from her daughter, Jesus obliquely replied, "Let the children first be fed, for it is not right to take the children's bread and throw it to the dogs." (Mark 7:27) It is a clear reference to the children of Israel, and that he, as the bread of life, had come first to Israel. It is probable that the first half of Matthew 7:6 derives from the same or a similar incident.

Yet casting pearls before swine has come to signify something far more practically significant—wasting treasures on those incapable of recognizing, using, and appreciating them for what they are. We might use the example of handing over a mansion to a poor uneducated jungle native. Incapable of the wise stewardship required, he proceeds to trash it. Neither mansion nor native is any better in the end for the unwisely given gift.

But there is a danger here. Which of us is capable of wisely judging with God's perspective who is worthy of what? Which of us is worthy *ourselves* for the riches God desires to bestow on us? We are all swine together in God's palaces. However, we are told that our rags will one day be replaced by white robes, and that we will be welcomed as the King's own sons and daughters. And though that day has not yet come, here we are commanded by Jesus occasionally to apply the discernment required not to cast pearls before swine. Therefore, let us be very prayerful as we judiciously apply his words.

The most practical reading may point toward truth itself. Is it wise to lavish truth on those uninterested in hearing it? Is it wise to force the Gospel on those who are not ready for it? Is it wise to force the imperative of the Commands on one whose inner journey has not yet resulted in that tilling of the soil so necessary for the words of Jesus to strike root? Is it wise to share God's eternal mysteries with those whose beliefs are ruled by formula, dogma, and cliché?

Premature eagerness to "share truth" may do more harm than good. We might paraphrase this Command as: Keep your powder dry. Safeguard the seeds of truth until the soil is ready.

> I will send out no theory of mine to rouse afresh little whirlwinds of dialogistic dust mixed with dirt and straws and holy words, hiding the Master in talk about him…Only eyes opened by the sun of righteousness, and made single by obedience, can judge…formulated thought. Say if you will that I fear to show my opinion. Is the man a coward who will not fling his child to the wolves? What faith…I have, I will have to myself before God, till I see better reason for uttering it than I do now.
>
> George MacDonald, *Unspoken Sermons, Third Series,* "Justice"

God, bring to my remembrance this day the Command of Jesus NOT TO CAST PEARLS BEFORE SWINE. *Let me not forget that truth is a sacred and holy treasure. May I treat truth with its due respect. Thus, heavenly Father, may I be an instrument in my small corner of the world for the ultimate salvation of mankind. Amen.*

108. Do Not Test the Lord

"You shall not tempt the Lord your God." (Matthew 4:7)

Back in the Jesus Movement days of the 1970s, putting out fleeces before the Lord, according to the example of Gideon in Judges 6, was a popular method of determining God's will. God can of course reveal his will by such means. But we actually may be flirting with danger by "testing the Lord" in this way, as is often the case when a single passage of Scripture is given too much prominence. Depending on "signs" leads to an erroneous perspective on one's entire relationship to God. This is the crux of what it means to test, or *tempt* God—taking matters into our own hands, trying to coerce him to march to our drum. Of course it's backwards. *We* make God march to *our* drum! Who do we think we are?

The word πειράζω (PEIRAZŌ—tempt/test) does not always denote temptation to *sin*. It is a word with a good *and* a bad meaning—test, try, prove in a way that strengthens faith and character...*or* to test or *tempt* in the sense of ensnaring in sin. Our faith is *tested*, and we are also *tempted*. The word used in Matthew 4:7 in Jesus' response is a much stronger form of the word. An accurate reading would be more along the lines of, "Do not *overtempt* the Lord your God."

Interestingly, even bad *temptations* can prove beneficial as strengthening *testings* of faith. Though Satan was trying to *tempt* Jesus contrary to his true mission, Jesus turned it into a *testing* that made him stronger. Using the same Greek, James calls these "trials" a benefit to faith and a cause for joy, adding, "The *testing* of your faith produces steadfastness." (James 1:3)

What Jesus is warning about here is specifically the sin of Satan. Whether Satan's words *tempted* Jesus to sin in the ordinary sense of the word is an open question. He said, "*If* you are the Son of God, throw yourself down..." It is that single word *if* where the evil lay. *Prove* that you are God...and prove it on *my* terms. It was an illegitimate test. It was a test Satan had no right to demand. As we saw, one of the "good" meanings of PEIRAZŌ is indeed prove. But we have no right to demand that God prove himself by *our* standards.

Yet how subtly we also place similar *ifs* before him. The common prayer we hear so often, and have likely prayed ourselves, "Lord, you have promised in your Word that...and so we take you at your word and ask that..." may be a subtle twist on Satan's own method. Are we quoting Scripture back to God in an attempt to coerce him to act according to *our* desires? In how many different ways do we say, "If God is God, then surely he..."

We must be very wary of raising the same *if* that Satan raised. God *is* God. His faithfulness *will* be proved. His goodness is eternal and will stand *every* test and *all* the tests of eternity. But there are no *ifs* with God. I cannot demand that he march to my drum.

> I think this will throw some light upon the words of our Lord, "If ye have faith and doubt not, if ye shall say unto this mountain, Be thou removed, and...cast into the sea; it shall be done." Good people...have been tempted to tempt the Lord their God upon the strength of this saying, just as Satan sought to tempt our Lord...Faith is that which, knowing the Lord's will, goes and does it; or, not knowing it, stands and waits, content in ignorance as in knowledge, because God wills...It is its noblest exercise to act with uncertainty of the result, when the duty itself is certain, or even when a course seems with strong probability to be duty. In the latter case a man may be mistaken, and his work will be burned, but by that very fire he will be saved. Nothing saves a man more than the burning of his work, except the doing of work that can stand the fire. But to put God to the question in any other way than by saying, What wilt thou have me to do? is an attempt to compel God to declare himself, or to hasten his work. This probably was the sin of Judas. It is presumption...either a forcing of God to act...or the making of a case wherein he shall seem to have forfeited his word if he does not act. The man...instead of acting by the divine will from within...acts in God's face, as it were, to see what he will do. Man's first business is, "What does God want me to do?"
>
> George MacDonald, *Unspoken Sermons, First Series,* "The Temptation in the Wilderness"

God, bring to my remembrance this day the Command of Jesus NOT TO TEST YOU. Wean me from interpreting your will through the lens of my desires, and then praying to bend your will to mine. Reveal to me the unwitting ifs I erect as roadblocks to your work. Thus, heavenly Father, by my submission to your will, may I be an instrument in my small corner of the world for the ultimate salvation of mankind. Amen.

109. Wash One Another's Feet

"If I then, your Lord and Teacher, have washed your feet, you also ought to wash one another's feet." (John 13:14)

The ongoing debate between how "literal" one is to take the accounts and Commands of the Bible is filled with pomposity, self-righteousness, and thorough inconsistency on all sides. Those of liberal bent tend to explain away the literality of the Garden of Eden, Noah's ark, the sun stopping in the sky, the virgin birth, even in some cases the resurrection. They scoff at what they consider the unenlightened views of those who persist in believing the Bible a *literal* account.

Yet these same free-thinking progressives will be the first to insist that we must absolutely take the Command to feed the hungry and give to the poor literally when it suits their political agenda.

Conservatives and evangelicals, with their insistence that the Scriptures are "literal" and "inerrant" are equally inconsistent. The televangelist who pompously asserts, "I'm a simple country preacher…I just take the Word of God as it comes and believe what it says," is fooling no one but himself. How *literally* does he take the Command to cut off hands and feet to prevent sin? How literally does he take Paul's words about circumcision of the heart? And how literally do most evangelicals in our day take the Commands that women should keep their heads covered and not speak in church? Intriguingly, it is many Catholics who read the communion passages "literally," while fundamentalists "explain them away" by preaching about the *symbolic* nature of the body and blood of Christ.

The fact is, we are all *literalists* and we all interpret the Scriptures *symbolically* when it suits us. Everyone reads the Bible with a thorough mix of both *literal* and *interpretive* approaches. We have to. The Bible can be read no other way.

No more interesting example of this dichotomy between the two ways of reading Scripture exists than with the simple Command Jesus gave his disciples in the upper room: *Wash one another's feet.*

Obviously this is a Command with ten thousand applications of humble service and ministry to our kind. Washing another's feet has come to symbolize in Christian terminology any act of selfless service.

Yet in very few fellowships within Christendom, neither among liberals nor fundamentalists, is this Command widely practiced *literally.* Most Christians, it seems, agree that this particular Command is to be read symbolically and interpretively.

Curious, is it not? Jesus actually got down on his hands and knees and literally washed and dried his disciples' feet. Then he said, "I want you to do what I have done and follow my example."

As I said, we are all *literalists* and we are all *allegorists* together. Therefore, we will all read this Command and interpret it in our own ways.

However…just *maybe,* Jesus occasionally means it to be taken more literally than has been our custom.

Nothing disciplines the inordinate desires of the flesh like service, and nothing transforms the desires of the flesh like serving in hiddenness. The flesh whines against service but screams against hidden service. It strains and pulls for honor and recognition. It will devise subtle, religiously acceptable means to call attention to the service rendered. If we stoutly refuse to give in to this lust of the flesh we crucify it. Every time we crucify the flesh we crucify our pride and arrogance.
Richard Foster, *Celebration of Discipline*, p. 114

God, bring to my remembrance this day the Command of Jesus to WASH ONE ANOTHER'S FEET. Give me opportunities to wash the feet of my brethren in Christ, figuratively but perhaps not only figuratively. Thus, heavenly Father, by the humility of my bent-knee servanthood, may I be an instrument in my small corner of the world for the ultimate salvation of mankind. Amen.

110. Be Wise as Snakes and Innocent as Doves

"Be wise as serpents and innocent as doves." (Matthew 10:16)

Here we encounter another of Jesus' well-known Commands. The parallel with snakes, however, is troublesome because we usually associate snakes with evil. The confusion is increased by the occasional translation "shrewd," which can be read almost any way one wants. This danger is amplified in its juxtaposition as the contrasting opposite of "innocence." Hence, the "wisdom of serpents" that Jesus is apparently advocating has come to imply in the minds of many what we might call "worldly-wisdom," typifying an individual whom we call *worldly-wise* (which has a touch of the naughty in it), or whom we might also say has *street smarts*.

Nothing could be further from what Jesus intended. Wisdom from *Proverbs*, especially the wisdom of *God*, is SOPHIA in Greek. It is this James speaks of when he says, "If any of you lacks wisdom (SOPHIA), let him ask God who gives to all men generously." (James 1:5) This wisdom, in *James* and through *Proverbs* has a supernatural element. We must *pray* for it, and *seek* it, then God gives it by obedience. We develop wisdom by living in the truths of wisdom. We especially develop it by childlike ("innocent") trust. Only the childlike can truly apprehend the wisdom of God, not those who are "wise in their own eyes" in the ways of the world.

This high thing that Proverbs says should be the highest goal of life is *not* the craftiness of the snake, the cunning of the street-wise con man. These are a revulsion to the Lord. It is the *innocence of the babe* combined with the *wisdom of God*—the very *mind of Christ*.

The word translated "wise" in Matthew 10:16, φρόνιμος—PHRONIMOS—is more accurately rendered "prudence." The *prudence* commanded here is more closely linked to those Commands exhorting to us mental diligence and understanding. It conveys the sense of *practical* wisdom, of being sensible, being an individual of discernment, discretion, and understanding, a wise manager of affairs. It will be seen that the book of Proverbs is a roadmap to *both* forms of wisdom—God's wisdom, and practical prudence in the daily affairs of life: *The wisdom of a prudent man is to discern his way.* (Proverbs 14:8)

> The wise and the prudent, with all their energy of thought, could never see the things of the Father sufficiently to recognize them…Their sagacity labours in earthly things…they cannot see…eternal foundations…They are proud of finding out…They do not perceive…any truth which the intellect cannot formulate…Terribly has his gospel suffered in the mouths of the wise and prudent: how would it be faring now, had its first messages been committed to persons of repute, instead of those simple fishermen?…Had the wise and prudent been the confidants of God…the letter would at once have usurped the place of the spirit…a system of religion, with its rickety, malodorous plan of salvation, would…have at once been put in the place of a living Christ…But the Father revealed the Father's things to his babes; the babes loved, and began to do them, therewith began to understand them, and went on growing in the knowledge of them and in the power of communicating them; while to the wise and prudent, the deepest words of the most babe-like of them all, John Boanerges, even now appear but a finger-worn rosary of platitudes. The babe understands the wise and prudent, but is understood only by the babe.
>
> The Father, then, revealed his things to babes, because the babes were…able to receive them…near enough whence they come, to understand a little how things go in the presence of their father in heaven, and thereby to interpret the words of the Son…No wisdom of the wise can find out God…The Son alone can reveal God; the child alone understand him. The elder brother companies with the younger, and makes him yet more a child like himself…He lets him see how he delights in his father, and lets him know that God is his father too. He rouses in…[him] the sense of their father's will; and the younger, as he hears and obeys, begins to see that his elder brother must be the very image of their father. He becomes more and more of a child, and more and more the Son reveals to him the Father. For he knows that to know the Father is the one thing needful to every child of the Father…To see the Father is the cry of every child-heart in the universe.
>
> George MacDonald, *The Hope of the Gospel,* "The Yoke of Jesus"

God, bring to my remembrance this day the Command of Jesus to BE WISE AS SNAKES AND INNOCENT AS DOVES. *I ask, as James says, for the childlike insight of your wisdom, the very mind of Christ. Thus, heavenly Father, as I mature to reflect your wisdom in ways the world perhaps does not see, or even looks down on, may I be an instrument in my small corner of the world for the ultimate salvation of mankind. Amen.*

SERIES TWELVE

"THE JOHN COMMANDS"

The Abiding Life

THIS IS MY COMMAND: LOVE ONE ANOTHER

The only personal reference John makes to himself in his gospel is as "the disciple whom Jesus loved." As noted earlier, this love Jesus had for John was likely the love of a cousin.

What we know of John from the Gospels reveals a man of quite different character than we might infer from the peaceful words of John 14-15, or the "love letter" of 1 John. He and his brother James were ambitious. In league with their mother, they had the gall to ask Jesus for the most honored positions in his kingdom. It would also seem that the two sons of Zebedee inherited their father's temper. For in Luke 9:54 the two brothers were ready to bring down fire and brimstone on a Samaritan village because it would not receive them. Furthermore, John angrily forbid a man casting out demons in Mark 9 because he was not one of their company.

And yet Jesus apparently *loved* John with a depth equaled only by his affection for Peter. Tradition has it that John lived to be a hundred and spent his last years in Ephesus, where he penned his gospel and letters. The length of his life has led to the conjecture that John was a very young man during the events of the Gospels. It is possible that Jesus' love for him was that of an older cousin for a young boy for whom he had always had a soft spot, a love which deepened as the lad grew to become one of his most intimate friends and disciples?

Like Judas, John *changed* through the years. But John's change was the transformation into Christlikeness that is God's objective in every man and woman. John put to death his ambition, his temper, his selfish motives, and learned to *love*. Specially loved by Jesus, John allowed that love to "dwell" in him and transform every fiber of his being. As a result, over a lifetime, John was given extraordinary insight into the very love of God himself. In John we observe the miraculous result of "abiding" and "remaining" intrinsically connected to the vine-life of Christ over a lifetime. That result is love. How prophetic were Jesus' words about the very man who wrote down his words: "He who abides in me…bears much fruit."

Whether it is legend or fact, Jerome tells a touching story of John's dying charge. It is in perfect keeping with the message for which John is primarily known. It is said that his disciples asked John if he had any parting words to leave with them.

"Little children," he replied, "love one another."

He repeated the words several times. Finally they asked if this was all he had to say.

"It is enough," John answered, "for it is the Lord's command."

μένω: MENŌ—*Abide*

Though the word μένω—MENŌ—and its various forms are commonly used throughout the New Testament (more than twenty-five times), it is translated into English in a variety of ways that give many nuances to its meaning: Dwell, remain, continue, endure, cleave, tarry, stand, persevere.

Its most memorable use comes in John 15 where Jesus describes the life of the disciple, and its interconnection to his own life and the Father's. The image of the vine and branches, the fruitful and unfruitful vine, the pruning and the fire, and Jesus and the husbandman. These images are so familiar to Christians that it is easy to overlook the profound scope of this passage. A lifetime's reflection is not enough to plumb its depths. John expounds on it further in his first epistle.

The most significant and eternal of many truths revealed in John 15 is also the most practical and down-to-earth. Jesus tells exactly *how* to remain, continue, dwell, and *abide* in him.

Verse 10. We abide by keeping his Commands.

Series Twelve

This Is My Command: Love One Another

111. Abide in me by obeying my Commands.

112. Don't separate what God has joined.

113. Love me by having my Commands and words and keeping them.

114. Count the cost of single-minded devotion to God.

115. Don't look back on your past life.

116. Don't call me Lord and not do what I tell you.

117. Do as I do and become like me.

118. Bear fruit as my disciples.

119. Practice my words.

120. This is my Command: Love one another.

111. Abide in Me by Obeying My Commands

"Abide in me, and I in you…If you keep my commandments, you will abide in my love." (John 15:4, 10)

The profound example of the Apostle John's life is as powerful as the words he recorded of Jesus' farewell conversation and charge to his disciples in the upper room. For John was no scribe, historian, or journalist merely recording events. In a sense, John was setting down for all time the very principles he had himself lived by, the truths that had changed *his* own heart. He was illuminating the way the Holy Spirit works in human life to transform a fallen, broken, sinful, selfish humanity into fruit-bearing individual vines in God's vineyard.

John 15, therefore comes to us with a wondrous double message. Between its lines we observe the progress and transformation of John himself—from a feisty, tempestuous, ambitious youth into the "Apostle of Love." John learned to "abide" in Jesus, and to "remain" in him over a lifetime. He learned to abide by obeying. Out of that obedience grew a deep understanding of God's very nature. In his long life he witnessed branches that did *not* bear fruit and were cast out and burned (Judas, Ananias and Sapphira, Demas, Hymenaeus, Alexander the coppersmith). And in the lives of Peter and his other fellow disciples he saw the fruitful results of a lifetime spent "abiding in the vine."

John 15 gives us a picture of exactly how it should be: John's *example* matches his *words*. His words come to us with power because they also illuminate the example of his life.

At first glance, the abiding life Jesus speaks about seems *passive*, as if there is little we must actually *do* other than let the sap, the *life* of the vine, flow through us. The very words abide, remain, dwell, stand, tarry, persevere are all passive words. This reveals the unfortunate fact that many read John 15 by skipping over verse 10. Indeed the entire upper room discourse from John 13 to 17 can be read dreamily and passively.

But this is anything but a passive passage. If we are paying attention, that all important verse 10 jumps off the page like an explosion of spiritual dynamite. It represents the climax of the Gospel—the culmination of Jesus' entire teaching in a few short words. It is both a *Command* and a *promise*. He is commanding us to abide in his love, he is telling us *how* to abide in his love, and he is promising that we *will* abide in his love if we follow that *how*.

If you keep my commandments, you will abide in my love.

As John said, "It is enough, for it is the Lord's command."

*Abide in me…*these three words have always flowed over my soul like a cool mountain stream, soothing and calming and filling me with peace...these few words have been among my favorite passages of Scripture. They seemed to represent the apex, the ultimate in the Christian experience, the most powerful biblical exposition of... Christlikeness...

But... how [was] this "abiding"...to come about...It seemed...like an ethereal process that perhaps stole over one gradually by spiritual osmosis...The command to *Abide*, and the description of the abiding life, filled me with peace, but left me with few ideas how it was to be done...

I'm sure my shortsightedness will already be obvious to you. I had not paid sufficient attention to the remainder of the passage...Why was Jesus one with his Father? What enabled this oneness to be, in MacDonald's words, the bond of the universe, the chain that holds it together, the one active unity, the harmony of things? Jesus tells us clearly. "If you keep my commandments, you will abide in my love, just as I have kept my Father's commandments and abide in his love..."

Jesus was one with his Father because he did his Father's will. *To abide is to obey. And to obey is to love.* John 15 offers us a doorway, therefore—and neither a cryptic nor an ethereal one, but one that is extremely succinct and practical—into the Christlikeness we seek...Of what is abiding in Christ comprised? Of nothing more nor less than being one with the Father as he was one with the Father—by doing his will...John 15 makes of the cross a moment by moment way of life, not an *end* to life.

Michael Phillips, *Make Me Like Jesus*, "The Prayer of Life"

God, bring to my remembrance this day the Command of Jesus to ABIDE IN HIM BY KEEPING HIS COMMANDS. *No amount of brute will-power can keep me abiding and dwelling in you. I need your help. As you abide in me, your Spirit draws me into your very life. Keep me in your life by obedience. Thus, heavenly Father, may I be an instrument in my small corner of the world for the ultimate salvation of mankind. Amen.*

112. Don't Separate What God Has Joined

"What therefore God has joined together, let not man put asunder." (Mark 10:9)

It will be unpopular, in this time when obedience to the marital commandments of Scripture has grown so lax within Christendom, to read this Command from the mouth of Jesus as strictly forbidding divorce. But there is no other way to read it. Those who would excuse it or explain it away are simply toying with the Commands of Jesus.

It is true that in the same passage Jesus explained that divorce was "permitted" by Old Testament law. But make no mistake—there was only one reason God allowed it: *For hardness of heart.* Divorce, all divorce, is clearly and unambiguously contrary to the *intent* of God.

Now let the arguments rage, let justifications begin, let condemnation of the above words rail, let legalistic interpretations be debated about when divorce *is* permitted in Scripture. But how else are we to interpret these direct words from Jesus' mouth: *Don't separate what God has joined.* We are either serious about the Commands or we are not. If we want to find reasons why, in such-and-such a case we do not have to heed one or another of the Commands, they are found easily enough.

So discussion and debate will continue—whether adultery invalidates marriage and makes divorce allowable, whether it matters which party commits adultery and which party is free to remarry, whether such a thing as "spiritual" adultery constitutes grounds for divorce, whether "abuse" can be found in Scripture as providing justification for divorce, whether separation without divorce is the more scriptural solution to an intolerable or dangerous marriage situation, whether remarriage is *ever* permitted except in the case of the death of a husband or wife, whether a marriage viewed in retrospect as *not* ordained by God is governed by the same rules or does it qualify for divorce under different circumstances…these and a host of other complexities will make divorce and remarriage heatedly contentious among Christians, probably forever.

Everyone has to weigh the factors, the scriptural evidence, and the words of Jesus, then decide for themselves how they are going to live their lives before a watching world.

But when all is said and done, Jesus' words are still staring us in the face demanding nothing more nor less than the obedience of all men and women who claim to be his followers: *For your hardness of heart he wrote you this commandment. But from the beginning of creation, "God made them male and female…and the two shall become one." So they are no longer two but one. What therefore God has joined together, let not man put asunder.*

May God give his church the wisdom and humility to take obedience to his Word seriously, knowing that the world is basing its response to the Fatherhood of God on the visible obedience of its adherents to the Commands of Jesus.

> Our Lord was not in the habit of explaining away his hard words. He let them stand in all the glory of the burning fire wherewith they would purge us. Where their simplicity finds corresponding simplicity, they are understood.
>
> George MacDonald, *Unspoken Sermons, Second Series,* "The Hardness of the Way"

God, bring to my remembrance this day the Command of Jesus NOT TO SEPARATE WHAT GOD HAS JOINED. *In all things, especially those that touch my life most closely, whether this Command or some other, bring me face to face with the mirror of my own self-deception when I try to explain away some one or another of the Commands in order to justify my own disobedience. Drive me to my knees. Show me the way forward, through repentance, into the truth in which you would have me live. Thus, heavenly Father, by my willingness to face my own sin, may I be an instrument in my small corner of the world for the ultimate salvation of mankind. Amen.*

113. Love Me by Having My Commands and Words and Keeping Them

"If you love me, you will keep my commandments…He who has my commandments and keeps them, he it is who loves me…If a man loves me, he will keep my words." (John 14:15, 21, 23)

At first glance, this may seem but a restating of the Command we considered previous to the last. Are we splitting hairs to differentiate between the two? In fact, though obviously similar, and though the difference may be a fine one, it is also an important distinction.

In one sense, Jesus is saying the same thing—to *abide* in me, keep my commandments…if you *love* me, you will keep my commandments. But then he adds this twist: *He who has my commandments and keeps them, he it is who loves me.* In other words, he is laying down a validating mark of love. The implied reverse half of the coin is sobering: *He who does not keep my commandments does not love me.*

What does it mean to *have* his Commands? The word "have" is easily overlooked because it appears so simple. But the usage here is not as a mere auxiliary to the tense of some other verb. HAVE is the verb—one full of power and energy. It is no passive verb. Jesus is speaking of possessing his Commands with strong active *having*. Interestingly, the transliteration of the Greek ἔχω (have) is ECHŌ. No significance can be attached to the similarity with our English word other than coincidence. Yet that coincidence points us toward the strength of possession required—a whispered word is not echoed back. Only a loud, vigorous shout returns to one's hearing. We must "have" Jesus' Commands with strength and force and vigor. No passive "have," but a vital, *echoed* have. The *have* of John 14:21, therefore, carries these implications in the Greek—hold fast, receive, keep firmly in the mind, cling to, wear, possess.

Moreover, what does Jesus mean when he tells us to *keep* his Commands. Briefly, to watch over, guard, preserve, then observe and heed them—the obvious implication being to *obey* them. We might also add, by extension and drawing upon the theme of Psalm 119, simply to *love* them: *I love thy commandments above gold, above fine gold.* (Psalm 119:127) We protect and preserve and hold fast to what we *love.*

Furthermore, this "keeping" of his Commands parallels Jesus' prayer of John 17 in which the Lord prays that the Father will *keep* us (of the same

Greek root) in his name in the same way that he *kept* and guarded his disciples in the Father's name. This unity between Jesus' prayer and his Command surely elevates "having and keeping" his words to holy ground.

> Thou hast commanded thy precepts to be kept diligently. O that my ways may be steadfast in keeping thy statutes! Let me not wander from thy commandments! I have laid up thy word in my heart. Make me understand the way of thy precepts. I set thy ordinances before me. I will run in the way of thy commandments when thou enlargest my understanding! Teach me, O LORD, the way of thy statutes; and I will keep it to the end. Give me understanding, that I may keep thy law and observe it with my whole heart. Lead me in the path of thy commandments, for I delight in it. Teach me good judgment and knowledge, for I believe in thy commandments. The law of thy mouth is better to me than thousands of gold and silver pieces. Give me understanding that I may learn thy commandments.
>
> Oh, how I love thy law! It is my meditation all the day. I have more understanding than all my teachers, for thy testimonies are my meditation. How sweet are thy words. Through thy precepts I get understanding. Thy word is a lamp to my feet and a light to my path. Thy testimonies are the joy of my heart. I incline my heart to perform thy statutes for ever. I love thy commandments above gold, above fine gold. Therefore I direct my steps by all thy precepts; I hate every false way. Thy testimonies are wonderful; therefore my soul keeps them. The unfolding of thy words gives light; it imparts understanding to the simple. Give me understanding that I may live. My tongue will sing of thy word, for all thy commandments are right.
>
> David, son of Jesse, excerpts from Psalm 119

God, bring to my remembrance this day the Command of Jesus to LOVE HIM BY *HAVING HIS COMMANDS AND WORDS AND KEEPING THEM. Fill me with simple love for your words, so that keeping them is a delight. May I possess your Commands with such vigor and energy that they shout from within me. Thus, heavenly Father, may I be an instrument in my small corner of the world for the ultimate salvation of mankind. Amen.*

114. Count the Cost of Single-Minded Devotion to God

"For which of you, desiring to build a tower, does not first sit down and count the cost…So therefore whoever of you does not renounce all that he has cannot be my disciple."
(Luke 14:28, 33)

Count the cost and *Don't look back* are in a sense two ways to say the same thing. In Luke 9, three men came to follow Jesus. He seems to turn them away. In fact, he is but holding a mirror up to their own half-hearted motives by saying, "Count the cost and don't look back."

Counting the cost is one of the most practical messages of the book of *Proverbs*. It has application in all areas of life, not merely discipleship. The parable Jesus uses of building a tower is a financial and business example. But the implications are far-reaching. The application to evangelism is probing, though perhaps to some unwelcome.

Jesus countenanced no cheap commitment. How different are the evangelistic methods of soul-counters who base their success on the number of "decisions" made. How at odds with the Commands are the priorities of ministers who carefully monitor congregational statistics. How often do we hear that such and such is "the fastest growing church on the block?" How often do we hear about the popular pastor whose church boasts five services every Sunday? Even Billy Graham, as much as we honor his service to God and the example of his character, succumbed to this lethally unscriptural mindset.

Accompanying the *numbers game* are the *persuasion folly* and the *urgency mirage*. Evangelists are obsessed with talking people into belief, pressing the imperative of a "decision" for Christ…a decision *now*, before it is too late. Conversion is a matter of incentives, cajolery, and exhortation. Many altar calls resemble the pitch of used car salesmen: "What would I have to do to encourage you to buy *today*?" This emphasis on urgency, persuasion, and numbers is completely contrary to Jesus' methods. He was *never* in a hurry. He *never* pressed. He *never* counted heads. He was not afraid to let people walk away if they were not ready.

How much worldwide acclaim would a man receive if he followed his altar calls with a sobering reminder of the reasons *not* to make a premature commitment, then concluded, "You think about this decision long and hard. Pray to God in private. Recognize that there is no turning back. Everything will change. This decision may bring joy and suffering in equal measure. No bed of roses will await you, only death to ambition, pride, and self. Servanthood not fame is the mark of the Lord's disciples. Therefore, count the cost. If in two weeks you still want to give your life to Jesus Christ, come back and talk to me."

Jesus spent much time making sure people knew the reasons they *shouldn't* follow him, and the hardships and suffering they were sure to encounter. What good are 5,000 people sitting in a worship service if they have come for "fellowship"? How many would be there the following week if they were told, "Next week, you are all invited back to die."

> That is why He warned people to "count the cost" before becoming Christians. "Make no mistake," He says, "if you let me, I will make you perfect. The moment you put yourself in My hands, that is what you are in for. Nothing less…You have free will, and if you choose, you can push Me away. But if you do not push Me away, understand that I am going to see this job through. Whatever suffering it may cost you in your earthly life. Whatever inconceivable purification it may cost you after death, whatever it costs Me, I will never rest, nor let you rest, until you are literally perfect—until my Father can say without reservation that He is well pleased with

you, as He said He was well pleased with me. This I can do and will do. But I will not do anything less."...As a great Christian writer (George MacDonald) pointed out, every father is pleased at the baby's first attempt to walk: no father would be satisfied with anything less than a firm, free, manly walk in a grown-up son. In the same way, he said, "God is easy to please, but hard to satisfy."

C.S. Lewis, *Mere Christianity,* "Counting the Cost"

God, bring to my remembrance this day the Command of Jesus to COUNT THE COST OF SINGLE-MINDED DEVOTION TO GOD. Give me a sober-minded realization that no country club life awaits me. Would I return to church next Sunday if the invitation was to death? Perhaps that is exactly the case—but not just on Sunday. That is the call on my life today. Thus, heavenly Father, as I count the cost of being a disciple of your Son, may I be an instrument in my small corner of the world for the ultimate salvation of mankind. Amen.

115. Don't Look Back on Your Past Life

"No one who puts his hand to the plow and looks back is fit for the kingdom of God." (Luke 9:62)

The image Jesus is alluding to here is familiar from many sermon illustrations. The farmer guiding his single plow behind donkey or horse or ox desires to plough a precisely straight furrow from one end of the field to the other. This he achieves by setting between the ears of his faithful beast of burden some object in the distance, whether tree or fencepost, then fixing his eyes upon it through the two ears, and never once looking away until the entire furrow is done. Let him glance behind, however briefly, and the animal will feel the shift and swerve. Even if the momentary change be ever so slight, the damage is done. The jog in the upturned line of earth cannot be repaired. There is only one way to insure a perfectly straight furrow from one end to the other—once setting the hand to the plow, the farmer must never look back.

Jesus is stating the same principle his brother would write years later. "He that wavereth is like a wave of the sea driven with the wind and tossed...A double-minded man is unstable in all his ways." (James 1: 6, 8—KJV)

Discipleship is for keeps. Jesus is not saying that God will reject those who look back. The point here is not acceptability or worthiness in *God's* eyes. The point of this image is what kind of shape are *we* in. Are we strong enough to hold the plow straight?

Jesus is speaking of spiritual muscle, of *fitness* for what kingdom living requires. What sort of man am I? Am I in shape for the rigors of discipleship? If it is with twinges of regret that I recall my former life, keeping one foot in both camps as I wistfully dream about what I gave up, or if perhaps I did not actually give up all that much and if my lifestyle is not so different than before, then I am spiritually flabby, not *fit* and *in shape* for discipleship.

Jesus regularly sat his disciples down, looked them in the eye, and told them exactly what they were in for and what would be required. "Look," he said, "I want you under no illusions. Following me means selflessness, sacrifice, and ultimately death." When people came up enthusiastically with eager words of, "I will follow you wherever you go," Jesus turned them back on their heels. He knew they weren't ready. He knew they would eventually fall away. He knew they hadn't counted the cost. They weren't fit for what they would face. He knew it was better for them not to follow at all—*yet*—than to try to follow—*prematurely*—on the basis of enthusiasm rather than single-minded devotion.

Modern evangelism does the kingdom of God no favors by sweetening its message with alluring inducements. By regaling the wavering with promises of blessing, luring people in with as many enticing activities as possible from the fun and games calendar of the church schedule, new believers are actually taught to *disobey* this fundamental Command. Those who encourage such disobedience by the country club atmosphere of their mega churches may one day face the reality of the warning against those who cause little ones to stumble. That man of God is more to be honored who preaches the Commands of Jesus from the pulpit, and has in his congregation six or eight dedicated followers of Jesus who can hold the plow straight, than all the mega-church pastors in the land who preach a palatable and easy gospel of purpose and blessing, but who never raise the standard Jesus raised: *Count the cost and do not look back.*

Neither Jesus nor a pastor who preaches such a message is passing judgment. They are simply stating a fact. It takes *fitness* and *strength* to hold the plow steady.

> The word *perfect* (Greek *teleios*) is derived from *telos*, meaning "end," "goal," "limit." It...signifies "attaining to the end, complete, mature."...the quality of self-disinterested love and kindness for others, even for those who deserve no kindness. This kind of "perfectness" consists in the...attitude of the believer, rather than in absolute sinlessness. This is perfectly possible for believers. (*Harper Study Bible* on Matthew 5:48)

God, bring to my remembrance this day the Command of Jesus NOT TO LOOK BACK ON MY PAST LIFE. *Keep my gaze steadfastly forward, my hands steady on the plow, that my life may be straight and the furrows of my character deep and unwavering. Thus, heavenly Father, may I be an instrument in my small corner of the world for the ultimate salvation of mankind. Amen.*

116. Don't Call Me Lord and Not Do What I Tell You

It was not until after much reflection that it slowly dawned on me what an intriguing and perhaps prophetic word this is from the mouth of Jesus. We have it recorded twice, in both Matthew's and Luke's versions of the same material, called the Sermon on the Mount and the Sermon on the Plain. The two statements obviously contain the same exhortation, and were probably repeated often with slightly different wording.

"Not every one who says to me, 'Lord, Lord,' shall enter the kingdom of heaven, but he who does the will of my Father who is in heaven. On that day many will say to me, 'Lord, Lord, did we not prophesy in your name, and cast out demons in your name, and do many mighty works in your name?' And then will I declare to them, 'I never knew you; depart from me, you evildoers.'" (Matthew 7:21-23)

"Why do you call me 'Lord, Lord,' and not do what I tell you?" (Luke 6:46)

What is positively fraught with interest is where this powerful and chilling word comes in both gospels—at the very *beginning* of Jesus' teaching! The application is easy to see throughout the history of Christendom. We could point to endless examples of the kind of hypocrisy Jesus is speaking of, in former times and in our own, of pretense Christianity, pretending to be Christians in name but without a life of obedient reality to back it up.

However, we tend to think of the early days of Jesus' ministry, especially the first exciting months and first year, as a time when crowds were swarming to him and, except for the scribes and Pharisees, were enthusiastically embracing his teaching. It is shocking to see how quickly this problem arose. The moment Jesus began to teach, many people flocked to him to worship him and call him *Lord*...but did not do what he told them. No wonder it is such a problem in our own time. This disease of Christian pretense originated in the *very first days* of Christianity. It is obvious that Jesus hates this masquerading belief more than unbelief itself

The "evildoers" who will not enter the kingdom of heaven aren't unbelievers. They are *Christians!* Again we have Jesus turning traditional theology on its ear. Those who will be cast into the outer darkness, the goats of Matthew 25, and those of this passage to whom he will say, "Depart from me," are the *religiously* disobedient. Jesus has very little, if anything, to say about what sort of hell might await unbelievers. The hell of the Gospels, however, from Jesus' own mouth, is a hell reserved for complacent non-doing *believers*. What plans God might have for unbelieving heathens we don't know. Matthew 25:46 has nothing to say about that.

This Command contains an imperative warning. Don't pretend with God. Don't call Jesus *Lord*, don't call yourself a *Christian*, don't put a bumper sticker on your car, don't wear a cross around your neck, don't sing worship songs, don't memorize proof texts, don't pray for blessing, unless you are in earnest about *doing* what Jesus says. It's a deadly game.

Jesus hates spiritual pretense. He loves the pretender, but he hates the games they play with spirituality. If they don't get their act together, his retribution against the hypocrisy will be severe...that the pretender may be saved, if need be, by fire.

> If you can think of nothing he ever said as having had an atom of influence on your doing or not doing, you have too good ground to consider yourself no disciple of his. Do not...waste your time in trying to convince yourself that you are his disciple...if, after all, he say to you, "Why did you not do the things I told you? Depart from me; I do not know you!" Instead of trying to persuade yourself...you can begin at once...to *be* a disciple of the Living One—by obeying him in the first thing you can think of in which you are not obeying him. We must learn to obey him in everything, and so must begin somewhere: let it be at once, and in the very next thing that lies at the door of our conscience!
>
> George MacDonald, *Unspoken Sermons, Second Series*, "The Truth in Jesus"

God, bring to my remembrance this day the Command of Jesus NOT TO CALL HIM LORD AND NOT DO WHAT HE TELLS ME. Shout to me through my conscience of the <u>*next*</u> *thing you would have me do. Thus, heavenly Father, may I be an instrument in my small corner of the world for the ultimate salvation of mankind. Amen.*

117. Do as I Do and Become Like Me

"For I have given you an example, that you also should do as I have done." (John 13:25)

The debate is long standing in Christendom about what exactly "sanctification" is and how it comes about. Some believe that we are automatically set apart and sanctified by God when we put our faith in Christ. Though still in the world and subject to the pull of the old Adam, we are positionally seen by God as washed in the blood of Jesus and therefore sanctified. Others believe that such transformation comes at death, when the sinful nature of the flesh falls away and we are instantly made perfect and like Christ. Clearly elements of truth exist in both perspectives. Something certainly changes when we believe. But the battle between flesh and Spirit continues. Paul's exposition of this mystery in Romans, and of the ongoing daily struggle between flesh and spirit (Romans 7) is illuminating yet complex beyond understanding.

But is there actually more to it than either of these perspectives fully reveal? What is "sanctification" but *Christlikeness*—becoming *like* Christ? The question is: *How* are we transformed into Christlikeness? Jesus says that he is our "example," and that we are to do as he has done. It may be that this obedience—not instantaneous transformation—is actually the key to sanctification. Transformation into Christlikeness is thus a lifelong *process.*

"What [does] God want to do in your life, and in mine, above *all*...things...the ultimate purpose that is in God's mind when he thinks of *you* and *me?* It can be simply stated: That we become sons and daughters...who are conformed to the image of Christ...his younger brothers and sisters, who are *like* him—who love like him, think like him, respond like him, resist the enemy like him, trust the Father like him, and who pray like him...When we give our lives to him...in the midst of our sinful and selfish natures, to the extent we yield to that remaking process...[He] begins to fashion children who will one day bear the image and reflect the nature of...Jesus Christ himself." (Michael Phillips, *Make Me Like Jesus,* "God's Ultimate Purpose")

Christlikeness comes not by magic wand. There is no pixie dust of sanctification the Holy Spirit sprinkles on a new believer that suddenly changes who he or she is. It is at the point of initial faith that the *example* of Jesus takes over. As we follow and conform ourselves to that example—doing as Jesus said, modeling our lives after his—we slowly, by degrees, become infinitesimally more *like* him. Over the course of a lifetime, that slow transformation (given power by the Holy Spirit) is hopefully substantial. There is no magic sanctification that *miraculously* makes us like Jesus. Obedience in the trenches, "a long obedience in the same direction," very *slowly* makes us like Jesus. Nothing is more beautiful than an aging saint of God whose countenance reflects the fruit of a lifetime following the example of Jesus!

> Humanity is already "saved" in principle. We...have to appropriate that salvation. But the...spiritual life...has already come down into the human race. If we will only lay ourselves open to the one Man in whom it was fully present, and who, in spite of being God, is also a real man, He will do it in us...
>
> It is not a question of a good man who died two thousand years ago. It is a living Man...really coming and...turning you permanently into a different sort of thing; into a new little Christ, a being which, in its own small way, has the same kind of life as God...
>
> The Church exists for nothing else but to draw men into Christ, to make them little Christs. If they are not doing that, all the cathedrals, clergy, missions, sermons, even the Bible itself, are simply a waste of time. God became Man for no other purpose. It is even doubtful...whether the whole universe was created for any other purpose...God became man to turn creatures into sons.
>
> C.S. Lewis, *Mere Christianity,* "Obstinate Toy Soldiers", "Let's Pretend", "Is Christianity Hard or Easy?", "Nice People or New Men"

God, bring to my remembrance this day the Command of Jesus to DO AS HE DOES AND BECOME LIKE HIM. *In all I do, may Jesus be not merely my teacher but my example of how life is to be lived. Every day, let me "put on Christ" and thus, in obedience, become like him. Thus, heavenly Father, may I be an instrument in my small corner of the world for the ultimate salvation of mankind. Amen.*

118. Bear Fruit as My Disciples

"By this is my Father glorified, that you bear much fruit, and so prove to be my disciples."
(John 15:8)

What is the "fruit" we are to bear as the Lord's disciples? How will our lives "glorify" God the Father? Is it "niceness"—goodness, kindness, unselfishness? Of course. It is these qualities of character and many more. Yet these are the "fruits" that result from something deeper—the intrinsic life that flows within the human tree and through its vines and branches. That deeper life which produces the fruits of character is quite literally the *life* of Jesus Christ himself, the very Spirit of God. The Fruit we were created to produce as sons and daughters of God is the fruit of Christlikeness. We are to become *like* Jesus in every way. This is God's intent. It is why he is transforming us, if we will let him, from mere children into mature sons and daughters. The prayer, "Make me like Jesus," is no exercise in presumption. It is prompted by the humble recognition of God's eternal purpose in the universe.

In his sermon "The Truth," George MacDonald illuminates this life of "fruitfulness," which he likens to the "blossom of humanity" and which is Christ in us as we grow into the sonship, and thus bring glory to God the Father.

"Man is man only in the *doing* of the truth, perfect man only in the doing of the highest truth, which is the fulfilling of his relations to his origin…

"When the man bows down before a power that can account for him…then the man is bursting into his flower…then the truth of his being…has begun to show itself. When he kneels before the God whose desire is to make of him a creature able to look up to Himself without shadow of doubt or anxiety or fear, confident as a child whom his father is leading by the hand…then his real nature…has begun to come alive. When the man feels his whole being in the embrace of self-responsible Fatherhood, then his nature is in harmony with itself…

"When with his whole nature, a man is loving and willing the truth, he is then a live truth…The one originating, living, visible truth, embracing all truths…is Jesus Christ. He is true. He is the live Truth. His truth, chosen and willed by him, the ripeness of his being, the flower of the sonship which is his nature, the crown of his one topmost perfect relation acknowledged and gloried in, is his absolute obedience to his father.

"The obedient Jesus is Jesus the Truth. He is true and is the root of all truth and development of truth in men. Their very being, however far from the true human, is the undeveloped Christ in them. His likeness to Christ is the truth of a man, in the same way that the perfect meaning of a flower is the truth of a flower...The truth of every man is the perfected Christ in him. As Christ is the blossom of humanity, so the blossom of every man is the Christ perfected in him." (*Unspoken Sermons, Third Series*, "The Truth," quoted from *The Truth in Jesus,* ed. Michael Phillips)

We must not suppose that even if we succeeded in making everyone nice we should have saved their souls. A world of nice people, content in their own niceness, looking no further, turned away from God, would be just as desperately in need of salvation as a miserable world—and might even be more difficult to save.

For mere improvement is not redemption...God became man to turn creatures into sons: not simply to produce better men of the old kind but to produce a new kind of man...a change from being creatures of God to being sons of God...To become new men means losing what we now call "ourselves." Out of ourselves, into Christ, we must go...

Now the whole offer which Christianity makes is this: that we can, if we let God have His way, come to share in the life of Christ...If we share in this kind of life we also shall be sons of God...Every Christian is to become a little Christ. The whole purpose of becoming a Christian is simply nothing else.

C.S. Lewis, *Mere Christianity,* "Nice People or New Men", "The New Men", "Good Infection"

God, bring to my remembrance this day the Command of Jesus to BEAR FRUIT AS HIS DISCIPLE. *I pray that the truth of my being, and the flower of my humanity will be Jesus perfecting his work in me. May that fruit of Christlikeness be visible to those who observe me. Thus, heavenly Father, may I bring glory to you, and be an instrument in my small corner of the world for the ultimate salvation of mankind. Amen.*

119. Practice My Words

"Therefore everyone who hears these words of mine and puts them into practice is like a wise man who built his house on the rock." (Matthew 7:24, NIV)

Throughout the Gospels, Jesus urges obedience to his Commands in many ways and with a great variety of words, phrases, metaphors, and parables. Concluding the Sermon on the Mount of Matthew 5-7, he uses the familiar image of two men—one who built his house on a rock, the other who built his house on sand. Only the house with a secure foundation was able to stand firm when the flood came. The wise builder, Jesus said, was the man who not only hears but *does* his words.

The Greek ποέω—POIEŌ...*do*—has been rendered many ways by biblical translators.

The King James and Revised Standard have it, "...and *does* them..." Many translate it, "...and *acts upon* them..." (NEB, NAS, Weymouth, Moffatt, Goodspeed.) Still others, like the NIV quoted above, have it, *practice* them, or, "...and *puts them into practice...*"

J.B. Phillips and Ken Taylor render the Greek differently for the wise and foolish man: "...Everyone then who hears these words of mine and *puts them into practice...*And everyone who hears these words of mine and *does not follow them...*" (Phillips); "All who listen to My instructions *and follow them...*But those who hear My instructions *and ignore them...*" (LB)

The many instances where forms of POIEŌ occur in the New Testament add still more to the above breadth of meaning by their varied shades of meaning: continue, observe, perform, fulfill, keep by habit, commit, abide.

Without getting lost in the translations of a single word of text, this variety illustrates that the DO Jesus always associates with the *hearing* of his words is much more than the simple word it appears. It is an all-encompassing, life-ruling *do.* Upon what we do in relation to the words of Jesus, the house of our life literally stands or falls.

It is the *do* of wisdom, the *do* of discipleship, the *do* of obedience, the *do* of constancy, the *do* of habit, the *do* of goodness, the *do* of love, the *do* of a life well-lived.

To hold a thing with the intellect, is not to believe it. A man's real belief is that which he lives by...Supposing your theories right, and containing all that is to be believed, yet those theories are not what makes you Christians, if Christians indeed you are. On the contrary, they are, with not a few of you, just what keeps you from being Christians...No opinion, I repeat, is Christianity...

Do you ask, "What is faith in him?" I answer, The leaving of your way, your objects, your self, and the taking of his and him...*and doing as he tells you.* I can find no words strong enough to serve for the weight of this necessity—this obedience. It is the one terrible heresy of the church, that it has always been presenting something else than obedience as faith in Christ...Ask yourself whether you have this day done one thing because he said, Do it, or once abstained because he said, Do not do it. It is simply absurd to say you believe...if you do not anything he tells you...

Oh fools and slow of heart, if you...do not set yourselves to do his words! you but build your houses on the sand. What have such teachers not to answer for who have turned your regard away from the direct words of the Lord himself...to contemplate plans of salvation tortured out of the words of his apostles...There is but one plan of salvation, and that is to believe in the Lord Jesus Christ; that is, to take him for what he is—our master, and his words as if he meant them, which assuredly he did. To do his words is to enter into vital relation with him, to obey him is the only way to be one with him. The relation between him and us is an absolute one; it can nohow begin to *live* but in obedience: it is obedience...

What have you done this day because it was the will of Christ? Have you dismissed...an anxious thought for the morrow? Have you ministered to any needy soul or body, and kept your right hand from knowing what your left hand did...Did you set yourself to judge righteous judgment...Have you forgiven your enemy...Are you hungering and thirsting after righteousness? Have you given to some one that asked of you? Tell me something that you have done, are doing, or are trying to do because he told you.

George MacDonald, *Unspoken Sermons, Second Series,* "The Truth in Jesus"

God, bring to my remembrance this day the Command of Jesus to PRACTICE HIS WORDS. *Only so will I grow into your obedient son or daughter. Only so will I understand your ways. Thus, heavenly Father, may I be an instrument in my small corner of the world for the ultimate salvation of mankind. Amen.*

120. This is My Command: Love One Another

"This is my commandment, that you love one another as I have loved you...
This I command you, to love one another." (John 15:12, 17)

"Little children, yet a little while I am with you. Where I am going you cannot come. A new commandment I give to you, that you love one another; even as I have loved you. By this all men will know that you are my disciples, if you have love for one another.

"Let not your hearts be troubled; believe in God, believe also in me. In my Father's house are many rooms; if it were not so, would I have told you that I go to prepare a place for you? And when I go and prepare a place for you, I will come again and will take you to myself, that where I am you may be also.

"I am the way, and the truth, and the life; no one comes to the Father, but by me. He who has seen me has seen the Father. Believe me that I am in the Father and the Father in me. If you love me, you will keep my commandments. Yet a little while, and the world will see me no more, but you will see me; because I live. In that day you will know that I am in my Father, and you in me, and I in you. He who has my commandments and keeps them, he it is who loves me; and he who loves me will be loved by my Father, and I will love him and manifest myself to him. If a man loves me, he will keep my word, and my Father will love him, and we will come to him and make our home with him. Peace I leave with you; my peace I give to you; not as the world gives do I give to you. Let not your hearts be troubled, neither let them be afraid.

"I am the true vine, and my Father is the vinedresser. Every branch of mine that bears no fruit, he takes away, and every branch that does bear fruit he prunes, that it may bear more fruit. Abide in me, and I in you. As the branch cannot bear fruit by itself, unless it abides in the vine, neither can you, unless you abide in me. I am the vine, you are the branches. He who abides in me, and I in him, he it is that bears much fruit, for apart from me you can do nothing. By this my Father is glorified, that you bear much fruit, and so prove to be my disciples. As the Father has loved me, so have I loved you; abide in my love. If you keep my commandments, you will abide in my love, just as I have kept my Father's commandments and abide in his love. These things I have spoken to you, that my joy may be in you, and that your joy may be full.

"This is my commandment, that you love one another as I have loved you. Greater love has no man than this, that a man lay down his life for his friends. You are my friends if you do what I command you. No longer do I call you servants, for the servant does not know what his master is doing; but I have called you friends, for all that I have heard from my Father I have made known to you. This I command you, to love one another."

"Father, the hour has come; glorify thy Son that the Son may glorify thee. I have manifested thy name to the men whom thou gavest me. Now they know that everything that thou hast given me is from thee; for I have given them the words which thou gavest me, and they have received them and know in truth that I came from thee. I am praying for them. And now I am no more in the world, but they are in the world. I do not pray that thou shouldst take them out of the world, but that thou shouldst keep them from the evil one. They are not of the world, even as I am not of the world. Sanctify them in the truth; thy word is truth. I do not pray for these only, but also for those who believe in me through their word, that they may all be one; even as thou, Father, art in me, and I in thee, that they also may be in us, so that the world may believe that thou hast sent me. The glory which thou hast given me I have given to them, that they may be one even as we are one, I in them and thou in me, that they may become perfectly one, so that the world may know that thou hast sent me and hast loved them even as thou hast loved me."

God, bring to my remembrance this day the Commands of Jesus and give me the courage, understanding, grace, humility, wisdom, selflessness, endurance, and good cheer to obey them. Thus, heavenly Father, may I be an instrument in my small corner of the world for the ultimate salvation of mankind. Amen.

THE COMMANDS

1. Obey my Commands (J 14:21,14:23,15:10,15:14)
2. Love
3. Love God (M 22:37; Mk 12:30; L 10:28)
4. Love man (M 19:19,22:39; Mk 12:31; L 10:28)
5. Love the brethren (J 13:34,13:35,15:12)
6. Pray (M 6:9-13,21:22,26:41; Mk 11:24,14:38; L 11:2-4,18:1,18:6,18:13,22:40,22:46; J 14:13,14:14)
7. Be careful and watchful (M 16:6,24:4,26:41; Mk 8:15,13:5,13:9,13:23, 13,33,13:35,13:37, 14:38; L 21:36)
8. Remain alert and on guard (M 24:32,24:42,24:44,25:13; Mk 13:5,13:9,13:23,13:28, 13:33,13:35,13:37,14:34,14:38; L 12:15,12:35.12:36-7,12:40,17:3,20:46, 21:8,21:34)
9. Take heart, take courage (M 9:22, 14:27; Mk 6:50; L 21:34; J 16:33)
10. Don't be afraid (M 8:26,10:28,10:31,14:27,17:7,24:6,28:10; Mk 4:40,5:36, 6:50,13:37; L 5:10, 8:50,12:4,12:7,12:32,21:9; J 6:20,14:1,14:27)

11. Be pure (M 5:8)
12. Guard against ambition (Mk 10:31,10:43)
13. Commit no sexual sins (M 5:32,5:33,19:9,19:18; Mk 10:11,10:19; L 16:18,18:20)
14. Be patient, enduring, persevering (M 10:22; L 21:19)
15. Repent (M 4:17; Mk 1:15,4:3; L 13:3,13:5)
16. Listen (M 7:24,15:10; Mk 4:3,7:14; L 6:47,8:21;11:28; J 5:24)
17. Listen carefully (M 11:15,13:9,13:15,13:18,13:43; Mk 4:9,4:23,4:24,7:14,8:18; L 8:8,8:18, 9:44,14:35)
18. Be clear-minded, thoughtful, mentally diligent (M 13:15; Mk 8:17)
19. Apply yourself to think, learn, understand (M 13:14,15:10,15:16,16:9, 16:11; Mk 4:13,7:14,7:18,8:17,8:18,8:21; J 8:43)
20. Think no impure thought (M 5:28,6:22-23; L 11:33)

21. Be humble (M 5:5,18:4,23:12; Mk 10:31; L 14:11,18:13,18:14)
22. Give when asked and do more than required (M 5:39,5:40,5:41,5:42,10:8; L 6:29, 6:30,6:34,6:35)
23. Follow me (M 4:20,8:22,9:9,10:38,16:24,19:21; Mk 1:17,2:14,8:34, 10:21; L 5:27, 9:23,14:27;18:23; J 1:43,8:12,12:26,18:22,21:19,21:22)
24. Care for the suffering (M 25:35-36,25:40; Mk 9:40; L 14:13)

25. Give to the poor (M 19:21; Mk 10:21; L 12:33)
26. Believe (Mk 1:15,5:36; L 8:50,24:25-6,18:22; J 12:36,20:27)
27. Believe in God (J 14:1)
28. Believe in me (Mk 1:15; J 3:16,5:24.5:46,5:47,8:24,12:46,14:1)
29. Don't be anxious (M 6:25,6:34; L 12:22,12:29,24:38; J 14:1,14:27)
30. Believe that you will receive what you pray for (M 21:22; Mk 11:23; L 18:1,18:6; J 14:13,15:7,16:24)

31. Be righteous (M 5:6,5:20,5:48; L 6:21)
32. If part of your body sins, get rid of it (M 5:29-30,18:8-9; Mk 9:43-47)
33. Be at peace, reconciled, and united with others (M 5:9,5:24,5:25,18:15-17; Mk 9:50; J 17:21)
34. Deny yourself (M 16:24; Mk 8:34; L 9:23)
35. Lose your life (M 10:39,16:25,16:26; Mk 8:35,10:21; L 9:24,14:33,17:33; J 12:25)
36. Be a servant (M 20:26,23:11; Mk 9:35,10:31; L 22:26)
37. Do not defraud (Mk 10:19)
38. Be a son or daughter of God (M 5:45; L 6:35; J 12:36)
39. Pray, fast, give, and do good in secret (M 6:2,6:6,6:16-18)
40. Beware of practicing piety to be noticed (M 6:1,6:5,16:6,16:11,23:3,23:27; Mk 8:15,12:38, 16:6,16:11; L 12:1,18:11-14,20:46)

41. Forgive (M 6:14,18:34; Mk 11:25; L 6:37,17:3,17:4)
42. Forgive 70 x 7 times (M 18:22; L 17:4)
43. Do good, be good (L 6:27,6:33,6:35)
44. Seek first God's kingdom (M 6:33; L 12:31)
45. Store up treasure in heaven (M 6:19-20; L 10:20,12:21,12:33; J 6:27)
46. Be kind (L 6:35)
47. Love and pray for your adversaries (M 5:44; L 6:27,6:35)
48. Do good to those who hate you (L 6:27)
49. Do not exalt yourself (Mk 10:31,10:43,23:8,23:10; L 9:48,11:43,14:8,14:10, 14:11,22:26)
50. Honor your father and mother (Mk 10:19; L 18:20)

51. Guard against hypocrisy (M 5:20,16:6,16:11; Mk 8:15,12:38; L 4:35,11:29,12:1; J 9:41)
52. Let your light shine before men (M 5:14,5:16; L 4:33; J 9:4)
53. If someone takes from you, do not demand back what you have given (L 6:34,6:35)
54. Seek no spiritual signs (M 12:39,16:4; Mk 8:12; L 11:29,17:20)
55. Be born again (J 3:4,3:5)

56. Do not justify or worry how to defend yourself (M10:19; Mk 13:11; L 12:11, 16:14,18:16, 18:17,12:14)
57. Learn of me (M 11:29; J 8:31-32)
58. Receive the kingdom of God like a child (M 19:14; Mk 10:14,10:15; L 9:48,18:16,18:17)
59. Have salt in yourselves (M 5:13; Mk 9:50)
60. Be a good steward over what God has given you (M 25:29; L 16:10,16:12;19:26)

61. Trust and have faith in God (Mk 4:40,11:22; L 5:4,12:28,17:6; J 20:27)
62. Do not be called teacher or leader (M 23:8,23:10)
63. Do not be diverted by externals, traditions, and doctrines, but look to the heart (M 15:6, 23:3,23:23; Mk 7:8,7:13, 7:18,7:20; L 11:41, L 11:42)
64. Don't fret about trifles (L 10:41)
65. Do not show goodness and hospitality only to those who are kind to you (M 5:46-47; L 6:32,6:33,6:34,6:35,14:12)
66. Worship the Lord and serve him only (M 4:10,23:9; L 4:8)
67. Do not desire more than God gives you (M 6:24,20:15; L 12:15,16:13)
68. Do not pray ostentatiously and with empty phrases (M 6:7; L 18:11-14)
69. Remain gratefully aware of your spiritual need (M 5:3)
70. Take up your cross (M 10:38,16:24; Mk 8:34; L 9:23,14:27)

71. Do and think toward others as you would have them behave toward you (M 7:12; L 6:31)
72. Don't judge (M 7:1; L 6:37; J 8:7)
73. Deal with your own faults before thinking of the faults of others (M 7:5; L 6:42)
74. Ask, seek, knock (M 7:7; L 11:9; J 16:24)
75. Enter through the narrow gate (M 7:13; L 13:24; J 10:9)
76. Come to me with your burdens and find rest (M 11:28-30; J 4:14,7:37)
77. Take my yoke upon you (M 11:29)
78. Don't swear (M 5:34-36,23:20-22)
79. Judge rightly not by appearances (L 12:56,12:57; J 7:24,8:15)
80. Give the world its due and give God the things that are his (M 22:21; Mk 12:17; L 20:25)

81. Love truth, speak truth, do truth, (M 19:18; Mk 10:19; J 3:19,3:21,8:32)
82. Do not speak carelessly (M 5:37,12:36-37)
83. Acknowledge your discipleship (M 10:27,10:32,11:6; Mk 8:38; L 9:26,12:8; J 5:23)
84. Let your yes be yes and your no be no (M 5:37)
85. Do not doubt (M 14:31,21:21; L 24:38)

86. Speak graciously with words of peace (M 10:13; L 10:5)
87. Let people injure you without retaliating (M 5:39; L 6:29)
88. Show mercy (M 5:7,9:13; L 6:36)
89. Proclaim the kingdom of God (M 10:7,10:27; Mk 5:19; L 8:39,9:60)
90. Don't insult or call anyone a fool (M 5:22)

91. Rule your life by the will of God (M 4:4; Mk 3:35; L 4:4,12:47; J 7:17,8:31,12:35)
92. Settle disputes promptly and privately (M 5:23-25,18:15-17; L 12:58,17:3)
93. Ask the Lord of the harvest to send workers (M 9:38; L 10:2)
94. Partake of the symbols of my body and blood (M 26:26-27; L 22:17; J 6:53,6:56)
95. Do for the least of humanity as you would for me (M 18:10,19:14,25:40,25:45; Mk 9:37; L 14:12-14)
96. Do not give way to anger (M 5:22)
97. Do not close your eyes to the Holy Spirit's work (M 12:32; Mk 3:29,9:39; L 9:50,12:10)
98. Give generously, and not merely from your abundance (M 10:8; L 6:38,21:4)
99. Don't heed false prophets (M 7:15,15:14,24:4,24:11,24:23; Mk 13:5,13:21-2; L 17:23,21:8)
100. Obey the commandments (M 5:19,19:17;19:18-19; Mk 10:19; L 18:20)

101. Be glad in all circumstances (M 5:12; L 6:23; J 16:33)
102. Give up everything (Mk 10:29-30; L 14:33)
103. Don't resist evil men (M 5:39)
104. Do not lead others into sin (M 5:19; Mk 9:42; L 11:46,17:1-2)
105. Teach the nations to obey what I have commanded (M 28:19-20)
106. Do not follow the example of those who preach but do not practice (M 15:14,23:3; L 20:46)
107. Don't cast your pearls before swine (M 7:6)
108. Do not test the Lord (M 4:7, L 4:12)
109. Wash one another's feet (J 13:14)
110. Be wise as snakes and innocent as doves (M 10:16,10:17; L 16:9,16:11)

111. Abide in me by obeying my Commands (J 15:4,15:7,15:9,15:10)
112. Don't separate what God has joined (M 19:6; Mk 10:9)
113. Love me by having my Commands and words and keeping them (J 14:15,14:21,14:23)
114. Count the cost of single-minded devotion to God (M 6:21.6:24; L 14:28,14:33,16:13)

115. Don't look back on your past life (M 8:22,10:37; L 9:60,9:62, 14:26,14:33,17:32; J 5:14,8:34)
116. Don't call me Lord and not do what I tell you (M 7:21; L 6:46)
117. Do as I do and become like me (M 10:24-25; J 13:15)
118. Bear fruit as my disciples (J 15:8,15:16, 21:15, 21:16,21:17)
119. Practice my words (M 7:24; L 6:46,6:47;8:21,10:37,11:28; J 8:51,12:47,13:17)
120. This is my Command: Love one another (J 13:34,15:12,15:17)

One question now to be put to the test is this: Can we have that contact with God all the time…fall asleep in His arms, and awaken in His presence…Can we think His thoughts all the time?…

I choose to make the rest of my life an experiment in answering this question.

Someone may be saying that this introspection and this struggle to achieve God-consciousness is abnormal and perilous. I am going to take the risks, for somebody ought to do it…If our religious premises are correct at all then this oneness with God is the *most* normal condition one can have. It is what made Christ, Christ. It is what St. Augustine meant when he said, "Thou has made us for Thyself, and our souls are restless until they find their rest in Thee."…

"Can a laboring man successfully attain this continuous surrender to God? Can a man working at a machine pray for people all day long, talk with God all day long, and at the same time do his task efficiently?"

"Can a merchant do business, can an accountant keep books, ceaselessly surrendered to God?"

"Can a mother wash dishes, care for the babies, continuously talking to God?"

"Can a politician keep in a state of continuous contact with God, and not lose the following of the crowds?"

"Can little children be taught to talk and listen to God inwardly all day long, and what is the effect upon them?"…

Do we really mean what we say when we repeat "the highest end of man is to find God and do his will" all the time?…

"Any hour of any day may be made perfect by merely choosing. It is perfect if one looks to God that entire hour, waiting for His leadership all through the hour and trying hard to do every tiny thing exactly as God wishes it done, as perfectly as possible. No emotions are necessary. Just the doing of God's will perfectly makes the hour a perfect one. And the results of that one perfect hour, I believe, will echo down through eternity."

Frank Laubauch, *Letters By A Modern Mystic*, March 23, 1930

We Western peoples are apt to think our great problems are external, environmental. We are not skilled in the inner life, where the real roots of our problem lie. For I would suggest that the true explanation of the complexity of our program is an inner one, not an outer one. The outer distractions of our interests reflect an inner lack of integration of our own lives…

For over the margins of life comes a whisper, a faint fall, a premonition of richer living which we know we are passing by. Strained by the very mad pace of our daily outer burdens, we are further strained by an inward uneasiness, because we have hints that there is a way of life vastly richer and deeper than all this hurried existence, a life of unhurried serenity…If only we could slip over into that Center! If only we could find the Silence which is the source of sound!…

I think it is clear that I am talking about a revolutionary way of living. Religion isn't something to be added to our other duties…The life with God is the center of life, and all else is remodeled and integrated by it. It gives the singleness of eye…

There is a way of life so hid with Christ in God that…from such a holy Center come the commissions of life…Life from the Center is a life of unhurried peace and power. It is simple. It is serene. It is amazing. It is triumphant. It is radiant. It takes no time, but it occupies all our time. And it makes our life programs new and overcoming. We need not get frantic. He is at the helm. And when our little day is done we lie down quietly in peace, for all is well.

Thomas Kelly, *A Testament of Devotion,* 1941,
"The Simplification of Life"

The three volumes of *The Commands* and the five volumes of *The Eyewitness Bible* present a unity of vision and outlook on God's work and purposes through history and in the individual lives of his people. Their themes and messages form a single tapestry-perspective of the Bible as God's revelation. They are most profitably read in conjunction with each other, and with that overarching unity in mind.

The Commands of the Prophets
The Commands of Jesus
The Commands of the Apostles

The Eyewitness Old Testament, Volume 1
The Eyewitness Old Testament, Volume 2
The Eyewitness New Testament, Volume 1
The Eyewitness New Testament, Volume 2
The Eyewitness New Testament, Volume 3

Special Editions:
The Commands of the Prophets Extra Large Print Edition
The Commands of Jesus Extra Large Print Edition
The Commands of the Apostles Extra Large Print Edition
The Commands of Jesus Journal Edition
The Prayers of the Commands
The Commands of Jesus Pocket Edition
The Commands of the Apostles Pocket Edition

The listings of commands from *The Commands of the Prophets* and *The Commands of the Apostles* follow

THE COMMANDS OF THE PROPHETS

1. WISDOM

1 Listen to your father's instruction.
2 Love, cherish, seek, and pray for wisdom.
3 Though it cost all you have, get understanding.
4 Let wisdom, understanding, and discretion protect you.
5 Exercise prudence.
6 Don't act or speak hastily, and listen before speaking.
7 Do not speak thoughtlessly, or carelessly pass on gossip.
8 Trust God with all your heart, and do not rely on your own understanding.
9 Acknowledge God in all your ways.
10 Find a husband or wife of noble character.

2. CHOICE AND CONSEQUENCE

11 Love God with your whole heart, soul, mind, and strength.
12 Seek God diligently.
13 Take heed not to forget God's commands.
14 Choose this day whom you will serve.
15 Walk in obedience to God's commands.
16 Do what is right and good in the sight of the Lord.
17 Do not let your heart become proud.
18 Do not be afraid or discouraged.
19 Remember blessings and consequences and choose life.
20 Set the desires of your heart Godward.

3. AUTHORITY

21 Acknowledge God's authority.
22 Embrace command.
23 Choose obedience.
24 Walk with God.
25. Do not let sin beguile you.
26 Run from sin.
27 Honor marriage and family.
28 Separate from the world.
29 Keep covenant with God.
30 Live as a manifestly distinct righteousness-choosing people.

4. COMMAND

31 Worship no other gods than the Lord your God.
32 Make no idols.
33 Do not speak the Lord's name carelessly.
34 Observe the Lord's rest.
35 Honor your father and mother.
36 Do not kill.
37 Do not commit adultery.
38 Do not steal.
39 Do not speak falsely about others.
40 Do not covet what you do not have.

5. OBEDIENCE

41 Love your neighbor as yourself.
42 Show kindness to widows, orphans, strangers, and aliens.
43 Help and be kind to the poor.
44 Keep your camp pure.
45 Work diligently and cheerfully in what you undertake.
46 Respect the property of others.
47 Make restitution for wrong.
48 Bear no grudge, seek no revenge.
49 Lend without interest.
50 Exercise wise stewardship over God's provision.

6. SEPARATION

51 Be strong and courageous not to walk in the world's ways.
52 Watch yourself closely so the world does not ensnare you.
53 Do not yield to the world's enticements.
54 Do not associate with worldly people.
55 Make no friends of fools.
56 Do not bring sin into your home.
57 Do not covet or imitate what the world's people have or do.
58 Women do not wear men's clothing, men do not wear women's clothing.
59 Do not be lured into worshiping false gods.
60 Do not follow others into sin.

7. Watchfulness

61 Keep watchful by knowing God's commands.
62 Read and re-read God's law.
63 Fix God's words in your mind and store his commands in your heart.
64 Apply your heart to understand God's purposes.
65 Do not help an evil man or woman.
66 Do not let sin become a thorn in your side.
67 Seek counsel, guidance, and advice.
68 Meditate on God's precepts.
69 Humbly listen and heed wisdom, insight, instruction, and correction.
70 Live by the truth you know.

8. Righteousness

71 *Pray with David:* Search me, O God, and know my heart. Try me and know my thoughts. See if there be any wicked way in me, and lead me in the way everlasting.
72 Incline my heart to your commands.
73 Teach me your ways.
74 Give me understanding and wisdom in my secret heart.
75 Help me not to stray from your commands.
76 Give me wise judgment and knowledge.
77 Protect me from falsehood, keep my steps steady, let no sin get dominion over me.
78 Create in me a clean heart and put a right spirit within me.
79 Guard my life—may integrity and upright-ness preserve me.
80 Guide me, lead me, and help me walk in truth.

9. Judgment and Forgiveness

81 Confess sin.
82 Forgive when you have been wronged.
83 Judge others fairly.
84 Overlook offenses and weaknesses in others.
85 Repent of unintentional sin.
86 Be honest and truthful in dealings and relationships.
87 Turn away anger with gentle speech.
88 Wear a cheerful countenance.
89 Spread peace.
90 Keep your word.

10. Renewal and Restoration

91 Be still and know God.
92 Consecrate yourself.
93 Circumcise your heart.
94 Continually renew covenant with God.
95 Destroy potential idols.
96 Make no rash decisions.
97 Do not chase fantasies.
98 Avoid people who talk too much.
99 Keep knowledge to yourself.
100 Do not engage in meaningless worship.

11. Legacy

101 Live a peaceable, responsible, domestic, and upright life.
102 Speak truth.
103 Claim and pass on your inheritance in God.
104 Instruct your children in God's commands.
105 Show respect to the elderly.
106 Succeed by planning.
107 Walk in patience.
108 Cultivate love for the Lord's statutes and commands.
109 Walk in integrity.
110 Act justly, love mercy, and walk humbly with your God.

12. Purity

111 Be pure in thought and behavior.
112 Do not be the cause of allowing sin to spread.
113 Engage in no sexual relations outside marriage.
114 Hate falsehood and do not circulate potential falsehoods.
115 Guard your tongue.
116 Purge temper, anger, bitterness, resentment.
117 Use honest weights.
118 Turn from all hint of impurity and impropriety.
119 Purge evil from your life.
120 Welcome God's furnace of purification.

The Apostolic Commands

1. JERUSALEM—*Pursue Godliness*

1 Yield yourself to God.
2 Present yourself as a daily living sacrifice to God.
3 Choose to be transformed by the renewal of mind.
4 Seek to grow in righteousness.
5 Train yourself in Godliness.
6 Be constant in prayer.
7 Abide in Jesus.
8 Lead a virtuous life.
9 Set your thoughts on high things.
10 Serve God and live for his glory.

2. ANTIOCH—*Nurture Personal Spirituality*

11 Obey the Lord's commands.
12 Be a doer of the word, not a hearer only.
13 Take your faith seriously.
14 Take heed to yourself.
15 Do not envy.
16 Do not be afraid or lose heart.
17 Keep watchful and alert.
18 Stand firm and courageous in God.
19 Be thankful in all circumstances.
20 Don't worry.

3. GALATIA—*Grow the Fruits of the Spirit*

21 Walk by the Spirit.
22 Make love your aim.
23 Rejoice in all circumstances, especially in your trials.
24 Walk in peace.
25 Respond with patience.
26 Be kind.
27 Do good, love good, be good.
28 Walk faithfully by faith, not by sight.
29 Be a gentle person.
30 Exercise self-control.

4. CORINTH—*Turn from Sin*

31 Repent.
32 Do not be conformed to the world.
33 Hate evil.
34 Sin no more—do not yield to sin.
35 Do not participate in the sins of others.
36 Do not associate with immorality.
37 Avoid worldly-minded believers.
38 Revere no idols.
39 Confess your sins.
40 Keep your conscience clear.

5. THESSALONICA—*Live God's Priorities at Home*

41 Christian leaders, live exemplary lives.
42 Honor marriage.
43 Husbands, love, honor and serve your wives.
44 Wives, respect and submit to your husbands.
45 Children, obey and honor your parents.
46 Practice hospitality.
47 Manage your households well.
48 Raise your children in the wisdom of the Lord.
49 Train young men to be self-controlled, young women to be chaste and domestic.
50 Care for widows and orphans.

6. LAODICEA—*Show Respect in Relationships*

51 Show honor and respect to all.
52 Seek the good of others.
53 Put others first.
54 Be merciful and full of sympathy.
55 Harbor no grievances or animosities.
56 Avoid the shallow and hypocritical who do not live their faith.
57 Control anger.
58 Don't judge.
59 Associate with the lowly. Show no partiality to the rich and powerful.
60 Place no stumbling blocks in the way of another's faith.

7. ATHENS—*Develop Wise and Gracious Habits*

61 Conduct yourself becomingly.
62 Be courteous and full of grace toward all.
63 Do not insist on your own way.
64 Don't be suspicious. (Don't yield to or allow suspicions to fester)
65 Live without guile.
66 Do not be irritable or resentful.
67 Do not be foolish.
68 Mind your own business.
69 Give generously.
70 Owe no one anything.

8. CAESAREA—*Speak with Grace*

71 Speak graciously.
72 Control your tongue.
73 Be quick to listen, slow to speak.
74 Say what you mean.
75 Do not grumble, complain, or speak against others.
76 Do not gossip, slander, or lie.
77 Do not swear.
78 Do not quarrel.
79 Speak to edify, encourage, and bless one another.
80 Speak not to flatter, impress, or please men.

9. PHILIPPI—*Reflect Christlikeness of Character*

81 Put on the character of Christ.
82 Seek God's will and live by it.
83 Pray for wisdom and walk in wisdom.
84 Be pure.
85 See through God's eyes by developing the mind of Christ.
86 Do not be covetous, greedy, or lover of money.
87 Clothe yourself with humility.
88 Eagerly rejoice in right and goodness.
89 Endure suffering with faith, fortitude, grace, and courage.
90 Wage vigorous spiritual warfare.

10. COLOSSAE—*Build Mature Beliefs*

91 Be mature in your thinking and wise in doctrine.
92 Increase your knowledge of God.
93 Build on a foundation of Jesus Christ.
94 Love truth.
95 Do not be ruled by legalisms.
96 Do not be shallow of belief.
97 Walk with discernment.
98 Do not dispute over doctrine.
99 Do not be deceived.
100 Equip yourselves for fitness to teach spiritual completeness.

11. EPHESUS—*Exemplify Unity and Servanthood in Church Life*

101 Do not be anxious to teach or place the immature in leadership.
102 Older men and women, teach younger men and women.
103 Pursue and emphasize what builds up the body of Christ.
104 Encourage one another.
105 Be sensitive to the weak in faith.
106 Use your gifts wisely.
107 Do all things decently and in order.
108 Deal with body conflicts in the church.
109 Don't neglect fellowship with your brothers and sisters.
110 Maintain unity.

12. ROME—*Evidence Discipleship in the World*

111 Live quiet peaceable lives.
112 Live in harmony with all.
113 Honor and submit to authority.
114 Honor, respect, and give your best to your masters and employers.
115 Be modest in dress, manners, and demeanor.
116 Aim at what is honorable in men's eyes as well as God's.
117 Work diligently and do not be slothful or idle.
118 Live your faith with zeal, good cheer, and steadfastness.
119 Consider your witness.
120 Recognize yourselves as a people set apart.

Made in the USA
Coppell, TX
20 January 2026

67063440R00155